CELTIC'S

CULT HEROES

DAVID POTTER

Know The Score Books Limited

www.knowthescorebooks.com

KNOW THE SCORE BOOKS SPORTS PUBLICATIONS

CULT HEROES	Author	ISBNHH
CARLISLE	Paul Harrison	978-1-905449-09-7
CELTIC	David Potter	978-1-905449-08-8
CHELSEA	Leo Moynihan	1-905449-00-3
MANCHESTER CITY	David Clayton	978-1-905449-05-7
NEWCASTLE	Dylan Younger	1-905449-03-8
NOTTINGHAM FOREST	David McVay	978-1-905449-06-4
RANGERS	Paul Smith	978-1-905449-07-1
SOUTHAMPTON	Jeremy Wilson	1-905449-01-1
WEST BROM	Simon Wright	1-905449-02-X

MATCH OF MY LIFE	Editor	ISBN
DERBY COUNTY	Nick Johnson	978-1-905449-68-2
ENGLAND WORLD CUP	Massarella & Moynihan	1-905449-52-6
EUROPEAN CUP FINALS	Ben Lyttleton	1-905449-57-7
FA CUP FINALS (1953-1969)	David Saffer	978-1-905449-53-4
FULHAM	Michael Heatley	1-905449-51-8
LEEDS	David Saffer	1-905449-54-2
LIVERPOOL	Leo Moynihan	1-905449-50-X
MANCHESTER UNITED	Ivan Ponting	978-1-905449-59
SHEFFIELD UNITED	Nick Johnson	1-905449-62-3
STOKE CITY	Simon Lowe	978-1-905449-55-2
SUNDERLAND	Rob Mason	1-905449-60-7
SPURS	Allen & Massarella	978-1-905449-58-3
WOLVES	Simon Lowe	1-905449-56-9

GENERAL FOOTBALL	Author	ISBN
2007/08 CHAMPIONS LEAGUE YEARBOOK		
	Harry Harris	978-1-905449-93-4
BURKSEY	Peter Morfoot	1-905449-49-6
The Autobiography of a Football God		
HOLD THE BACK PAGE	Harry Harris	1-905449-91-7
MARTIN JOL: THE INSIDE STORY	Harry Harris	978-1-905449-77-4
OUTCASTS	Steve Menary	978-1-905449-31-6
The Lands FIFA Forgot		
PARISH TO PLANET	Eric Midwinter	978-1-905449-30-9
How Football Came To Rule The World		
MY PREMIERSHIP DIARY	Marcus Hahnemann	978-1-905449-33-0
Reading's Season in the Premiership		
TACKLES LIKE A FERRET	Paul Parker	1-905449-47-X
(England Cover)		

TACKLES LIKE A FERRET	Paul Parker	1-905449-46-1
(Manchester United Cover)		
UNITED THROUGH TRIUMPH AND TRAGEDY		
	Bill Foulkes	978-1-905449-78-1
2006 WORLD CUP DIARY	Harry Harris	1-905449-9

CRICKET	Author	ISBN
ASHES TO DUST	Graham Cookson	978-1-905449-19-4
GROVEL!	David Tossell	978-1-905449-43-9
The Story & Legacy of the 1976 West IndiesTour of England		
MOML: THE ASHES	Sam Pilger & Rob Wightman	1-905449-63-1
MY TURN TO SPIN	Shaun Udal	978-1-905449-42-2
WASTED?	Paul Smith	978-1-905449-45-3
LEAGUE CRICKET YEARBOOK	Andy Searle	978-1-905449-70-5
North West edition		
LEAGUE CRICKET YEARBOOK	Andy Searle	978-1-905449-72-9
Midlands edition		

RUGBY LEAGUE	Editor	ISBN
WIGAN WARRIORS	David Kuzio	978-1-905449-66-8

FORTHCOMING TITLES

MATCH OF MY LIFE	Editor	ISBN
ASTON VILLA	Neil Moxley	978-1-905449-65-1

GENERAL FOOTBALL	Author	ISBN
ANFIELD OF DREAMS	Neil Dunkin	978-1-905449-80-4
MANCHESTER UNITED RUINED MY WIFE		
	David Blatt	978-1-905449-81-1
THE DOOG: The Incredible Story of Derek Dougan - Football's Most Controversial Character		
	Gordos & Harrison	978-1-905449-02-9
THE RIVALS GAME: Inside The British Derby		
	Douglas Beattie	978-1-905449-79-8

RUGBY LEAGUE	Editor	ISBN
MOML LEEDS RHINOS	Phil Caplan & David Saffer	978-1-905449-69-9

CELTIC'S

CULT HEROES

DAVID POTTER

Editor: Ivan Ponting
Series Editor: Simon Lowe

www.knowthescorebooks.com
First published in the United Kingdom
by Know The Score Books Limited, 2008

Know The Score Books Limited
118 Alcester Road
Studley
Warwickshire
B80 7NT
Tel: 01527 454482   Fax: 01527 452183

www.knowthescorebooks.com

A CIP catalogue record is available for this book from the British Library
ISBN-13: 978-1-905449-08-8

Jacket and book design by Lisa David

Printed and bound in Great Britain
By Cromwell Press Ltd

Photographs reproduced by kind permission of Action Images, Colorsport, Getty Images and the Scottish Football Museum, Hampden Park.

Mixed Sources
Product group from well-managed
forests and other controlled sources
www.fsc.org Cert no. TT-COC-2082
© 1996 Forest Stewardship Council
FSC

Author's Acknowledgements

In a book like this, it is impossible to thank everyone personally who gave their assistance to me, but I feel I should single out the following people for their help and encouragement – Tom Campbell, that Celtic polymath; Craig Mcaughtrie, the editor of the *Keep The Faith* website; Marie Rowan, who supplied the female insight into how women loved the "bad bhoy" Dan Doyle; Danny Leslie and the other "bhoys and ghirls" of the Joseph Rafferty Celtic Supporters club; Jack Marshall, who I met by chance one day at Parkhead and who supplied me with interesting information about Malky MacDonald; and Philip Hulme-Jones, who supplied his own dignified and detached perspective on my occasionally rabid view of things. In addition Tom Greig, Sean Quinn, Pat Woods, Tony Griffin, John Traynor, John Fallon, Douglas Simpson, Alex Petrie, Alan McCreadie and David MacDonald have all in their own quiet way supplied encouragement, as have the Watson and the Hepburn families of Falkland Cricket Club.

But two men, sadly no longer with us, have supplied most of the inspiration. Eugene MacBride, that grand old Celt with an encyclopaedic knowledge and love of the club, sadly passed away in 2006, and my own father Angus Potter has now been dead for almost a decade and a half – but still manages to talk to me about his beloved Celtic every day. My posthumous thanks to both of them. Heaven will not be dull with these two around.

David Potter
December 2007

Jacket Photographs
Front centre: Shunsuke Nakamura celebrates after netting yet another glorious free-kick, this time to defeat Manchester United.
Left: Celtic fans had a love affair with Champagne Charlie Nicholas; in love one minute after yet another goal, out of love the next when he left to join Arsenal .
Right: The legend that was Jock Stein; manager of the 1967 Lisbon Lions.
Inset: Henrik Larsson celebrates with another piece of silverware - the 2004 Scottish Cup.

Rear
Left: Jinky Jimmy Johnstone was a dribbling genius, who had his finger paused regularly over the self-destruct button.
Right: The Coronation Cup winning team who defeated Hibs in 1953 were packed with cult heroes.

Contents

Introduction

'Football without fans is nothing.'

Jock Stein

CELTIC ARE A TEAM of legend, and of legendary characters. And from among their band of brave, skilful and exciting players it is no easy matter to choose 20 Cult Heroes, for the truth is that, in a sense at least, every player who dons a green-and-white jersey automatically becomes a cult hero for the sizeable community that is proud to call itself "Celtic-daft" - that hereditary, endogenous, irreversible and terminal condition which throws up so much happiness and so much pain in its wake.

Some of us fans have tried to shake off this yolk of serfdom. In the gruesome days of the early 1990s before Fergus McCann, things were so bad that I tried to associate myself with other organisations, to support smaller and therefore less painful outfits, even to stop watching football altogether and trying pursuits like swimming, dog walking, reading and even shopping... but Saturday afternoon could never rid itself of that gnawing away at the vitals that is so much part of loving the Celtic, and 4.40pm would always find me in front of a television or with my ear to a transistor radio, agonising over how the team got on.

So what exactly is a cult hero in the context of this "not so much a football club more a way of life" that is Celtic? Clearly the effect that the man has on the support is a crucial factor. It is not necessarily the best player who is a cult hero. Kenny Dalglish, for example, was one of Celtic's greatest ever in terms of being both a footballer and goalscorer, but he never really became a cult hero - simply because he was so good and so professional. On the other hand Henrik Larsson, by some distance in my view the best player that Celtic have had in recent decades, did become a cult hero with masks of his features, Swedish flags and dreadlocks visible among the support, and songs sung in his honour - "You are my Larsson, my Henrik Larsson" - among many others. In short, it is the supporters who decide which players become a Cult Hero. It is we, the fans, who place these players on a pedestal and change them from mere mortals into Gods.

Sometimes cult heroes disappoint and let the fans down. Pat Crerand and Charlie Nicholas, for example, both arrived at the club with impeccable Celtic credentials, played brilliantly for the club for a time, but then departed in a way which reflected little credit on anyone and took their talent elsewhere. The effect of their departure devastated and drained the support as disorientated youngsters tried to make sense of it all, and wondered why anyone would, in any circumstances, ever turn their back on Celtic.

Yet the brand mark is always there. Charlie Nicholas, so vilified and hated after his departure in 1983, was working for *Sky Sports* more than 20 years later. Celtic had just scored a vital European goal, and Charlie was caught off camera (as he thought) going bananas with joy. *Sky Sports* then played it back to the public hoping, presumably, to embarrass Charlie, who should, like all good sports commentators, have been unbiased (some hope!). In fact it went a great way to redeeming Charlie in the eyes of Celtic fans, and even perhaps to earn him a degree of forgiveness.

Some Cult Heroes are obvious ones. The three Jimmies - Johnstone, McGrory and Quinn - were the deserved heroes of successive generations. How nice it would have been to have been born in 1890 and to have died in 1980 and thus have been able to enjoy all three of them! But other less obvious heroes are included. Joe Cassidy, Bertie Thomson, Peter Wilson and Malky MacDonald are less talked about these days as the generations which saw them play begin to dwindle, but as they were much loved in their time, it is only right that those of you too young to have seen them should nevertheless have the opportunity to hear about them and to read of their exploits in the days when they wore the green.

The only current Celt among the 20 is Shunsuke Nakamura, the man of the free-kicks and the oriental wizardry who has charmed the hearts of the Celtic faithful, particularly the maternal ladies in the support who love his apparent vulnerability as well as his brilliant play. He, too, has changed the Celtic support in that Japanese flags can be seen among the crowd when he is playing, and he is clearly responsible for the large amount of young Oriental boys and girls who now appear adorned in the green-and-white, and thus lending even more credence to founding father Willie Maley's much quoted dictum that "It is not his creed or his nationality that counts, but the man himself".

A high proportion of those selected are centre-forwards and goalscorers. This is hardly surprising in the context of this club, whose supporters absolutely crave those moments of ecstasy when the back of the net balloons and another celebration begins. Sandy McMahon possible started this love affair with goalscoring in the 1890s, but others have carried on the tradition. Quinn, McGrory and Larsson have already been mentioned, but there is also, for the fifty-something generation, Dixie Deans, whose hat-trick in the 1972 Scottish Cup final has perhaps even been overtaken in supporters' memory by his somersault of rapture on that same occasion.

There are also one or two bad bhoys in the collection. Dan Doyle, for example, more than once went AWOL, yet remained a much loved and revered figure. Then there was the man who could have been the greatest Celt of them all, Tommy McInally, who brightened up the 1920s for a spell, but was finally laid low by his own follies, which were self-destructive in nature and freely admitted to by the loveable rogue that Tommy was.

Great commanding figures are also well represented. Sunny Jim Young, Jock Stein and Roy Aitken all had their moments of captaining the team, and in Stein's case also becoming a legendary manager. John Hughes remains an enigma. He was much discussed and argued about by the supporters in his day, for he could be infuriating and inspiring in equal measure and within minutes, love and admiration could become anger and bewilderment. Charlie Tully could do likewise. "Cheeky Charlie's capers" had often to be balanced with Tully's tantrums.

Not everyone will agree with my choice of 20, but no matter who your own particular Cult Hero or whenever your own halcyon days as a Celtic fan were, there will be someone for you to remember fondly in this book and also players to learn of anew. I have tried to pick heroes who animated and excited the support in their own time. I have also tried to give some sort of indication of what the love of the Celtic has meant and will continue to mean for the 60,000 who turn up on match day, proud to wear the colours and to be identified with what for us remains the greatest show on earth.

David Potter
December 2007

Dedication

To all my wonderful family, in this world and the next,
and not least to my grandson, little Callum Weir, who has
suffered terribly through illness, but has fought back with
all the tenacity of a true Celt.

DAN DOYLE

'NED'

1891-1899

BHOYS CAREER

Games	133
Goals	6
Caps	8

MAGIC MOMENT

Having an outstanding game in the 1892 Scottish Cup final when Celtic won the trophy for the first time, leading to prolonged street parties in the poverty stricken East End.

'In the wild rover that was Dan Doyle, the Celtic faithful had a man who was the embodiment of their own hopes of rising above the mundane whilst remaining independent of soul.'

Marie Rowan

DAN Doyle was one of those who created Glasgow Celtic as a great football team. It was because of personality players like Doyle that Celtic did not go the way of so many other clubs which started in the 1880s and 1890s. Celtic did not disappear. The fact that Celtic stayed was, of course, due to good management and the undeniable fact that they had a huge captive audience in the Glasgow Irish, but also because they had players like Dan Doyle.

Tall, handsome, curly-haired, Dan was an immediate hit with the Celtic fans, and very soon he became a cult player, associated with so much spectacular success. It is often said that crowds, particularly Celtic crowds, love a small player like Patsy Gallacher or Jimmy Johnstone with whom they can identify as being the underdog, just like they perceived (and possibly still do in some cases) themselves to be against the wicked, powerful bully, referee or landlord. But they also love to identify with someone who has clearly "made it", who has got a lot going for him, who is clean-cut, tall, handsome and well dressed in the image of Willie Maley or Billy McNeill. An early example of this role model was Dan Doyle.

Dan was born in Paisley on 16 September 1864 and played for many teams, some of them with quaint names like Slamannan Barnsmuir and Broxburn Shamrock (as well as a more familiar one called East Stirlingshire) before he joined Hibs for a spell. In fact he played for Hibs in the first game to be played at Old Celtic Park on 8 May 1888 against Cowlairs. He tried his luck in England (where professionalism was legalised) with Newcastle East End, Grimsby Town and Bolton Wanderers before this happy mercenary arrived at Goodison Park to play for Everton in August 1889.

While he was with Grimsby, he was involved in a tragic incident which plagued him the rest of his life. It was a total accident, but it did give some indication of the strength that he had. It was 12 January 1889 when Grimsby were playing against Staveley, who featured a player called William Cropper, better known as a cricketer with Derbyshire. He and Doyle went for a ball together and Cropper was unfortunate enough to receive the full impact of Doyle's knee in his stomach. Cropper was carried off unconscious and was diagnosed to have a ruptured bowel. In those days before preventive measures could be taken routinely, infection set in so quickly that he died the following day, still in the dressing room, the medical authorities having not deemed it wise to move him to an infirmary.

Doyle was blameless in this incident, and no charge was brought against him. Indeed, there had been a certain amount of dither and delay on the part of the medical services, which was probably more responsible for the death than anything else, but those who did not like

Doyle were not likely to allow him to forget it, in the same way that there were those who shouted "Killer" and "Murderer" at Sam English for his part in the accidental death of John Thomson in 1931. It was probably because of this that Dan was keen to move on to Everton, although there was also the undeniable fact that Everton paid more!

IT WAS WITH EVERTON that Doyle made his name, attracting a great deal of attention in both the English and the Scottish press when Everton won the English League championship in 1891, wresting it from "Proud Preston" who had won it for the previous two years. Everton were a great club and played good football. They had a large support, mainly Irish immigrants, and identified with this flamboyant Scotsman with Irish connections. He was called "Scottie" Doyle, and his presence in the Everton defence was a mighty one.

But happy though he was with Everton, he hankered after a return to Scotland, particularly when feelers were put out to him by this new Glasgow Irish club who seemed so ambitious and contained fine players like Willie Maley and James Kelly. But the problem was that Celtic were, theoretically at least, an amateur team and could not be seen to pay him. Doyle would make out that he was homesick and wanted to return to Scotland, but there seems little doubt that the perspicacious John Glass and other Celtic founding fathers were prepared to break laws in order to attract Dan Doyle.

Willie Maley would later admit that Celtic were far from an amateur club even before professionalism was officially recognised in Scotland in 1893. Maley would justify this by stressing the charitable origins of the club and declaring: "Charity covereth a multitude of sins". Even when Doyle came to Glasgow in 1891, newspapers like the Scottish Referee were asking pointedly: "How can an amateur club like Celtic outbid a very wealthy professional club in Everton?" According to that magazine: "It is easier to comprehend the weaving of one of Mr Gladstone's speeches" (a reference to the increasingly senile octogenarian politician) "than to find out how this was done, for it has imposed too great a strain on our credulity".

With Doyle now in Glasgow, Everton were furious, threatening legal action for breach of contract, offering him £5 and the managership of a public house in Liverpool. But Celtic had already trumped that one, for they had installed him in his own public house. This was always a successful way of attracting a footballer in Victorian Britain, for there was a great deal of money (as always) to be made in drink, particularly when patrons were very happy to spend money just to see Dan, or "Ned" as he quickly became known, behind the bar in his hostelry in Airdrie. Everton made one last attempt to lure him back. A director appeared in Dan's pub one day and asked him to name his price. "The Mersey Docks" was the answer! In the meantime, the English club's legal action came to nothing, for it was clear that Dan was at last where he really wanted to be.

On the field, Doyle was an instant success. Season 1891/92 saw Celtic win three Cups – the Scottish Cup, the Glasgow Cup and the Glasgow Charity Cup – and had it not been for a reverse on the opening day of the season to Hearts and a crucial 0-1 defeat to the eventual champions Dumbarton towards the end of April, then the League would have been won as well. Doyle settled into this team instantly, turning out to be all that a left-back could be expected to be. He was a strong tackler, and good kicker (meaning he could clear the ball accurately) and he was also a fine taker of free-kicks. He was the first of the attacking full-backs for which Celtic would later become famous and, very importantly for Victorian football, he was a good "charger".

This meant that he was not easily bundled off the ball, and for his part, he was able to send an opponent into touch. This was, of course, legal in the 1890s as long as it was done by the shoulder and not by the elbow. Dan could certainly look after himself, and it was soon clear that opponents would treat him with a great deal of respect. The reputation that he had acquired in England had gone before him.

SPRING 1892 WAS A heady time for Celtic and for Doyle. With the Glasgow Cup won in a 7-1 thrashing of Clyde the previous December, the scent of victory was in the nostrils of the club, and the phenomenally large following was in a perpetual state of excitement and euphoria, especially with the added thrill of the new stadium being built to the south east of the original one. On the playing side everyone was talking about Sandy McMahon, Willie Maley or James Kelly. But the hero of them all was Dan Doyle.

On 6 February 1892 Celtic beat Rangers 5-2 to reach the Scottish Cup final for the second time in four years of history. Their opponents were Queen's Park on 12 March, but the game had to be abandoned and played out as a friendly because of the huge Celtic crowd turning up at Ibrox and catching the authorities by surprise. But Celtic's joy would only be delayed.

But before the Scottish Cup final could be played again on 9 April, there were at least two other big events in Doyle's life. One was the planting of shamrocks at the still uncompleted New Celtic Park by the famous Irish patriot Michael Davitt on 19 March, before everyone went across to Old Celtic Park to watch Celtic draw with Clyde, and the other was Doyle's selection to play for Scotland against England at Ibrox on 2 April.

It was Doyle's first full cap, but it was a sad disappointment as Scotland went down 1-4 to a very strong England side. Ibrox was a very exposed ground in these days, and this game, like many others, was spoiled by the strong wind. It was also windy at the same ground the following week, but this time it was a far happier occasion for Doyle, as Celtic lifted the Scottish Cup for the first time in their history. The enthusiasm of the Celtic fans surprised the watching journalists, but it was nothing to the ecstasy which prevailed in the underprivileged East End for days afterwards as Doyle and company brought home the Scottish Cup. The barefooted urchins stood to get a glimpse of the horse-drawn charabanc containing mighty men like Dan Doyle, who had done so much to make their life worth living. When Doyle raised his hand to acknowledge the cheers, it was as if he were a conquering hero from Waterloo or Crimea.

And it hadn't finished there, for Celtic then went on to win the Glasgow Charity Cup as well, beating Rangers 2-0 in the final held on the somewhat late date of the first day of June. Thus Doyle's first season ended with three medals to be shown off to patrons of his public house, and there could not have been the slightest doubt that he had made the right decision in coming north. But it was no greater a decision than that of Celtic, who had enticed Doyle back to Scotland.

He was a well-known personality in Victorian Glasgow. Being the hero of the ethnic minority was one aspect of him, but he was also well respected by others who were not of the same persuasion. The 1890s was the first decade of the almost total domination of football over any other aspect of life, and players were recognised and pointed out in the street.

Dan's full-back partner Jerry Reynolds was similarly famous, and the phrase "Reynolds and Doyle" became as much a catchphrase as "Gilbert and Sullivan", the writers of Victorian opera.

Naturally Doyle, being such a clean-cut, handsome man, was good copy for newspapers and was much admired by women. Media coverage was nothing like what it would become 100 years later in the Beckham era, but it was substantial nevertheless, and gossip was not slow to attach stories, apocryphal or otherwise, to the name of Dan Doyle. The frequent trips made by Celtic to England merely added to his reputation. Like many a Scotsman in England, his behaviour off the field was not always a credit to Scotland, but this did little to take away his "tourist attraction".

The story is told about the time when he was sitting with the rest of the Celtic team in a posh London hotel the night before a friendly game with one of the local teams. Always elegantly dressed, Dan was puffing a cigar, and suddenly he put one of his legs on a table to display a multi-coloured sock. This naturally attracted some attention to him – Victorian London sometimes despised ostentation, but at other times was attracted by it. Dan then said that it was the only sock of its kind in all London: "I bet you can't find another like it!" A wager of £10 (a huge amount in the 1890s) was then struck between Dan and a punter that another like it couldn't be found. The bet struck, the punter, a wide guy, said that he could find another, and that it would be on Doyle's other foot. Dan calmly lifted up his trouser leg to reveal a simple black sock. The man had been fooled and was compelled to cough up the £10.

Whether this story is true or not, nobody will know, but Doyle was famous enough to have it attached to him as the reputation of the Celtic team continued to grow apace with his own. In 1893, Celtic won the Scottish League championship for the first time. Their successes included impressive victories over Dumbarton, Hearts, Third Lanark and Rangers, and the press talked grandiloquently about "Dandy Dan" or "Dynamite Doyle". He won his second Scottish cap that year in an 8-0 win over Wales at Wrexham, and he might have expected to be given a game against England at Richmond. But his place went to a Queen's Park man with the unlikely name of Robert Smellie. If he was disappointed, he did not show it and, indeed, the folly of Scotland not playing their best full-back was shown in the 2-5 scoreline.

There was one other major disappointment in 1893 for Doyle and Celtic and that was the failure to retain the Scottish Cup. Queen's Park gained a little revenge for the previous year's defeat in the final, but Celtic were sore about what happened. The wind was dreadful (again), Queen's Park indulged in questionable tactics which caused many injuries to Celtic players, not least to Willie Maley, who lost a few teeth in the game. To crown it all, Dan Doyle conceded what looked to all the spectators like a corner, but the Queen's Park players were convinced that the ball had passed on the other side of the post (there were no goal nets in 1893). One of them said to the referee: "It's a goal, Mr.Harrison", and the goal was given! Then in the last part of the game, when Celtic had pulled a goal back from Jimmy Blessington, and Dan Doyle was committed to the attack, Queen's Park persisted in kicking the ball out of play, in spite of protests from the crowd who had paid to watch some football. Willie Maley, however, in his series of articles that he wrote for the *Weekly News* in 1936, singled out the "immense courage" of Doyle in what was "a forlorn hope" as "(Doyle) inspired the rest of us to put up a glorious fight right to the end."

But Dan had one major success that season, and that was in the Charity Cup final against Rangers when Celtic beat them 5-0, thus avenging their defeat in the Glasgow Cup final in February. Doyle played right-back that day, but it mattered little for he could play equally well on either side, and it was he who orchestrated the massive victory with his runs down the wing and long, accurate crosses which "perpetually brought applause and approbation" from the crowd. The game itself was remarkable for the 5-0 scoreline at half-time, followed by a second half in which Celtic toyed with their opponents without adding to the score. Indeed, it was the opinion of many that the referee shortened the second half, for Celtic had no real desire to score any more goals, and the supporters were beginning to sing, a clear sign that boredom was setting in. Perhaps the song being sung was the Doyle adaptation of the Music Hall favourite *Clementine*:

Oh my darling, oh my darling, oh my darling Danny Doyle
How I love that football champion, my darling Danny Doyle!

The honours were similarly distributed in the 1893/94 season, with Celtic once again proving their consistency by winning the League and the Glasgow Charity Cup, but falling a little short in the Glasgow Cup and the most prestigious trophy of all, the Scottish Cup. The League was won very comfortably in spite of a 0-5 defeat from Rangers in September on Doyle's first day back from injury. After that reverse Celtic, inspired by Doyle, did not lose again until after the League had been comfortably won. The Scottish Cup saw Rangers' first success in that tournament. It was a wet, slippery day at Hampden Park, and Rangers were quite simply the better team, and although Celtic would get their revenge the following week in a League match, this defeat hurt especially as the Cup had been lost for two years in a row to different Glasgow teams.

However, Doyle was given a great honour on 7 April 1894 when he was invited to captain Scotland against England. It was strange that he was asked to skipper the international side, for he had only captained Celtic on the rare occasion when James Kelly was not playing, but perhaps the fact that the game was being played at the new, smartly completed Celtic Park had a great deal to do with it. Indeed Celtic Park presented a wonderful sight that bright but breezy afternoon with 45,000 there to see Scotland, led by the redoubtable Dan Doyle, take on England. For 1894, 45,000 was a phenomenal crowd, quite clearly a world record, and even the well-built Celtic Park could not contain all the spectators, some of whom spilled on to the cycle track round the field of play.

Scotland played very well. Their forwards missed a few chances, but even so they were well pleased with themselves to be leading 2-1 as the game entered its final stages, with only an inspired performance by Leslie Gay of Old Brightonians in the England goal preventing the hosts going further ahead. Dan would have been imagining himself as the first Scottish captain to beat England since his old rival Bob Smellie of Queen's Park did it in 1889, but then disaster struck in the final minute, when John Reynolds of Aston Villa shot through a ruck of players and beat the unsighted Davie Haddow of Rangers in the goal. The 45,000 were stunned into silence, and Doyle and the rest of his team were shattered. It cannot have been easy for Dan to call for the traditional three cheers for England that night.

Strange goings-on occurred, however, the following year when Scotland went to England to play at Goodison Park. Doyle travelled down to Liverpool on the Friday with the rest of the party, but suddenly disappeared. He had, of course, played for Everton four years previously and it was assumed that he was visiting an old acquaintance. The "old acquaintance" may or may not have been a member of the opposite sex, but certainly Doyle failed to reappear at the team's hotel on the Friday night.

In the morning the selectors had little option. Although aware that Doyle's absence might cause a riot among the many Scottish fans who had travelled down, but nevertheless seriously concerned for his whereabouts and dabbling with the idea of contacting the police on the grounds that he may have been kidnapped by some criminals or anarchists, they asked reserve Bob Foyers of St Bernards to take over at left-back and appointed Jimmy Oswald of the same team as captain.

Then suddenly Doyle reappeared, apparently none the worse for his disappearance, which he was remarkably shy about discussing. The instant reaction of the selectors was to keep him out of the team because of his irresponsible behaviour, but then they realised that he was such a big name, and such a great player, that the cause of Scotland would be much diminished without Dan. Foyers was accordingly told that he would not be required after all, although Oswald remained the captain.

Clearly it was the wrong decision. Doyle had a shocker of a game, playing very badly (and such a good player having an off-day did matter) as Scotland went down 0-3. He and Neil Gibson were involved in a dreadful mix up which led to an own goal, and the Scotland forwards, missing Doyle's long passing, never really got themselves into the game.

Rightly or wrongly, Doyle was held responsible by the nation for this fiasco, and it would be another two years before he was invited to don the Scotland jersey again. The 1894/95 campaign had been a bad year for Celtic, certainly the worst of their seven-year history, and there had been clear indications of player unrest. Some of this had been caused by Doyle who was often seen as the leader for discontented factions who resented the incompetences of the often inept committee; at other times, there was the feeling that Doyle was a prima donna, and that he was no great team man.

For whatever reason, that term Celtic lost the Scottish League to Hearts, and departed anonymously from the Scottish Cup in the early rounds. They did win the two Glasgow tournaments, but that was scant consolation for the large and unhappy support. Yet Dan, for all his faults, remained a personality figure, attracting crowds wherever he went. Celtic went to Kirkcaldy, for example, one Friday night in late May to play a friendly, and there were reports of traffic congestion as fans in horse-drawn carriages made their way to Stark's Park, hoping to see the "bould Celts" and such cult heroes as Sandy McMahon and the great Dan Doyle. Doyle knew how to milk this hero worship, clearly revelling in the adulation and making a point of talking to supporters, particularly the youngsters. The local newspaper refers simply to "Dan".

Like many Victorian footballers, he also played other sports – bowls, quoits, cricket, athletics and billiards. He was a superb athlete with broad shoulders, flat chest and long legs, very fast, supple and lithe, and he had the common sense to realise that although he could occasionally indulge in some of the earthly pleasures, the necessity to keep fit was paramount. Professionalism meant that he simply had to keep fit, for all the opponents that he faced were at least as fit as he was. They may have lacked some of the ability that Doyle possessed, but they were all as athletic. There really was no excuse for someone not being fit. Doyle, now into his thirties, realised that he would have to work all the harder. Yet, having his own public house in Airdrie, the temptation was there.

The 1895/96 season was a better one for Celtic, who won three out of a possible four trophies. Doyle had been injured in the early part of the season but was fully fit by the end of September (interestingly the three games that Celtic lost were all when Doyle was out) and he took part in the record 11-0 thrashing of Dundee in October, a 7-0 beating of Third Lanark in November and a 6-2 win over Rangers in December, by which time the League championship was virtually won.

Queen's Park had also been put to the sword 6-3 in the Glasgow Cup final, and would also bow the knee in the Charity Cup final at the end of the season, but the one discordant note of an otherwise fine campaign was when Queen's Park removed Celtic from the Scottish Cup at the first time of asking. Doyle did score that day on a difficult pitch at Parkhead in wintry conditions, but Celtic went down 4-2 to the amateurs.

This would have caused deep disappointment to Doyle, but no more than his failure to get back into the Scotland team, especially as the "big" international against England was once again to be played at Celtic Park. But the events of the previous year had not been forgotten or forgiven, and Doyle was not included in the Scotland team for any of the three Internationals that year, even though he was given a game for the Scottish League against both the English and the Irish Leagues.

It was the following season which saw the biggest mystery of Dan Doyle. It was 9 January 1897, the date of Celtic's infamous defeat at Arthurlie in the Scottish Cup – the biggest act of giantkilling in Scottish football history until the demise of Rangers at Berwick in 1967– and one of the reasons was that Dan Doyle did not turn up. Why he didn't, no-one can say. Reports at the time mentioned a great deal of "stuff going on" before the turn of the year, with a players' strike – three men withdrew their labour because of heavy press criticism – and a bad run of form in December. One game in particular, against Rangers, seemed to indicate that certain players were simply not trying, but whether this was connected with Doyle's non-appearance is not clear.

It may be that Dan, sensing the vulnerability of the team and also aware that his own playing career was approaching its twilight, now that he was well into his thirties, chose this moment to turn petulant with a request for more money. If this was so, it reflects very badly on him, but there may have been other reasons. Perhaps Doyle was ill, he may have "hit the bottle", perhaps he became lucky with a young lady; but for whatever reason, Doyle simply did not appear. Annoyingly, Willie Maley, who certainly would have known the reason, remained very reticent about Doyle's non-appearance.

That absence was crucial and the team went down to a defeat which would haunt them for many decades. Even more surprising about this whole affair was his almost immediate restitution to favour. He was fined £5, but then played for Celtic for the rest of the season. And 1897 did see his return to international duty, and this time, Dan was on the winning side. This was a famous occasion at the Crystal Palace when Scotland beat England 2-1, their first win on English soil for eight years. "Lambie (of Queen's Park) captained the side, but Doyle bossed it" was the comment in one newspaper, and there was no doubt that Doyle's presence was a hugely positive factor for the Scots, as he played a large part in the build-up to the goals scored by the Rangers pair of Jimmy Millar and Tommy Hyslop.

The Arthurlie disaster of 1897 was the catalyst for a seismic change in the structure of management at Celtic Park. The old committee system of picking a team was abolished and Willie Maley effectively became manager. Willie was, of course, an old team mate of Dan, holding him in great respect and friendship, but he was not blind to the left-back's faults. One presumes that there was a clear-the-air meeting between the two of them, because for a spell Doyle's form and attitude showed a marked inmprovement. Anno Domini however was beginning to catch up on Dan.

IN 1897/98 CELTIC regained the Scottish League crown, this time without losing a game, but their knockout campaigns were all failures. As luck would have it, the team were back at Arthurlie in the Scottish Cup. This time Doyle was there in all his glory and Celtic thumped the hapless amateurs 7-0, only to go down to Third Lanark in the next round. The feature of the season, however, was the emergence of Rangers as a strong force. They won the Scottish Cup and also beat Celtic in the final of the Glasgow Cup after a prolonged struggle.

At international level that season, Doyle played twice. Once was against Ireland in a 3-0 canter in Belfast at the ground with the unlikely name of Solitude, but then Dan suffered the personal disaster which brought his career to a close. Some 70,000 were at Celtic Park to see the Scotland v. England game, the ground having had to undergo several changes to accommodate the huge crowd. Scotland had gone two goals down, but pulled one back and looked as if they might go on to equalise, until Doyle made a gross mistake with a pass which was directed into the path of the great Steve Bloomer, who put England 3-1 up.

It was, of course, an honest mistake, the sort of error that any professional will make once or twice in his career, but the unsympathetic crowd turned on Doyle. Dan was distraught, and the unfortunate name of the England forward (Steve Bloomer went on to become one of their most famous forwards of all time) meant that Glasgow talked about Doyle's "bloomers" for a long time.

Crowds can be fickle, and heroes can be fragile and prickly. Doyle never played again for Scotland and, indeed, played only sporadically for Celtic in the next season, 1898/99, before disappearing from the game altogether. In truth, Celtic had unearthed another fine full-back in Davie Storrier from Arbroath, and with John Welford and Barney Battles around, Celtic were not short of flank defenders. Noticeably, in the Scottish Cup triumph of 1899, Doyle does not feature.

Dan's later years (like those of many footballers) were far from happy. He now owned two drinking shops in Bellshill, but they both came to grief – he was his own best customer, the cruel ones said – and he had to take a labouring job. Even that didn't last long. Alex James, the famous Raith Rovers, Preston North End and Arsenal forward, who hailed from Bellshill affirmed: "Dan didn't keep his pubs many years. He started on the bottle himself and the inevitable end came. There's a story told of Dan that, some years later, after his collapse, he was wandering about the East End of Glasgow – down and out – picking up a drink here and there on the side. He was in a bar one day when the man who was standing the drinks dropped a coin from his change on to the floor among the sawdust and got down to scratch in the dust for it. Dan, noticing the searching, said 'Whit are ye lookin' for, Willie?' Said Willie: 'I've lost a thrupenny bit amang the sawdust, Dan' Said Dan: 'A widnae worry owe much aboot it, Willie, a've lost twa pubs, sawdust an a', an' it's no botherin' me noo!'"

Towards the end of the First World War, Dan, having suffered serious ill health for some time, contracted cancer and died on 8 April 1918 at the age of 53, just at the time when it began to appear that Germany might yet win the war with the success of Ludendorff's spring offensive, which broke the Allied line at several points. Willie Maley, still the manager of Celtic, was summoned to attend Dan's bedside.

Although Maley, with his love of romance and maudlin obsession with death, tells the story of Doyle on his deathbed rolling back the bedclothes and showing the legs that had done so much for Celtic – this story must be treated with extreme scepticism, for it is told of other players as well! – the truth is that Doyle, great player though he was, might have achieved an awful lot more had it not been for the fatal Scottish and Irish trait of self-destruction. Yet four Scottish League medals, one Scottish Cup medal and eight caps for Scotland is hardly a failure.

What he did do, however, was to give the under-achieving ethnic minority that the Glasgow Irish certainly were in the 1890s something to be proud about. He was a role model with his good looks, curly hair, straight back and heavy shoulders. Like many role models, he occasionally fell from grace, but all that proved was that he was mortal, and therefore fallible. In terms of Celtic history, however, Dan "Ned" Doyle must surely be listed as one of the immortals.

SANDY MCMAHON

'THE DUKE'

1890-1903

BHOYS CAREER

Games	217
Goals	171
Caps	6

MAGIC MOMENT

Scoring two goals in Celtic's 5-2 victory in the first Scottish Cup win in 1892 - one when he walked through the defence and the other in the final minute when he "rose like a bird" to head home a corner kick.

'Sandy McMahon was one of the club's earliest stars and certainly one of its brightest, and was regarded as the most marvellous header of the ball of the period.'

Willie Maley

IT is true that Willie Maley was the "Man Who Made Celtic", but Maley was lucky in that he had around him an abundance of men who helped him in the beginning of this awesome tradition. James Kelly was a fine defender, for example, and John Glass was a great administrator off the field, but the man who was most responsible for the launching of Celtic as an attacking force, playing the game as it was meant to be played and scoring plenty of goals was Celtic's first famous marksman – Sandy McMahon.

Celtic have always been famous for their goalscoring abilities – and great Celtic teams have always been blessed with great goalscorers. Three super-heroes immediately spring to mind in Jimmy Quinn, Jimmy McGrory and Henrik Larsson. There are others like Jimmy "Sniper" McColl, Joe Cassidy, the McPhail brothers, Dixie Deans and (possibly) Scott McDonald, but the man who started it all was Sandy McMahon.

Yet Sandy does not fit the popular image of a prolific sharpshooter. Photographs show a moustachioed, magisterial Victorian gentleman with a kindly but perhaps boring expression, not at all the aggressive, competitive demeanour of other strikers of that (or indeed any) age. But appearances are deceptive. Rather like Clement Attlee, the unlikely-looking Labour Prime Minister who was responsible for the social revolution of the late 1940s, what one saw was not necessarily what one got.

NOT A GREAT DEAL is known of Sandy's life outside football. Tradition has it that he was born in Selkirk in 1871, but the exact day of his birth has been hard to trace. On the other hand there was an Alexander McMahon born in Dundee in 1871, the son of the licensees of a tavern. Is this perhaps our Sandy? Certainly the Irish had arrived in strength in Dundee throughout the 1850s and 1860s, and there are a few local indications in Dundee and Angus folklore that Sandy might have sprung from that source.

It matters little. He played his early football in the late 1880s in Edinburgh for teams like Harp Juveniles, Woodburn, Leith Harp and the great Hibernian football club themselves. Hibernian were, of course, the natural club to which the young Sandy would have gravitated. Avowedly and even exclusively Irish, the Hibernian team won the Scottish Cup in 1887 to the great joy of the large Irish community. The only problem with that (as far as Hibernian were concerned) was that it planted a seed among Irishmen in Glasgow that they, too, could form an Irish team, one that would supplant and take over from the Edinburgh Hibs. This one would be called the Celtic.

Sandy had been with Hibernian – indeed, he had been a reserve in their Scottish Cup victory in February 1887 – then moved for a brief and unhappy time to a team called Darlington St.Augustine's, before returning to Edinburgh in September 1888. He played for Hibernian for two years but then in December 1890 he joined Celtic. Hibs were at that time imploding as a result of the rise of this new Irish team in Glasgow, and they also had major difficulties with their ground. Legally, there was no problem about McMahon jumping ship like this without any indication of a transfer fee because Scottish football until 1893 was, at least in theory, amateur.

It does, however, stretch our belief more than somewhat to say that McMahon received no money from this young and ambitious Glasgow team. Money would indeed have been a strong factor, but as potent a pull, one would imagine, would have been the clear indications that this Celtic side, which from the start and (unlike Hibernian) would welcome Catholics and Protestants alike, were the one that was going to win trophies. Indeed, they had already been in the Scottish Cup final in 1889.

His debut was in a friendly against Dumbarton at Old Celtic Park on New Year's Day 1891. Dumbarton had beaten Celtic ten days previously to put them out of the Scottish Cup, and would go on to share the Scottish League that season with Rangers, but on this day they were held to a 1-1 draw. The Glasgow Observer newspaper, sometimes called the "Catholic Observer" and with no real claims to objectivity as far as Celtic were concerned even in the early days, was satisfied with the draw but described McMahon in curious terms: "Arms held high, spread out like ostrich wings, head down, back slightly bent forward, enormous feet". It is from such slender indications of brilliance that a mighty career was to be launched.

Sandy's competitive debut for Celtic was against Vale of Leven in Alexandria, near Dumbarton, on 24 January 1891. Sandy may or may not have been a professional, in theory or in practice, but the general amateurishness of Celtic's approach in the early days is evidenced by the fact that a player missed his train and Celtic had no reserves available. So Sandy actually had to play left-back until the man arrived! The team lost 1-3, thereby losing what little chance they had of landing the League championship in 1891.

McMahon did not play in the club's big success that season, namely the winning of the prestigious Glasgow Cup, but he did play sporadically at first and later regularly for the team, hitting the highlights on 5 May with four goals in a spectacular 9-1 drubbing of Vale of Leven at Old Celtic Park. He was now settled at inside-left and could interchange brilliantly with Johnny Campbell on the left wing. The passing game was, of course, the trademark of Scottish football, and he had an almost telepathic understanding with Campbell. But he was also noted for his individual play, and the coming season of 1891/92 was to indicate the arrival of Celtic's first superstar. It would also be the first great year in the history of the club.

Celtic retained the Glasgow Cup in December and this time Sandy won a medal, scoring a goal in a 7-1 thrashing of Clyde at Cathkin, and by the turn of the year the team was going well in both the Scottish League and the Scottish Cup, with the crowd beginning to appreciate the inspired play of McMahon. In the Scottish Cup Cowlairs fell in the quarter-final and Rangers in the semi, with McMahon's name on the scoresheet on both occasions. The Scottish Cup final was at Ibrox on 12 March against Queen's Park, but although Celtic won 1-0, the game was declared a friendly, such were the chaotic conditions with the huge crowd. The cause? Principally the widespread enthusiasm to see the now-famous left wing combination of McMahon and Campbell.

Not only were the Celtic fans impressed by Sandy, so too were the Scotland selectors, and he found himself in his country's team on 2 April at Ibrox. It was a sad day, however, for both Scotland and McMahon, as they were engulfed 1-4 by a strong England team. Sandy never got going, but as he left Ibrox that night, he knew he would be back a week later for what he hoped would be a happier occasion. This would be the replay of the Scottish Cup final.

We all know, don't we, that the first hat-trick to be scored in a Scottish Cup final was by Jimmy Quinn in 1904, a feat emulated by Dixie Deans in 1972? But was Jimmy's truly the first? A certain amount of evidence came to light recently to indicate that perhaps it was Sandy McMahon in 1892 who scored the first Scottish Cup final hat-trick. It is, of course, the task of the historian to evaluate evidence and to make up his mind on what is in front of him.

The disturbing (if that is the right word) evidence comes in the shape of The Scotsman's report of the 1892 Scottish Cup final. The game against Queen's Park was played (after the first encounter had been declared void because of overcrowding and crowd encroachment) on 9 April 1892 and Celtic won 5-1. The edition of The Scotsman concerned is that of Monday 11 April 1892, clearly written (anonymously in the style of Victorian journalism) a matter of hours after the final whistle.

The key goal is the first one. Willie Maley, who played in the game, and all orthodox Celtic historians give this to Johnny Campbell. It was the goal which levelled the scores, as Celtic played with the wind which was blowing towards the west goal at Ibrox (i.e. towards what is now called the Broomloan Road Stand or the "Celtic End" of Ibrox). The Scotsman had this to say: "The Irishmen's (sic) efforts were at length rewarded, as after some smart play in front of the goal, McMahon with a wonderful overhead shot, put through the first goal for his team".

The scribe of The Scotsman then comments on the "outburst of enthusiasm from the Parkhead club's followers" and after a short period the second goal "was put through for the Celtic from the left wing". Curiously, he does not mention who scored it other than obliquely, but the "left wing" presumably means that Johnny Campbell scored it.

Then comes the third goal. Having praised Dan Doyle, who was "simply unpassable", the reporter says: "McMahon (was) playing up in surprising fashion, and through his instrumentality, Baird was beaten for the third time". This is the goal which Maley describes thus: "McMahon, indulging in one of those mazy runs – head down, arms outstretched – simply walked through the Amateurs' defence to register the third goal". No doubt about that one – it was Sandy McMahon who scored it and "the Celtic followers were now quite beside themselves with delight".

The fourth came from a deflection by a defender from a James Kelly free-kick, and then Sandy McMahon scored Celtic's fifth with a header from a corner. But was this Sandy's second or his third? Everyone seems to agree that Sandy scored numbers three and five, but is the writer of The Scotsman right in attributing the first goal to McMahon?

On balance, probably the historian will conclude that The Scotsman's reporter may have made a mistake, because the term "hat-trick" is not used in his summing up of McMahon's performance. Sandy is described as "showing astonishing dash and resource which marked him out as the best of the forward line". One would have expected "hat-trick" or even "three goals" to be mentioned.

What is certain, however, is that Scottish football was never the same again. The rejoicing in the East End of Glasgow that night was legendary. The Celtic had arrived. "Our Bhoys Have Won The Cup!" cried the urchins, the destitute and the ill-fed, as everyone swirled round the charabanc to the music of the bugles and the flutes, (Yes, flutes!) hoping to catch a glimpse of their heroes. Queen's Park, the team of the avowed amateur ethics, the middle class, the rich, the privileged, had been beaten in a Scottish Cup final. The talk of Scotland was now of men like James Kelly, "Dan" (Doyle, but now simply referred to as "Dan") and, of course, "Sandy" or "The Duke" after the French President Duc de Mac-Mahon, although some say that Sandy was being compared to The Iron Duke, the Duke of Wellington.

The impoverished Irish in Glasgow had been given a boost to their morale. They now had a standard around which they could rally. They could now hold their heads up when football was mentioned, and even if they had not previously been interested in this new thriving Scottish game, they certainly would become so now. Sneers about being Irish could now be counteracted by mention of Sandy McMahon.

But did McMahon score a hat-trick, the first ever in a Scottish Cup Final? Or did the type-setter of *The Scotsman* simply make a mistake with the first goal? Certainly, the writer was very definite that it was a "wonderful overhead shot". In some ways, one hopes that *The Scotsman* was right. It would certainly be no slur on Jimmy Quinn or Dixie Deans to compel them to share the same spot in the Celtic Valhalla as Sandy McMahon. And what a pity Jimmy McGrory and Henrik Larsson did not emulate that mighty feat as well! McGrory scored two in the 1931 replay, and Larsson two in 2001 and 2004. How many did McMahon score in 1892?

Of more concern in 1892 was whether Celtic could do the Grand Slam and win all four Scottish trophies. For a long time they were neck and neck with Dumbarton, but lost the crucial fixture at Boghead (soon to be called "fatal Boghead" because of the amount of times Celtic and Rangers lost there) on 23 April and the League slipped away to the Sons of the Rock. But Celtic lifted their third trophy of the season when they beat Rangers 2-0 in the Glasgow Charity Cup final on 1 June. Three trophies out of four is not bad, and legend has it that a Celtic committee man, Ned McGinn, sent a telegram to the Vatican asking the Holy Father to light candles in St.Peter's. His Holiness apparently refused, although had he seen the brilliance of Sandy McMahon, the Glasgow wags said, he would have been hard pressed to refuse canonisation.

BUT THAT SAME SUMMER brought disturbing news of McMahon. He and Neil McCallum had apparently joined Nottingham Forest. Professionalism was, of course, legal in England, and McMahon was clearly neither the first nor the last to be "bought and sold for English gold". There then occurs one of the most famous stories in Celtic mythology, namely that a group of committee men spearheaded by the energetic John Glass hastened to the Midlands and persuaded Sandy to return home. Words like "kidnap" and "coup" have been used, and we are expected to believe that the still-amateur Celtic persuaded him back for no reason other than the love of the club.

Clearly we will never establish the entire truth of this matter, but some suggestion that Celtic (illegally) offered more money than Nottingham Forest did to the homesick Sandy, and that he accepted, would not appear to be entirely wrong. Yet it is an indication of the reputation and prestige of the man that we hear stories of tables being knocked down as the raiding party rushed to the station, of someone detaining the Forest delegates while Sandy escaped, and a great reception organised by Willie Maley back in Glasgow. Such stories could only accrue to the charisma of Sandy McMahon.

Maley, who both played with and managed Sandy, said that "of speed he had little", but such were his other attributes that this was hardly noticed. There were possibly three aspects to McMahon's greatness. One was his goalscoring ability with both feet and head, one was his dribbling (not for nothing was he called "The Prince of Dribblers") and the third was his telepathic understanding with left-wing partner Johnny Campbell.

Johnny was indeed lured away to England, to Aston Villa, for a couple of years (no adequate rescue operation having been arranged for him) and in his absence Sandy struggled for the want of an adequate partner, with 1897 proving a particularly low ebb in the club's short history. Campbell and McMahon, however, remained good friends to the extent that when McMahon married Annie Devine in May 1896, Campbell returned from England to do the honours as best man. The marriage, incidentally, took place on a Tuesday. On the previous Saturday, McMahon scored as Celtic beat Rangers 6-1 in the Glasgow Charity Cup semi final and on the following Saturday he scored again as they beat Queen's Park 2-1 in the final.

But before the departure of Campbell, the club had won the Scottish League in 1892/93 and 1893/94, also losing the Scottish Cup final in both those years. Sandy scored 11 goals in 13 League games in 1892/93 and ten in 15 in 1893/94. Twice he scored hat-tricks against Third Lanark and St Bernards, and the fans of the green-and-white vertical stripes (which Celtic wore until 1903) talked about little other than Sandy McMahon.

Celtic fans in the 1890s were small in number (but growing) and it would be some time before they extended their base beyond the East End of Glasgow. But McMahon's fame spread to other parts of Scotland as well and on 7 April 1894, it was Sandy who, on his own pitch at the recently built New Celtic Park, scored the goal that put Scotland ahead against England, only for their hopes to be cruelly denied in the last minute.

Football was a rough game in those days and Sandy, like many forwards, was prone to receive more than a little hacking from none-too-gentle opponents. He was out for a long time on several occasions, notably in the bad season of 1896/97 when Celtic finished trophyless for the first time in that decade. He was injured on 21 November 1896 as Celtic went down to Rangers in the final of the Glasgow Cup, and never reappeared that term. His supporters must have wondered whether he was finished. They might well have asked the same question about Celtic themselves. Of course, 9 January 1897 was the day that Celtic shocked Victorian Scotland by going down to Arthurlie in the Scottish Cup. It would have been hard to imagine that happening if Sandy had been on board.

McMahon's value to the Celtic cause was underlined in the 1897/98 season. The team swept all before them in the Scottish League. They were undefeated, they drew on three occasions and won against everyone else. This included a spectacular defeat of Rangers at Ibrox on the Monday September holiday, competent victories against other challengers like Hearts and Hibs, and there was a particular relish for Clyde, who were put to the sword 6-1 and 9-1. In all of this McMahon, playing at inside-left, was a goalmaker rather than a goalscorer, supplying the ammunition for George Allan, a Celtic centre-forward whom history has curiously undervalued. Johnny Campbell, too, had returned, and was now playing at inside-right to complete a prodigious inside trio.

But things came to a shuddering halt for Celtic in the Scottish Cup when they went down to Third Lanark in late January 1898, the significant factor being the absence through injury of McMahon, and the consequent necessity to rejig the forward line. Even at this early stage of the club's history, the Scottish Cup was considered a vital tournament. Celtic had exited two years in a row in January. On both occasions, McMahon was not playing.

All this was made good in the Scottish Cup of 1899 when Celtic beat Rangers 2-0 to lift the trophy for the second time. League form had not been good. Rangers now had a great side and went through the 1898/99 League season with a 100-per-cent record, and on both occasions that they beat Celtic, they put four goals past them. They had also defeated Celtic in the Glasgow Cup final in October, so the green-and-whites had little reason to approach the Scottish Cup final on 22 April with any degree of sanguinity. No team had ever as yet managed to win both the Scottish Cup and the Scottish League in the same season, but the smart money would have been on Rangers to do it that year.

But Celtic still had McMahon. He had scored in every round on the way to the final, including two in the quarter-final as Celtic edged past Queen's Park 2-1. In fact, he had also scored the previous week, but the game had had to be abandoned because of "bad light", although the cynics suspected that the light was good enough, whereas an abandonment would lead to another large gate – such was the desire to see the great Sandy McMahon, who was now talked about incessantly in the ale houses of Glasgow.

The final would be played at Second Hampden, a ground that would be called Cathkin Park when Third Lanark took it over. The Third Hampden Park would not be built until 1903, and it was probably the massive crowd at Second Hampden to see this Scottish Cup final in 1899 which persuaded Queen's Park that another stadium was necessary. Some 25,000 turned up – a huge crowd, and possibly a record for a game other than Scotland against England. One says "possibly" because crowd counting was not necessarily an exact science at the time, and it was estimated that 40,000 attended the 1892 Scottish Cup final at Ibrox, which had to be declared a friendly because of repeated crowd encroachment. In addition, there had been several claims that season that 35,000 or 40,000 had attended a game but "attendances", then as now, were often little other than the guess of a newspaper man.

This time the *Glasgow Herald* reported that the crowd was orderly and well behaved, and that although the weather was worthy of a Scottish Cup final, the standard of play was less so. Rangers had the better players (as their League form indicated) but Celtic's defenders marked their forwards tight. By no means as tight, however, as Rangers' notorious Nick Smith, whose coarse challenge severely disabled McMahon's left-wing partner, Jack Bell.

Half-time came with no score, then in the early part of the second period, the game swung decisively in favour of Celtic. Rangers had a goal chalked off, allowed themselves to be flustered about it, and Celtic took the initiative. They forced a corner, then for once McMahon eluded the eager attention of the two Rangers defenders detailed to mark him and rose "like a bird to meet the dispatch" and head home brilliantly. Celtic now took charge with McMahon on song, winning balls, dribbling and "passing to a degree of excellence". It was no surprise when Hodge added a second, although Rangers claimed offside.

The game finished with Celtic 2-0 ahead, and Rangers were sporting enough to admit that, on this occasion, their Glasgow rivals were worthy winners. Thus Celtic had won the Scottish Cup for the second time, and McMahon had earned himself another niche in the club's history for having scored a glorious header. Of course, Sandy had had a point to make as well. He had been dropped from the Scotland team after the draw in 1894, and had felt that he was good enough to regain the spot. In 1899, two weeks before the Scottish Cup final, Scotland had lost 1-2 to England at Villa Park. McMahon still felt that he could do a job for his country.

ANOTHER SCOTTISH CUP WOULD come Celtic and McMahon's way a season later. The year was 1900, and the new century was bringing in a new order to Scottish football. Rangers, having won the Scottish League in 1898/99, had done so again in 1899/1900 and were now quite clearly emerging as the rivals to Celtic. Rangers were never likely to take support away from Celtic, for Celtic's support was firmly anchored in the Glasgow Irish, but the Ibrox club was definitely, in this respect, getting the better of Queen's Park.

Queen's Park had stayed amateur and refused, at first, to join the Scottish League. They were thus left behind with their middle-class support, whereas the Protestant working class turned more and more to Rangers. Sectarianism had not yet arrived to foul Scottish football, but the seeds were there.

McMahon, however, defeated both these outfits in spring 1900. The semi-final at Ibrox was drawn (another sinister and suspicious dynamic at work in those days was the tendency for Rangers and Celtic to draw Cup-ties, leading to the necessity of a replay and another big crowd!) but then in the re-match, Celtic chose to turn on the style. They defeated Rangers 4-0, with McMahon "ubiquitous, ambitious and dominant", scoring two goals from the inside-left position.

It was a mighty forward line of Hodge, Campbell, Divers, McMahon and Bell, when they were all on song. They were on this occasion and the 32,000 fans left Celtic Park that day singing paeans of delight and clamouring for the inclusion of the whole Celtic forward line in the Scottish team for the game against England. In the event, Jack Bell and Johnny Campbell got the nod, albeit not in their normal Celtic positions, but McMahon was once again sidelined to the annoyance of the fans.

Any feelings of frustration, however, had to be tempered when Scotland played brilliantly on 7 April and beat England 4-1, with Robert McColl of Queen's Park scoring a hat-trick. In any case McMahon had a chance to prove his point the following week in the Scottish Cup final when Queen's Park faced Celtic at Ibrox. It was a game played in a gale blowing in from the west. McMahon scored twice in the first half as Celtic went in at half-time 3-1 up, but that was with the benefit of the wind.

Realising the necessity of keeping the ball on the ground as much as possible against the wind, McMahon was instrumental in Celtic scoring early in the second half, releasing Divers to find the net. From then on, however, it was backs to the wall, with McMahon having to play his part in defence as Queen's pressed and pressed. They did score twice, but too late in the game to have any effect, and when Mr Walker of Kilmarnock blew for up for time, the green-and-white vertical stripes had captured their third Scottish Cup, and Sandy McMahon and Johnny Campbell had participated in all three triumphs.

This was the zenith of McMahon's fortunes with Celtic. He was now nearly 30, and although he earned a Scotland recall against Ireland in 1901 and Wales in 1902, he never made it for the games that really mattered against England. Ireland and Wales seldom troubled Scotland in those days, and it was common practice for them to play virtually a reserve side.

YET FOR ALL THAT, Sandy McMahon can claim to be part of a Scottish record. The game against Ireland at Celtic Park – it was also widely believed and scarcely denied that for games against Ireland at Celtic Park, the Scottish team was full of Celtic players for reasons of attracting a large crowd – ended up in an 11-0 win for the Scots over a woefully inadequate visiting team. This still stands as a Scottish record. Sandy scored four goals that day, as did Bob Hamilton of Rangers.

But the Celtic team were now ageing, McMahon as much as any of them. In addition, the Rangers teams of 1900/01 and 1901/02 were as good as had ever previously come from Ibrox, and Celtic also had the misfortune to lose two successive Scottish Cup finals to Hearts in 1901 and Hibs in 1902. McMahon had reason to feel ill done by on both occasions. He scored in the Hearts final – a game that Celtic would have won but for dreadful goalkeeping errors –and the Hibs final also proved to be unlucky. It was played at Celtic Park only three weeks after Glasgow had been stunned by the Ibrox disaster, in which 26 people had been killed and many more injured at the Scotland v England game. In this unfortunate atmosphere, Hibs scored the only goal of the game with a backheeler.

There would have been less justification for self-pity on New Year's Day 1902. It was Celtic's last game of the Scottish League campaign (the Scottish League usually finished at the turn of the year in those days) and Celtic were two points ahead of Rangers, who had a game in hand. Thus a Celtic victory would have won the League, and a draw would have guaranteed at least a play-off. Around 40,000 were at Parkhead, and Celtic, without the impressive young Jimmy Quinn, played very badly, losing 2-4. McMahon scored one of the goals, but then, infuriated by one or two eccentric decisions by the referee, Mr Nesbit of Cowdenbeath, he got himself sent off in a melée in which he seemed to push and trip the official. Celtic never recovered from this blow, and Rangers won their fourth consecutive Scottish League title when they beat St Mirren in their remaining game.

It was now becoming clear to the energetic manager, Willie Maley, that changes were required. This involved the gathering of young talent from which would emerge the mighty and virtually unchallengeable forward line of Bennett, McMenemy, Quinn, Somers and Hamilton. This meant that the old guard had to be gradually and gently pushed out the door. McMahon, in any case, missed a large part of the 1902/03 season through injury and his last big game was the dreadful Scottish Cup quarter-final against Rangers at Parkhead, when the team went down 0-3.

He finished his playing days with Partick Thistle. It was perhaps appropriate that the Celtic team changed its jersey to the horizontal hoops rather than the vertical stripes round about the time that McMahon left and the new Celtic began to take shape. Thus McMahon never wore the hoops, but he had certainly worn the stripes. He, as well as Maley and others, certainly laid the foundation for the new Celtic.

McMahon lasted barely a year with Thistle, but then he did what so many other ex-footballers did in those days – he bought a pub. It was at 209 Great Eastern Road, not far from Celtic Park, and became know as "The Duke's Bar",where he proved to be a genial host. McMahon had the advantage as well of being a well-read man, who recited Shakespeare and Burns at Celtic soirees. Like so many great men and great Celts, McMahon was not snobby, conceited or big-headed. He was proud of his achievements, but he also relished the glory of his successors, delighting for example in the goalscoring exploits of Jimmy

Quinn, the wiles of Jimmy McMenemy and continuing success of his old colleague and friend Willie Maley.

Sandy lost his wife, Annie, in March 1908 in the most tragic of circumstances, in child-birth. She was only 33, and from then on Sandy's own life and health went downhill. Too old for war service in 1914, he found employment in the munitions industry as an iron-borer, a job he tried to combine with his interests in the licensing trade, but this did not last long. He suffered from nephritis, a chronic complaint of the kidneys, a condition which compelled his removal to the Glasgow Royal Infirmary in late 1915. It was left to Willie Maley, who had attended him assiduously, to tell the story of what happened a few days before his old friend's death on 25 January 1916. One Sunday night at the height of a dreadful war saw the great Maley in tears as Sandy rolled back the bedclothes, pointed to his emaciated legs, bruised and scarred by many injuries sustained on the playing field. "Willie", he said, "at least these two legs have done their bit for the Celtic".

This tale, also told of Dan Doyle, perhaps owes a little to Maley's romantic story telling, but it is an indication of the cult hero status of Sandy McMahon.

1901-1915

JIMMY QUINN

'THE BISON'

BHOYS CAREER

Games	331
Goals	216
Caps	11

MAGIC MOMENT

Becoming the first ever scorer of a hat-trick in a Scottish Cup final, in the most memorable fashion. Jimmy bagged his historic treble against Rangers in 1904, helping his side recover from 0-2 down.

'Look at him! Look at him! Walking back there as cool as hell!'

Spectator at the 1904 Scottish Cup final after Quinn had scored his third goal

A hundred years have now passed since the floruit of the great Jimmy Quinn. He still remains a potent legend in the impressive pantheon of that great Celtic club. Indeed, it is significant in the Willie Maley song that the first verse referring to the early days of the club states that "Gallacher and Quinn have left their mark". The Gallacher was, of course, Patsy Gallacher, and the Quinn was the miner boy from Croy.

Jimmy came out of the pits to play for Celtic and, after his career was over, that was where he returned. He was a simple working miner, like so many Celtic heroes, whose life differed from so many others only in that he was a great football player. No pretentiousness, no snobbery, not even a noticeably wealthier lifestyle. He was simply Jimmy Quinn of Croy.

Croy was an Irish village, deliberately created by the William Baird Company to house the Irish immigrants and to keep them apart from the Protestants of Kilsyth. There was a tradition every 12 July that the barricades were manned at a spot called Finger Post corner on the out-skirts of the village to keep out those intent on attacking adherents of the Catholic faith. To this day, it will be hard to find anyone in the village who does not love the Glasgow Celtic.

QUINN JOINED CELTIC IN early January 1901. Symbolically at the start of a new century, the great Willie Maley was embarking on a new beginning for Celtic. He had been manager since 1897, and although the Scottish League had been won in 1897/98 and the Cup in 1899, he was worried about the massive strides taken by this other Glasgow team, the Rangers, who seemed as if they would mount a long-term challenge to the likes of Celtic, Hearts and Queen's Park. The men from Ibrox had won the League in 1898/99 and 1899/1900, looked like doing the same in 1901, and it was really up to Celtic to stop them.

But for that, Maley needed youngsters. His spies scoured the country, and consistent reports reached his ears about this youngster called James Quinn of Smithston Albion. Maley met him, was impressed by his earnestness, enthusiasm and build, took a chance and signed him on as a left winger in the first instance.

Jimmy was unlucky in 1901 and 1902 to be on the losing side in Scottish Cup finals, but he did have one great day at the Glasgow Exhibition Trophy final of 1902 when his hat-trick beat Rangers.

Some say the Rangers are guid at fitba'
That Smith and Gibson and Speedie are braw,
But Jimmy Quinn, he diddled than a'
At the Glasgow Exhibition, oh!

Yet consistent success was hard to come by for the youngster. Maley could not really make up his mind what Quinn's best position was, nor could Quinn himself, for although he was always willing to play anywhere he was told, the brawny youngster never seemed able to settle on to a consistent seam of form.

Season 1903/04 was a pivotal one for Jimmy. It was the first in which Celtic wore the green-and-white horizontal stripes (in time they would be called the Hoops) as distinct from the vertical ones, and it was also the first season of the new Hampden Park, opened on 31 October 1903. The grand venue's first Scottish Cup final would be staged on 16 April 1904, and appropriately the teams taking part would be Celtic and Rangers.

Quinn's appearance in the centre-forward position for that final was fortuitous. Alec Bennett had been the centre-forward, but had also been the centre of speculation over a possible transfer to Rangers, a club for whom the player, a non-Catholic, had a certain sympathy. Maley decided to drop Bennett from the final, play Bobby Muir on the right wing, and move Jimmy Quinn, who had hitherto been all over the forward line, to the centre-forward position.

The Scottish Cup final was Quinn's big chance. He seized it, determined to make a name for himself as a spearhead. He had been more than a little dispirited by his failure to hold down any position and had been thinking of going back to the mines in Croy, but this was a Scottish Cup final. He had twice experienced the bitterness of defeat in that gala encounter, and at one point in the first half may well have felt that a similar thing was about to happen.

Celtic were two goals down, and it was beginning to look as if Maley's idea for the forward line was not going to work. Maybe it would have been better for Bennett to have played after all; maybe Quinn, who had thus far been overcome by nerves any time the ball came near him, was not really a centre-forward at all. But there was a great deal of the game to go yet, for half-time had not even been reached. Quinn got the ball on the halfway line and kicked it forward. It held up in the wind and Jimmy charged forward, using his mighty bison-like shoulders to barge two Rangers defenders out of the way before drilling home a great goal. Minutes after that, fine work from Bobby Muir on the right enabled him to fire a ball into the goalmouth where Quinn hammered home a second.

Thus at half-time things did not look all that bad. Two goals each. Indeed, looking at the large crowd of 65,000 in the new stadium, the managements of both teams might well have settled for a 2-2 draw, a replay and another big gate. But destiny called on Jimmy Quinn. Ten minutes remained when a ball came to him from the left. He was about 30 yards from goal. He feinted to pass out to the right, but instead charged head down towards the Rangers goal. Using his weight, he once again shouldered the Rangers markers out of his path, reached the edge of the box, and drilled the ball past the advancing Watson.

Celtic supporters went mad, Jimmy was surrounded by joyful team-mates, but, aware that ten minutes remained, the marksman simply walked back to the centre-line, face on the ground, determined that the team should not now lose the Scottish Cup. Indeed, they did not and Jimmy Quinn was the hero of the hour, having scored a hat-trick in a Scottish Cup final, an unprecedented feat.

It was Celtic's first national honour of the 20th century. It was also the springboard for total domination of Scottish football for the next six years, with Jimmy Quinn the centre-forward of the mighty attack comprising Bennett, McMenemy, Quinn, Somers and Hamilton, which can still be recited like a litany by most Celtic supporters today. Alec Bennett had been talked out of his departure for Ibrox. He would go there eventually, but played his full part in the successes of the next few years.

BUT THERE WAS A sting in the tail of that 1903/04 season. In the Glasgow Charity Cup final, Quinn was the victim of a nasty challenge from Rangers' Nick Smith and was carried off to hospital and reduced to a cripple for the rest of the summer. This incident did little to endear Rangers to Quinn, and would perhaps be a significant backdrop to a couple of incidents later in his career.

The first came on 25 March 1905 in the Scottish Cup semi-final at Parkhead (there were as yet no neutral venues for semi-finals). It was raining, and Celtic were having a bad day. In fact, they were 0-2 down, and showing little signs of getting back into the game as time slipped away. But Quinn had once before rescued Celtic from being 0-2 down and there was still hope.

A steepling ball came into the penalty area, but it was too high for anyone. Rangers full-back Alec Craig had jumped for it, but on landing slipped on the wet turf and, to break his fall, grabbed Jimmy, ending up holding his leg. Jimmy naturally shook his leg to rid it of such unwelcome, if accidental, attention, and in doing so his foot came into contact with Craig's head.

Referee Tom Robertson of Queen's Park thought this was deliberate, and Quinn was ordered off for violent conduct. Craig, a decent and honest man, intervened on Quinn's behalf but Robertson was adamant. The crowd, meanwhile, outraged by this decision, and perhaps seeing a little class prejudice in their hero being sent off by the referee who had such connections with the middle-class, snooty Queen's Park, invaded the field and the game had to be abandoned.

Celtic conceded the tie, for there could be no justification for such an attempt at mob rule, but contested the decision against Quinn. Although two Rangers players, Craig himself and Jamie Stark, said that there was nothing deliberate in Quinn's action, the SFA backed up the referee and suspended Quinn for a month, a decision sustained and upheld when Quinn later appealed.

This was bad news for Jimmy, for it deprived him of a chance to play for Scotland against England at the Crystal Palace. He had already impressed on his International debut against Ireland, and had looked likely to be picked for the trip to London. Sadly he was suspended, and the feeling that Celtic players were discriminated against and not welcome to play for the Scotland international side began to grow. But Jimmy still had one last laugh in 1904/05. Celtic and Rangers finished joint top of the Scottish League, and instead of using goal average or goal difference (Rangers would have won on both methods) a deciding game was played at Hampden. In fact, a Glasgow League encounter had already been scheduled, and the Scottish League decreed that the winner would be the Scottish champions. Quinn did not score that day, but was instrumental in both the Celtic goals as they won 2-1. Quinn had won the first of his six consecutive League titles that he and Celtic would collect between 1905 and 1910.

The other violent clash involving Quinn and Rangers came on New Year's Day 1907. This one concerned Rangers' Joe Hendry, who had just fouled Celtic's Jimmy McMenemy. Quinn came charging across to remonstrate and, in so doing, slipped on the wet turf, knocked Hendry to the ground and accidentally collided with his face. The referee, an Englishman called

Kirkham from Burslem, thought that it was all deliberate, Quinn was sent off and eventually suspended for two months.

The merits of the case however paled into insignificance in comparison with the reaction of the Celtic support. They felt that this was all a deliberate ploy by the authorities to prevent Celtic from becoming the first team to win the Scottish League and the Scottish Cup in the same season, and Quinn, already a hero, now became a demigod in the eyes of the Celtic fans. A campaign was started to compensate him for loss of earnings, and a grand total of £277 was raised as money poured in from Scotland, Ireland and the United States. Concerts were held, and Jimmy was presented with the money a gold watch, and his wife Annie was given a gold pendant.

The rest of Scotland gaped in amazement at this treatment of the Celtic cult hero. But it had already been obvious for some time that Quinn was a special player in the eyes of the Parkhead faithful. For example, he was referred to as "Jimmy". Everybody knew who was meant.As the saying went: "What is the difference between King Edward and Glasgow Celtic?" Well, the King has his Queen, but Celtic have their Quinn!" Brake clubs (the primitive equivalent of supporters buses) would call themselves the "Jimmy Quinn Charabanc", the horses which pulled them would be named "Jimmy" and "Quinn" and even the village of Croy itself suddenly found itself the object of national attention because that was where Jimmy Quinn came from.

Yet in spite of this, Jimmy remained a quiet man, embarrassed by all the accolades, but nevertheless determined that he would continue to fulfil his destiny playing the game he loved and for the team that he loved. He would be seen walking from the railway station to get the tram for Celtic Park, head down trying to avoid people's gaze, but if someone did recognise him, he would smile in acknowledgement before moving on.

In 1907 his stock rose dramatically after his suspension. He was not picked for Scotland in any of their three games – to the absolute fury of his fans and to the puzzlement of many non-Celtic lovers of the game – but he did help Celtic to their first national double. In fact, the key game was Quinn's first back after suspension. It was a Scottish Cup tie, as luck would have it, against Rangers at Ibrox.

"Masterly inactivity" would perhaps sum up Quinn's contribution that day to Celtic's 3-0 win. He was content to retain a low profile, carefully refusing to retaliate when his old enemy Joe Hendry "accidentally" stood on his stomach, and drawing Rangers defenders to himself while the rest of the forward line did the scoring. This was, of course, the heyday of the mighty half-back line of Young, Loney and Hay, but it was also clear to most spectators that Quinn's mere presence on the field was enough to spook the Rangers.

This Celtic won the double in 1906/07. (They had also won the League in 1905/06). The myth that this was not possible had been shattered. The only thing that spoiled a perfect season was Scotland's inability, without Quinn, to beat England at St.James' Park, Newcastle, in an insipid international in which Jimmy's presence might well have made all the difference. The England defence would not have relished his strength and "the vehemence of his charging" to which the newspapers kept alluding.

BUT IF 1906/07 WAS good, 1907/08 was superb. It was the season in which Celtic won everything they entered, a feat not paralleled until Jock Stein's team did the same in 1966/67.

Basically it was the year in which Maley's young team all matured at the same time, they got on marvellously well both on and off the field, and they played marvellous football. Jimmy Quinn was at the epicentre of it all, and it was probably about this time that he earned his nickname "The Equator", because everything revolved round him!

Quinn scored 24 goals that season, a fair amount considering that he was out for a long spell immediately after the New Year with a toe that turned septic, and caused complications. Still, it was this term that revealed the other side of Quinn's play. Previously it had been claimed by his detractors that he was simply a "rumble-them-up" sort of centre-forward, relying on brute force and using a great deal of shoulder-charging. Now his admirers saw another side to Jimmy.

He was now a great passer of the ball as he gave a master-class in leading the line. He could distribute to his wingers Bennett and Hamilton, he could interplay with the prodigiously talented inside-forwards Somers and McMenemy, and he could be a partner for centre-half Willie Loney, who would frequently join the attack, particularly for set pieces. In such cases, Quinn could hang back and help out the defence. He was a complete player, and totally deserving of the accolades that the *Glasgow Herald*, in particular, would hand out to him. "Quinn is a very master." "Quinn leads the Celtic forward line with panache and vigour." "Quinn is simply Quinn – and that sums it up!" These offer a telling example of the tributes during that tremendous season.

"Charging" is a word that one reads often in Edwardian football reports. A player was allowed to shoulder-charge an opponent, particularly a goalkeeper, as long as the goalkeeper's feet were on the ground and he held the ball in his arms. The charge had to be with the shoulder, not the elbow. This practice, barbaric as it sounds, continued in Britain up to the 1950s and although we wince at the thought of it in these softer, gentler times, no-one seemed to criticise its use in Jimmy Quinn's day. Quinn, of course, with his bison-type shoulders, excelled at it.

There was, however, a fine line between legal charging with the shoulder and fouling with the elbow, and it was the task of the referee to distinguish. On one occasion in October 1907, Jimmy was sent off for illegal charging by an infamous referee, J B Stark of Airdrie. Celtic fans and Quinn sympathisers now held their breath. Quinn's last suspension was two months. Would this one be more? Could it even be sine die ?

Fortunately, the SFA decided that Jimmy should be let off with a warning. The referee himself had been in trouble previously. The game concerned – Hibs v Celtic at Easter Road – had been a shambles in which other players had been sent off and carried off in the dreadful, internecine, fratricidal atmosphere that sometimes occurred when the Edinburgh Irish met the Glasgow Irish. Moreover, there had been a certain excuse for Jimmy's "charge" on his opponent. It had been to avenge a wrong previously done by the Hibs player to the diminutive Jimmy McMenemy.

It was as well that Quinn was not suspended, for 1907/08 would not have been the same without him. Not only were Celtic advancing comfortably on all fronts, but Jimmy revisited the international scene. In particular, he returned to the land of his forefathers, to Dublin on 14 March 1908, when Scotland beat Ireland 5-0. Jimmy Quinn scored four of them – a shot from the edge of the box, two tap-ins and a "charge through" – and the *Glasgow Herald* praised his unselfishness and distribution. Not to the extent that the Dublin press did, though. Stressing that Jimmy's parents were Irish, they reported that the talk in the Dublin hostelries that night was "Quinn, Quinn and more Quinn" with one newspaper even declaring: "Not since the days of Charles Stuart Parnell was a man talked about so much in this city".

All this meant that Quinn could hardly be passed over for the "big" international against England at Hampden on 4 April. But vast was the consternation among the Quinn faction when it was announced that Jimmy would switch to the left wing to accommodate Andy Wilson of Sheffield Wednesday. Wilson was another fine centre-forward, but hardly in the Quinn class. To be fair, Quinn had experience of playing on the left flank – indeed, he had appeared there once or twice for Celtic that season when team circumstances demanded it – but it did seem strange to play the mighty man out of position in such an important game.

Criticism of this move tended to die away, however, when early in the game Jimmy charged down the left wing and crossed for Wilson to score. The crowd, a record 120,000 (at least), erupted in raptures at that. Yet after that magnificent goal, England came into the game and earned a debatable equaliser near the end. The conventional wisdom after the game was that if Jimmy Quinn had been in the centre and someone like Bobby Templeton had been on the left wing, Scotland would have won comfortably.

Quinn had no reason to be disappointed about that and the rest of 1907/08 saw Celtic mop up the Scottish League, the Scottish Cup (in a very one-sided final against an overawed St Mirren) and the Glasgow Charity Cup to add to the Glasgow Cup that had been won in the autumn. Celtic had climbed Parnassus, and although the motivating forces were the mighty half-back line of Young, Loney and Hay, as well as the tricky inside-forwards Peter Somers and Jimmy "Napoleon" McMenemy, the player who made it all happen for Celtic was the spearhead Jimmy Quinn, now quite clearly the most talked-about man in Scotland, and possibly England as well.

The Prime Minister, Sir Henry Campbell-Bannerman, died at about this time in April 1908, and there were repeated rumours of the ill health of King Edward VII. Who would replace both these men? Well, Jimmy Quinn, of course! But if the Pope died as well, then he might have to ask for a little help from his friend Willie Loney! Croy became famous. Charabancs would arrive there on a Sunday and disgorge passengers, hoping that they might get a chance to see this mighty man. There was no-one in Scotland vaguely like Jimmy Quinn, often referred to simply as "Jimmy" "Jamie" or "Jeemy".

Yet all this adulation sat ill with a profoundly shy man. He had the next campaign to think of. There was no time to rest on laurels. The 1908/09 season remains a dreadful one in the annals of Scottish football, for that was when the lovely new Hampden Park was ripped to shreds after the Scottish Cup final – and all, indirectly, through Jimmy Quinn. It was Jimmy who was responsible for Celtic's late equalising goal in the first game, when goalkeeper Harry Rennie stepped over the line, ball in hand, to avoid Jimmy's shoulder charge. It was Jimmy who scored Celtic's goal in the replay and it was Jimmy whom all the hotheads clambered over the fence to see when he and some other Celtic players stood waiting in vain for extra time, and before things got so tragically out of hand.

In vain did Quinn try to wave them back before realising that safety considerations were of the essence, and that a speedy return to the pavilion was the better option. But although much has been written of the Hampden Riot (which was not, in spite of what some have said, a sectarian disturbance but rather a feeling of having been cheated out of extra time so that a third and even more profitable game could be played), comparatively little has been said of the immediate aftermath when Celtic had to play eight games in 12 days in order to win the Scottish League and pip Dundee.

Jimmy played in all eight games and scored seven goals, never shrinking, never "wanting a break, Boss", never avoiding the draining and exhausting experience. He was determined that Celtic would win their fifth title in a row, which they duly did on the evening of Friday 30 April 1909 by beating Hamilton Accies 2-1 at Douglas Park, Hamilton. Incredibly, the next day they played again in a pre-arranged tour game in the Highlands! These men were made of steel and Jimmy Quinn was the symbol of them all, ruggedly determined and with no little skil,l either.

However, he had seriously disappointed his fans in Scotland's game against England at the Crystal Palace the week before the first instalment of the 1909 Scottish Cup final. England beat Scotland 2-0 with two early goals, and Quinn was exceptionally unlucky when a shot from the edge of the box went just past, then his header hit the bar. But Quinn's moment for Scotland would come.

SEASON 1909/10 SAW CELTIC win the League for a phenomenal sixth time in a row, although they would lose in the Scottish Cup semi-final to Clyde. Quinn scored two absolutely sensational goals that term. One was in the Glasgow Cup final at Hampden, when Jimmy, already limping from a slight knock and three Rangers players (one of them the goalkeeper) went up for the same ball. No-one in the 55,000 crowd quite knew what happened but the ball ended up in the net and Jimmy finished with three Rangers men on top of him. It was the only goal of the game.

The other goal that was still the talk of Ayrshire during the war – not only the 1914–1918 war, but the 1939–1945 war as well! It happened on Christmas Day 1909. In Edwardian Scotland, Christmas Day was no big deal. The Presbyterian Church frowned on its adherents doing anything to enjoy themselves. But those who were at Rugby Park, Kilmarnock, got a Christmas treat that they were never likely to forget. It was a muddy day, the overnight frost having thawed suddenly. The pitch was anything but suitable for football; passing accurately was well nigh impossible in such energy sapping circumstances.

Celtic were struggling, with defender Alec McNair injured, and Jimmy was helping out the defence. Suddenly the ball came to him when he was still ten yards inside his own half of the field. His marker slipped on the wet surface. Jimmy saw his chance. There was no point in trying to find a colleague as the ball might stick in the mud, so Jimmy, head down, charged on goal with four Kilmarnock defenders trailing behind him. He was about 25 yards from his target when he feared that one of the defenders was catching up on him. He did what he liked doing best. He shot and scored a brilliant goal into the top corner of the net. "Even the lovers of Kilmarnock applauded vigorously" reported one newspaper.

There would be even more cause to laud Jimmy Quinn by the end of the season. Jimmy had long been a cult hero with Celtic fans, but now this hero-worship spread to all Scotland as well after the international match on 2 April 1910. Scotland's performances hitherto in 1910 had been none too impressive, but this game against England was widely recognised as the best ever. The scoreline was 2-0. The first goal arrived when Quinn hit the bar and Celtic colleague Jimmy McMenemy netted the rebound, then the man from Croy scored the second himself. Deftly avoiding a crushing sandwich between two England defenders, who banged into each other, he charged through and found the net. The very impressive forward line of Bennett, McMenemy, Quinn, Higgins and Templeton (only Higgins of Newcastle United had no Celtic connections, although Bennett now played for Rangers and Templeton for Kilmarnock) toyed with the panic-stricken England defence throughout, to the cheers of the Scottish crowd.

It was the apotheosis of Jimmy Quinn. Everyone in Britain now knew who he was. Trains on the Glasgow-to-Edinburgh line would see passengers leave their seats to view the village of Croy, where resided the hero. And yet, he was anything but a hero in his demeanour, going to chapel on a Sunday, talking to his neighbours, inquiring after the health of someone's ill mother, talking to the children of the village. The press might have called him "King James" and "Jamie the Great" (strong stuff that in Edwardian days!) but Jimmy was unaffected by it. He was, as someone put it rather well, just "an ordinary man".

The story is told about how, in another Scottish town on 6 May 1910, word was being spread about the death of King Edward VII. A boy overheard the bad news as the word went around along the lines of "He's deid" and "The Great Man's awa'" and so on. Automatically he assumed that the only great man it could possibly be was Jimmy Quinn. Fortunately, Jimmy still had a few years left in him yet!

QUINN WAS 32 IN 1910 and, inevitably given the amount of injuries that he had suffered – many of them deliberately inflicted by despairing defenders – he began to slow down and missed games through fitness problems. The great Celtic team had reached its peak as well, although Quinn did manage another two successful Scottish Cup finals in 1911 and 1912. In 1912, as well, Quinn played for Scotland against Wales, scoring the late winner and rendering the 31,000 Tynecastle crowd "demented with joy". He also played his final international game against England in 1912, but the selectors once again put him on the left wing, where he was not a failure, but no great success in the mundane 1-1 draw.

After 1912 injuries, an operation to his leg and general decline meant that he did not appear for Celtic very often, although it was not until 1915 that he played his final game, against Hearts at Parkhead in front of large crowd which contained many men in khaki, and already, a few severely disabled soldiers home from France and Belgium. He played little part in the great 1913/14 season, although he was very much part of the set-up, being willing, for example, to be seen helping to carry the kit hamper off the train at away fixtures. On such occasions, he would smoke a clay pipe, and star-struck locals would nudge each other and say "That's him", but then they would remark how true it was that he looked just like an ordinary man.

When his career finished, it was back to the pits at Croy, where every man was required for the war effort. He continued working there through the trauma of the general strike in 1926 and the tragic aftermath, the depression of the early 1930s. Then, late in his life, came the horror of his son John being killed in Holland in 1944.

Jimmy Quinn died on 21 November 1945 and he was buried in Kilsyth cemetery. His funeral was attended by almost everyone in Scottish football, and he had a surprise mourner, the great Billy Meredith of Wales, against whom Quinn had played in 1910 and 1912.

Great footballers never die, of course, for they live on in memory and tale. It is often said by the sneerers that nothing gets lost in the telling of the epic deeds of great men. Yet one only has to look at the contemporary accounts of Jimmy Quinn to find out that nothing had been exaggerated, and that he was the hero of thousands of Celtic fans, and not a few Scotland fans as well. No-one would ever have heard of Croy, if it hadn't been for the mighty Jimmy Quinn.

There is also the undeniable fact that Jimmy Quinn was a household name to people other than football fans. There is, for example, the true story of the Latin teacher whose star pupil was mispronouncing the Latin word "quin", which should have been pronounced as in "queen", rather than "Quinn". "No, no, it's 'quin' said the erudite sage – 'Quinn' was a football player!" I'll say he was!

JIM YOUNG

1903-1917

BHOYS CAREER

Games	443
Goals	13
Caps	1

MAGIC MOMENT

Captaining Celtic to a League and Scottish Cup double in April 1914.

'SUNNY JIM'

THERE could be no greater Celt than the legendary "Sunny" Jim Young, who played for the team throughout the great days between 1903 and 1917. He was a remarkable footballer who epitomised Celtic when they were good, when Maley's young side came to fruition and swept all before them. The record speaks for itself – six League titles in a row, then a break for three years as the team re-invented itself, then another four titles in a row, in spite of the rude intervention of the Kaiser.

There can be little doubt that without Jimmy, the Celtic history of those glorious years would have been so much the poorer. Yet although he was a great individual player, earning the adulation of all Celtic fans for his total commitment and unswerving loyalty to the cause, he was very much part of a unit, the awesome half-back line of Young, Loney and Hay. Along with Willie "No Road This Way" Loney and the inspirational captain Jimmy "Dun" Hay, Sunny dominated the middle of the field. A Celtic fan entering a hostelry in Edwardian Scotland would ask for a "Young, Loney and Hay". The barman would look at him quizzically before the fan would say he was wanting three "halfs" of whiskey, for Young, Loney and Hay were "three halfs of the best"!

Yet Young's origins were not connected with Celtic. Not to put too fine a point on it, he was a Protestant. This may have been a problem with a few bigots on the committee or in the support, but it mattered not one iota to the visionary Willie Maley, who was pledged to build the greatest team in Great Britain, irrespective of people's religion or anything else. "It's not a man's creed or his nationality that counts. It's the man himself" said Maley as he set about this ingathering of young talent in the early years of the 20th century.

JIM YOUNG WAS 20 and homesick. He played for Bristol Rovers but had not really made an impact in the past year, and he was missing his native Kilmarnock. The other Bristol team, the City, had shown an interest in him, as indeed had West Bromwich Albion, but he was really wanting a Scottish team. Fate then decided that Celtic committee man Mick Dunbar came to Bristol to ask Bobby Muir to join Celtic. Muir was keen, and possibly mentioned that his friend Jimmy Young was interested in going back to Scotland as well. Young himself confirmed this, and Dunbar, apparently acting on his own initiative but impressed by the strong athletic physique of the Kilmarnock man, signed both Young and Muir in the Black Swan hotel at Eastville, then the home of Bristol Rovers, in early May 1903.

Young was a centre-half in his early career, and it was in that position that he played his first few games for Celtic, helping to win the Glasgow Charity Cup a few weeks after joining the club, impressing in victories over Hibs in the semi-final and St Mirren in the final. It was the harbinger of things to come. Celtic had been having a fairly unfortunate time in the past few years, losing Scottish Cup finals to Hearts in 1901 and Hibs in 1902 (unluckily in both cases) and not having won the League championship since 1898. The only big success had been the

Glasgow Exhibition Trophy (otherwise known as the British League Cup) in a one-off tournament in June 1902.

But this was a new, young Celtic team in which Maley had made a great investment, and proof that change was in the air came on the rainy day of 15 August 1903, in the opening game of the season against Partick Thistle, when the team ran out in a new strip – green-and-white horizontal stripes, as distinct from the previous year's vertical ones. No-one knew then that this would very soon become the most famous and most readily identified strip in the world.

Success did not come instantly. The talent was there. Jim Young would note with approval the runs of Alec Bennett, the wiles of Jimmy McMenemy, the passing ability of Peter Somers and the strength of that shy and brooding introvert from the mining village of Croy, Jimmy Quinn. Young played well enough at centre-half, although he was never totally at home there, being frequently caught out of position and clearly stronger on his right side than he was on his left.

It was not until 27 February 1904 that Maley made a momentous decision before a difficult Scottish Cup replay at Dens Park, Dundee. Young would play at right-half instead of centre half which would be left to Willie Loney, and Jimmy Hay would be left-half. Thus Young, Loney and Hay came together, this time through the manager's choice rather than through compulsion forced by injuries as had happened on one occasion previously at Airdrie.

A few weeks later, Maley would have another brainwave and that was the deployment on a permanent basis of Jimmy Quinn in the centre-forward position, rather than the left wing where his play had been inconsistent, to put it mildly. It was at centre-forward that Quinn had scored a hat-trick in the Glasgow Exhibition Trophy of 1902, and his career now took off.

Quinn notched the hat-trick which won the Scottish Cup of 1904, but there is a danger that people might think that Jimmy Quinn was a one-man team. Not so. Behind Quinn, it was the mighty half-back line which supplied the ammunition as the team came from behind to win 3-2.

This success fired the fans to great levels of enthusiasm as the young team began to be spoken about in eulogistic terms. Celtic fans of all ages have always loved a trier, and this was what Jim Young always was. It was about this time that he earned the nickname Sunny. There were several reasons why he was so called. Some said it was because of his radiant smile. This was, of course, sarcastic, for on the field Jim was grim, determined, focused. Others said that it was given to him because of a song which was very popular in the Music Hall:

"Oh, Sunny, Sunny Jim,
Oh how I envy him!"

But the most likely explanation was the contemporary advertisement for a breakfast cereal called Force, seen widely on billboards and in newspapers. The central character was strong and energetic, and underneath pictures of him swimming rivers and climbing mountains – something that would strike a chord in those consumptive, undernourished Edwardian days – the slogan ran:

"Vigor, Vim, Perfect Trim
Force made him – Sunny Jim.
High o'er the fence leaps Sunny Jim,
Force is the food that raises him"

From now on, all the world would know who Sunny Jim was.

Willie Maley, reminiscing in a book entitled *The Story of the Celtic*, summed Young up: "Celtic have never had a more whole-hearted player. He was a half-back of the rugged type, but there was class in his ruggedness, whilst for stamina he stood in the first rank. His enthusiasm inclined him sometimes to excesses, but a kinder-hearted fellow never wore a Celtic jersey . . . In time he became captain of Celtic, and a splendid one he made. A player of dauntless courage, he served Celtic faithfully and ably for many seasons."

This was great praise, indeed, for Maley could be grudging with his plaudits, and was occasionally off-hand and even rude to great Celts like Delaney and McGrory. He clearly felt that Young was one of the cornerstones of his great teams of the pre-First World War era. Sunny was not the only one of course, for this was a truly outstanding side.

One of the many bones of contention between Sunny's fans and the rest of Scottish football was the gripe that he earned only one cap, against Ireland in Dublin in 1906. It was a poor game, won 1-0 by Scotland with a goal from Tommy Fitchie, and Young gave an ordinary display. But Celtic fans felt that he might have scraped into the team for the next game against England, such was the strength of his performances for Celtic, and also for the way he had played for the Scottish League against the English League. But the nod for the right-half spot went to Andy Aitken ("The Daddler" as he was known) of Newcastle United, a fine player in an era when Scotland seemed to produce fine players off a conveyer belt.

Young's under-representation at international level may well, however, have owed something to the very robustness of his play. Edwardian football in Scotland was certainly tough, and Sunny could dish it out with the best of them. He was routinely booed by opposition crowds, but such was his character that he revelled in it, smiling and waving back to them as they hurled vacuous insults at this Ayrshire Protestant.

James Handley, the author of *The Celtic Story*, waxes poetic about the Celtic team of that period. Having talked about the forward line, he then goes on to affirm " . . . and behind them ready for the cut and thrust of the game stood the Porthos, Athos and Aramis of the football field – Young, Loney and Hay. The two lines drew equilateral triangles between them with the ball or moved forward with the smooth and forceful precision of piston rods, the diesel-powered Quinn in front thundering along the track to goal".

The record of that team speaks for itself. Under captain Jimmy Hay, six consecutive League championships were won, the Scottish Cup found its way to Celtic Park in 1904, 1907 and 1908 and might have done so as well in 1909 had it not been for the Hampden Riot which rendered the game unfinished and forced the SFA to withold the trophy that year. In 1907 Celtic became the first Scottish team to win the double of the Scottish League and the Scottish Cup in the same season, and in 1908 they became the first team in world history to win every competition that they entered, namely the Scottish League, the Scottish Cup, the Glasgow Cup and the Glasgow Charity Cup.

Sunny Jim was well to the fore in all that. His blond hair made him instantly recognisable and he was the icon of that Celtic side. He was out occasionally with injury or suspension, but never for very long and was always willing to do anything for the club. On one famous occasion, Sunny played in the goal.

It happened on 2 January 1909 at Kilmarnock. Sunny had been injured in the game against Clyde on Boxing Day, and missed the New Year's Day game at Parkhead against Rangers. Celtic, without Sunny, won 3-1, but goalkeeper Davie Adams was injured. The next game was the following day, and Maley had a problem, with the reserve goalkeeper also being injured. He dabbled with approaching a junior club for the loan of a goalkeeper, but Sunny Jim offered his services, saying that he was still a bit stiff after his injury, but would be able to play in the goal as "Ah widnae hae to run around sae much".

In fact, in 1909 the delineation between a goalkeeper and an outfield player was not as sharp as it is now. A goalkeeper did not wear a different colour of jersey, and was allowed to handle the ball anywhere inside his own half. He seldom did this, of course, but this implies that a goalkeeper was little more than an extra defender. Still, it was a specialist position and goalkeepers did need special training.

Maley considered Sunny's offer. He was a wholehearted fellow, and the manager knew that he would not deliberately let the side down, even though what he was proposing was a little unusual, not to mention bizarre. But Sunny was persuasive and did have a way of swaying Maley. In any case, there was little option, as there was not really a great deal of time to find another custodian. Maley, after a while, accepted Young's offer.

The move was not a success, as Kilmarnock won 3-1, and for the following week Maley approached Morton and hired Jimmy Oliver, their reserve goalkeeper, while Young was restored to his right-half position. But it does show that Young was prepared to do anything for the club. The fans, who may well have disapproved of this odd move, nevertheless admired Sunny Jim for his willingness to try.

THE YEAR 1909 WAS a remarkable one in Scottish football. There was the Hampden Riot after the replay of the Scottish Cup final, when fans turned nasty because they were denied extra time, but even more remarkable, at least in footballing terms, was what happened next. The Scottish League insisted that their fixtures had to be completed by the end of April. Celtic, because of several replays and postponements, found that they had to play eight games within 12 days.

It is at such moments that mighty men like Jimmy Young stand up and are counted. He played in seven out of the eight games, and performed magnificently in them all. Loney was out injured, so it was the young Joe Dodds who took the centre-half spot in those momentous days. Dundee were the other team who were likely to win the League, but could do little other than stand in amazement and awe as Celtic completed this gruelling schedule, losing only one of these eight games, the second-last one to Hibs. They drew another two and won the remaining five. It was a remarkable achievement, and the Sunny Jim breakfast cereal advertisement looked particularly apt as Celtic's man of the moment covered every blade of grass for the cause.

It was the following year, 1910, that saw the end of an era. King Edward VII died, and Celtic's run of six League titles came to an end. There were also a few changes in personnel. Alec Bennett, the right winger, had moved to Rangers in 1908 and inside-left Peter Somers was now with Hamilton Accies. Then, at the end of 1910/11 (a difficult season in which Rangers had at last struck back and won the League, although the Scottish Cup had been won by Celtic after a struggle) captain Jimmy Hay moved on to Newcastle United following a dispute about wages.

There had been a certain amount of speculation that Sunny might also move on to an English team, but he had been homesick when he was in Bristol before his great days with Celtic, and in any case he loved Celtic, even the occasionally difficult-to-please supporters. Furthermore, another carrot was presented to induce him to stay, and that was the captaincy, which Maley had little hesitation in offering to him in the wake of Hay's departure.

Young was a fine choice as skipper. He had worked well with his friend Hay, whom he respected as a captain, but he had hankered after doing the job himself. He had a fine stentorian voice, heard all over the field and even in the stands as he encouraged his men, clapping his hands, giving the occasional rebuke but always applauding the good play of his men. With the opposition he was as tough as old boots, but always polite and courteous at the beginning and end of the game.

At this stage of his life, he had a set of false teeth, many of his originals having been lost in incidents on the field. He would remove his dentures before the start of a game, and would often remark that this was a symbol that the aggression and the toughness had to start now and would continue until the end of the game, when he could put his teeth back in again. Then he would be a gentleman with the opposition, but not before!

YOUNG'S FIRST YEAR AS captain was a difficult one. For one thing, Rangers were on a high, and Celtic were in a period of transition. Loney, Quinn and McMenemy were out for a long time, and not all the youngsters brought into the side were instant successes. There were two who were, however – left-half Peter Johnstone, who was the replacement for Jimmy Hay, and a spindle-shanked youngster who looked as if a good plate of soup (or indeed the "Sunny Jim" Force cereal!) would not be a bad idea. The boy was called Patrick Gallacher, but very soon he became known as Patsy.

Both these players needed careful handling, albeit for different reasons. Johnstone was big, strong and aggressive, and Young would need all his strong-mindedness to keep him in his place. Gallacher, on the other hand, looked as if he could be easily intimidated by coarse defenders like the infamous "dirty Galt" of Rangers, and he might need a little protection. Fortunately Sunny Jim was up to both tasks, and at the end of his first year as captain in 1912, Celtic had repeated the previous term's success by winning the Scottish Cup on a windy day at Ibrox against Clyde.

A fallow season followed, something that had not happened for a decade, but in 1913/14 a truly exceptional Celtic team had evolved with Sunny Jim as the captain. This side, in the opinion of contemporary observers, might have become even better than the 1908 vintage, had it not been for the intervention of the Great War. Certainly, four League titles were won in a row, but the circumstances were unusual and even a little unreal, given the wholesale slaughter and carnage that was going on in other parts of the world.

That season saw Celtic lift a League and Cup double with captain James Young well to the fore, the booming Ayrshire bark prominent and often heard clearly at the back of the stand. A replay was needed to win the Scottish Cup final against Hibs, but the campaign was not without its incident for Sunny. Celtic were drawn at Forfar. Even in that rural backwater, everyone had heard of men like McMenemy, Gallacher and Sunny Jim. Indeed, Forfar had unearthed their own genius, a wee man called Alec Troup, who after the war would go on to be capped for Scotland in a distinguished career for Dundee and Everton.

Sunny was now well into his thirties and young Troup was still in his teens. The nimble, slight figure of "Wee Troupie", playing at inside-left that day in direct opposition to Sunny, was giving the veteran the runaround, to the delight of the locals and even the amusement of some of Sunny's own team-mates and supporters.

In truth, however, this was a mere sideshow, for Celtic won 5-0, but there was a certain amount of humour in the sight of the nutmegs, the trickery and the dexterity of Troup getting the better of the somewhat more ponderous Sunny Jim. Such things did not often happen to Sunny and, once or twice, he "even got close enough to foul him" as a local put it. On one occasion, however, Troup ended up among the spectators in the tight little provincial ground.

Sunny was lectured by the referee, and the crowd bayed for blood, none more so than a middle-aged lady brandishing an umbrella. This was Troup's mother, who took it very ill that a mighty man like Jim Young was so abusing her son. At the end of the game, handshakes were exchanged and Sunny made a few apologies to Alec. This was not good enough for Mrs.Troup, however. As Sunny walked off the field, the good lady leaned over the barrier and, with her umbrella, made as if to hit Sunny, shouting dreadful execrations like "Tak that, ye durty Glesca bugger" before wiser elements of the crowd pulled her away.

Sunny and the rest of the team had a good laugh at all this, and indeed there was a great deal to smile about that year. The half-back line was now Young, Johnstone and McMaster, only marginally less effective than Young, Loney and Hay. The back three of Shaw, McNair and Dodds were reaching legendary status, and up front there were men like the cannonball shot Andy McAtee, the evergreen Jimmy McMenemy and, above all, the great Patsy Gallacher, now giving clear, visible and consistent indications of why he would become the "most talked about man in the trenches" in years to come, and why no-one who ever saw him would say anything other than that he was the greatest of them all.

But no matter how great the team was, there still needed to be leadership. Clearly Maley provided that off the field, but on the pitch there was no doubting the authority of Sunny Jim. He went out to play convinced that he was going to win, and very seldom did his convictions let him down. His own play, apart from the odd encounter with such as Alec Troup, remained consistently powerful. There was perhaps a touch of arrogance in him, but it was an arrogance rooted in the constant belief that there were very few like him, and it was motivated by the desire to win as many trophies and medals as possible.

His own crowd loved him and, always a sign of a great player, the opposition crowds hated him. "Let them hate, as long as they fear" might have been Sunny's motto, and in truth everyone feared Celtic, of whom Sunny, with his grim determination and desire to win, was the symbol and flagship.

IT WAS CELTIC'S FORTUNE to tour Europe in the early summer of 1914. They had been there several times previously, and this year seemed no different. Manager Maley would write later that he was a little perturbed by the amount of men in military uniform that he saw in Austria and Germany, but one suspects that he was merely being wise after the event. The war itself hit the world suddenly. Celtic were comfortably back in Scotland long before the assassination in Sarajevo, but even after that event, there was another month before things became serious. Even the word "war" did not conjure up all the horrors that it does now. It could have been translated as "adventure", and was certainly looked upon in such terms by many men, only too glad to get away from their boring jobs and dreadful housing conditions.

The football season started as usual, even though the outbreak of war preceded it. There were to be vital differences, though, in that there would be no Scottish Cup or International matches, players would only be part-time and would have to have another war-related job. Games were allowed only on Saturdays or the occasional Monday holiday. The Scottish League would continue, and the only really noticeable difference at football matches at the start of the war was that there would be a few men in khaki, and that there would almost always be some sort of recruiting drive at half-time, as rasping-voiced sergeants told everyone how nice it was to serve King and Country.

As far as Celtic were concerned, Maley was particularly careful to ensure that all his fine side had a reserved occupation and that they could avoid joining up without any accusations of war-dodging, or of receiving the white feather of cowardice from any woman who believed that a man was not doing his bit. Hearts, on the other hand, enlisted almost en masse – a noble sacrifice – but Sunny was happy to work in the Ayrshire mines for five and a half days per week, and play for Celtic on the Saturday afternoon. Most of Celtic's players had similar arrange-ments, although a few volunteered and Peter Johnstone paid with the ultimate sacrifice.

It would be a mistake to think that because football was played in these unconventional circumstances, it was taken any less seriously. On the contrary, as always happens when vital and dreadful things are going on, people need something to take their minds off the horror of it all. It was here that Celtic played a crucial part for their supporters, producing the excellent play that they had been famous for before the war, and giving those fans, at home and abroad, something to raise their spirits. It was, after all, the Celtic philosophy, and Sunny Jim was happy to be part of this outlook.

Celtic lost their first game in the first wartime season to Hearts at Tynecastle, but only on another two occasions in the League that term were the green-and-white colours lowered. Young played in every game. By this time his fair hair had turned a little darker, but he was still the same Sunny, shouting at his men and dominating the game. "Face the ball, Celtic!" became his watchword. By the turn of the year, the Celtic team really turned on the style, and with Patsy Gallacher in his glory and a new centre-forward called Jimmy McColl ("the Sniper" as he was nicknamed) taking the place of Jimmy Quinn, nothing could stop them winning the Scottish League and the Glasgow Charity Cup. What a pity there was no Scottish Cup that season!

Further delight was provided for the supporters at home and abroad the following season when Celtic, under Young's reliable, unspectacular, yet inspiring leadership managed to win all three competitions that they were entitled to enter, namely the Scottish League, the Glasgow Cup and the Glasgow Charity Cup. The Scottish League achievement included the famous occasion on 15 April when Celtic played two games in one day and won them both, beating Raith Rovers at Parkhead, then getting into a charabanc to motor to Motherwell to defeat the home team.

SUNNY WAS NOW 34, and showing no signs of slowing down. Indeed in war-time football, 34 was not particularly old, because players who should have retired previously were often prevailed upon to keep going. Thus the summer of 1916 saw Sunny Jim at the peak of his powers, a man who enjoyed the full trust of Willie Maley, a performer whose contribution was still utterly dependable and who was playing for a team and a support who adored him. If there had ever been the slightest problem about Young's religion, it had long gone.

Yet 1916 saw the beginning of the end of Sunny Jim. It was that year in which the realities of war began to bite. Even British propaganda could not entirely hide the fact that there had been a serious rebellion in Ireland, quashed only at the cost of much blood, that many ships had been lost in an indecisive naval battle at Jutland, and that the British Army had sustained its biggest ever calamity at a place called the Somme in France.

All the more reason, then, for fans to immerse themselves in football. The first day of the season saw Celtic at Love Street on 19 August. Celtic won 5-1, but Sunny injured his knee and hobbled off near the end. He missed the next game, but after that there was a partial recovery. Wiser counsel in more normal times might have suggested that a prolonged rest was in order to consolidate that recovery. But those were not normal times, and Sunny himself, hating any enforced idleness, maintained that he should be back. He then played another four Saturdays, clearly toiling but determined to keep going. Self-pity never featured very highly in Sunny's make-up and the team kept winning.

But the Saturday of 30 September 1916 saw the end of his career. A hard tackle on a Hearts player at Parkhead caused Sunny's knee to swell to a grotesque size and and he was carried off to hospital. He would remain there until after the New Year, enduring several operations, but it was soon obvious that the great Sunny Jim would never play again. This was made public in February 1917, and he officially retired at the end of the season, a victim, in a funny way, of the war which was doing so much damage to everyone else. It was no accident that the first year of Sunny's retirement saw Rangers win the Scottish League championship, and from then on hegemony passed slowly, reluctantly yet inexorably to the Ibrox club.

Now Sunny returned to work in war-related tasks. He also joined in partnership with his old friend and team-mate Bobby Templeton to run a pub in George Street, Kilmarnock, and when Bobby died suddenly in November 1919, Sunny became the sole owner. He was now married and had two daughters and one son. He was always a genial "mine host" and although he had a permanent limp, he laughed it off and would show his customers that he could still dance. "I can do a bit of a step dance with the old chap yet", he would say, before regaling his clientele with tales from his past life, notably his trips to England and abroad with Celtic. He was summed up by the *Weekly News* reporter as "a cheery likeable chap"

But he was not destined to live long, meeting his death in a motorcycle accident in 1922. It was Monday 4 September when the motorcycle on which he was a pillion passenger was in collision with a tram on the Wellington Bridge between Hurlford and his native Kilmarnock. Sunny sustained head injuries from which he never recovered. It had all come about when two friends of his, Joseph Deans and Andrew Shearer, had been in Kilmarnock for ammunition, went into Sunny's pub and asked him if he fancied some rabbit shooting at a spot near Darvel. Sunny agreed and travelled on the pillion behind Deans, while Shearer was in the sidecar.

The collision at a spot where the road narrowed suddenly left Shearer only shaken but Deans and Young were sent flying. Deans was thrown into grass at the side of the road and survived, but Sunny's head hit the road. He probably never regained consciousness and died later that evening in hospital.

He had just reached his 40th birthday, and his death was a tragic loss of life. Celtic supporters were plunged into mourning, with manager Maley, who had looked upon Jim as a son, almost – sometimes, by a Freudian slip, Maley misspelt his nickname as Sonny – was particularly distraught. But they never die if they leave something immortal behind them. Nine League championship medals, six Scottish Cup medals, one Scottish cap (and there should have been a great deal more) and six Scottish League caps was enough for Eugene MacBride in An Alphabet of the Celts to claim that Sunny Jim was the greatest Celt of them all.

But perhaps the greatest indication of the love and respect in which he was held comes in the way that a good century after his floruit, he is still remembered affectionately by his nick-name. He is not the dry or dusty James Young that he might have been in reference books. No, even those who never came within 50 years of seeing him play still refer to this cheery soul as Sunny Jim.

JOE CASSIDY

1912-1924

BHOYS CAREER

Games	204
Goals	104
Caps	4

MAGIC MOMENT

New Year's Day 1921 at Ibrox; Joe scored both goals in the 2-0 victory which lit up the Celtic community and led to part of the city being named "the Cassidy cavalcade".

'TROOPER'

IN the desperate days of the 1990s, the beleaguered Celtic board appointed a front-man called Terry Cassidy who would be their spokesman for the media. The cynics said that they were hiding behind him, and in truth the man was a lightweight who had the annoying habit of answering a direct question with another question. A veteran supporter watched his television in disgust before saying that it would have been better if they had resurrected old Joe to save us.

Joe Cassidy was one of the cult heroes of the early 1920s. The times were grim in the aftermath of the Great War, with the ongoing problems in industrial relations and in Ireland, both of which affected Celtic fans intimately as everyone struggled with the problems of adapting to a new life. In many cases this happened without the breadwinner, who was lying in the fields of Flanders or who was sitting in a wheelchair, effectively a parasite in a situation where the Government was cynically indifferent to his plight.

Joe Cassidy played his part in alleviating suffering. Joe had been a soldier himself – he was called "Trooper Joe" – in the Great War and had won the Military Medal in the last few days of the conflict in November 1918, while serving with the Black Watch. Born in 1896, he had made an insignificant impact for Celtic, both before the war and, whenever he had the opportunity, during it. But in the years immediately following the Armistice, he really began to make his mark.

He was not properly demobbed until summer 1919, although while home on leave he did manage a few games in the 1918/19 season. He was an inside-left and there was brisk competition for the inside-forward positions at Celtic Park in 1919/20, with Patsy Gallacher and Jimmy McMenemy consistently and impressively brilliant. But McMenemy left for Partick Thistle, Maley having erroneously considered that he was past his best, and opportunity knocked for the charismatic young Cassidy in 1920/21.

The inside trio of Gallacher, McInally and Cassidy was a formidable one, and the team would have won the Scottish League that term had it not been for the fact that they were up against a top-class Rangers team. But they did win the Glasgow Cup and the Glasgow Charity Cup, and for Joe there was one particular occasion when he captured both the imagination and the hearts of the faithful.

It was New Year's Day at Ibrox when Joe scored both goals in Celtic's 2-0 victory in front of 70,000 fans. The goals were well taken and many contemporary accounts exist of the scenes in Glasgow after the game, as the horse-drawn carriages and charabancs returned from the game. The revellers were blowing bugles, roaring Celtic songs and singing the praises of their hero Joe Cassidy!

If Joe had not been a cult hero before, he was now. A very handsome man with a touch of shyness about him, Joe was exactly what any mother would have wanted for her daughter. He was clean-cut, kept himself fit, was a war hero and, in footballing terms, he was a perfect foil for the wilder elements of McInally and Gallacher. Being an inside-left, he did not score as many goals as he might have (22 in that season), but he was very definitely the purveyor, the hard worker, the accurate passer and the man who could occasionally bring a cheer by the odd piece of football trickery.

ONLY A DISAPPOINTING defeat at Raith Rovers on a day towards the end of the campaign when Celtic had a few players missing (as we shall see) prevented the winning of the League, but there would be better luck for the Celts the following season. Still, Joe's success in 1920/21, particularly his high-profile performance on New Year's Day, earned him international recognition. He had already played for the Scottish League when he was invited to play his first game for Scotland.

This was on 12 February at Pittodrie when Scotland took on Wales. Joe was chosen to play alongside the tricky Alec Troup of Dundee, a man with whom he had struck up a rapport. Such games were big business in those days, and a crowd of more than 22,000 appeared at Pittodrie to see the first full International match of the season. Some reports of the game are hard on Joe; *The Scotsman* in particular singling him out for criticism, but the team won 2-1 with goals from Andy Wilson, and Joe retained his place for the next game.

This was a far more tricky proposition, but not for reasons that had anything to do with football. It was against Northern Ireland in Belfast. That year saw the War of Independence, as it is sometimes called, in full spate in Ireland, and for a Celtic footballer this might cause problems. The word "war" is no exaggeration. There were assassinations, bombings and a general atmosphere of terror and intimidation, as the Protestant North did its utmost to avoid home rule and protect their Protestant ascendancy, while the Roman Catholics were determined to join the South in independence. Was it a coincidence that no Rangers players were picked for Scotland that day? On the other hand, Joe Cassidy and Willie McStay of Celtic were in the Scottish team for the game that was to be played at Windsor Park, Belfast.

There was an additional complication for Joe in that he was an ex-serviceman, as indeed were many others in the Scottish team. Thus it could be that he was regarded as a legitimate target for both the Catholic side, in that he could be associated with the Army and the Black and Tans, and for the Protestant side in that he played for Scotland's perceived Catholic team, the Glasgow Celtic.

While jokes could be made about this by some of the less sensitive members of the Scottish side, and while most members of the team like Alec Troup and Joe Harris shook their heads in amazement and bewilderment at what was going on, there seems little doubt that the security of McStay and Cassidy had to be taken seriously. In fact, the game was played before a mainly Protestant 30,000 crowd who did little other than behave in the way that most crowds do, namely cheering on their own men and booing their opponents.

For reasons that were never satisfactorily explained, Scotland wore white that day with navy blue shorts (if this had some connection with the political situation it was hard to fathom), and defeated Ireland 2-0, with Cassidy scoring the late clincher which killed off what little hope the hosts might have had of getting back into the game. The left-wing pairing of Cassidy and Troup was given a good press after the game, and both men confidently expected the call for the "big" international that year, namely Scotland against England at Hampden on 9 April.

But the call never came. The team was chosen in those days by selectors, normally directors of various clubs. This was amateurish, to put it mildly, and not infrequently led to claims of favouritism and corruption. There were, therefore, many howls of anguish when the team to play England was announced and the left-wing pairing was not the expected and successful one of Cassidy and Troup, but the Rangers duo of Andy Cunningham and Alan Morton.

Celtic fans were frequently accused of not supporting Scotland, preferring the land of their forefathers. On the other hand, there were times when they had a definite feeling on injustice about them. It would be more pointed a few years later when Jimmy McGrory was frequently passed over in spite of his phenomenal goalscoring, but there were also grounds for complaint on this occasion. Joe himself maintained a dignified silence about it all. But he was clearly upset and did not play his best at Stark's Park, Kirkcaldy, when Celtic went down to Raith Rovers on the same day that Scotland beat England 3-0 at Hampden, with both Cunningham and Morton playing well and scoring, thus justifying the opinion and trust of the selectors.

But in spite of the disappointment of the end of that season, including the double blow on 9 April of losing the League and not playing in the international, Joe continued to enjoy massive popularity with the Celtic fans. Cassidy scored 23 goals that season from the inside-left position, but he did a lot more than that for his team. He was an excellent harrier and forager, and provided many opportunities for that controversial and charismatic character Tommy McInally.

In early 1922 Tommy was going through a bad spell. Crowds turned on him, berating him for not using his undeniable ability to the full. Cassidy offered a contrast. Clearly Joe possessed less natural talent, but showed far more spirit, working hard, training hard and, unlike Tommy, not indulging in the more earthly pleasures, particularly drink, which was a mammoth social problem in Glasgow and all of Scotland. If alcohol is a problem in the early years of the 21st century (as undeniably it is) it was 100 times worse in the 1920s. Joe took a drink, but in extreme moderation, and was looked up to as one of the icons of society as a result of his sober demeanour, his handsome features and his good sense of dress.

McInally got injured and vanished from the first team in the wake of the Scottish Cup defeat at Hamilton in late February. This necessitated a change in formation, and Maley hit upon the idea of making Joe the centre-forward while bringing the immensely gifted young John (nicknamed "Jean") McFarlane to the inside-right position. He was certainly fast, could take a goal and knew how to force his way through a defence. In the run-in to the 1922 championship, Joe was the mainstay of the Celtic attack, scoring goals against Hearts and Falkirk and two each in the difficult fixtures with Queen's Park and Dundee.

Joe did not score in the game which decided the League title on the last day of the season at Greenock, but only because he was double-marked. In fact, it was his friend Andy McAtee who scored the goal which earned Celtic the draw and the championship.

It was, indeed, a fine side with Gilchrist, Cringan and McMaster having now taken over the mantle of Young, Loney and Hay as the half-back line which dominated the field, sprayed passes and fed the hungry forwards. Behind them stood Shaw, McNair and Dodds, great men all who had formed the defence of Celtic for almost a decade now, and in the case of Eck McNair not far short of 20 years. In the forward line, as well as Cassidy there was Andy

McAtee from Croy, Patsy Gallacher, quite clearly one of the best players of all time, and on the left wing Adam McLean was also making his mark.

It was, however, a far from happy atmosphere in that ground at Cappielow on that day of 29 April 1922. The troubles of Ireland had clearly been imported for the occasion. Ireland itself had now voted in favour of accepting the Free State (and allowing the British to keep control of the North) but the situation there was far from settled and a civil war between the two factions would last until well into 1923. A nation was being born but the pangs of parturition were long and grievous.

To say that this had nothing to do with Scottish football is true, but it also avoids the issues that were likely to arise whenever Celtic were playing. Here the Morton support, whose team had won the Scottish Cup two weeks previously, turned on Celtic viciously, and the play was stopped more than once to clear the pitch of invaders and missiles thrown by those whose years in the khaki of the British Army had taught them rather too much aggression and violence.

Once again, it is difficult to imagine the feelings of Trooper Joe, who had done so well in the British Army during the Great War, but now found himself the target of abuse by those who accused him of being in league with Sinn Fein. One hopes that he was able to smile at all that, and he certainly did have the last laugh as Celtic's draw was enough to win them the Scottish League by one point over Rangers.

Cassidy would be thankful that he was a successful professional footballer. A wage that was more than adequate (unlike so many in those times), a steady job as long as he was young and uninjured, perks like foreign tours in the summer, and above all, the love and adulation of his many fans. He was playing for the team that he loved, he enjoyed the favour of the autocratic Maley, and life, for the moment, was sweet.

JOE'S ANNUS MIRABILIS IN a Celtic jersey was to come in the next season, 1922/23. It was all the more remarkable a campaign for Joe because the team itself was going through a transformation, and there were quite clearly a few players who did not fit in well with Maley's rigid demands on discipline. Joe Dodds had retired (perhaps prematurely); Tommy McInally, after a series of arguments with Maley, was transferred to Third Lanark to his own dismay and that of the Celtic supporters, and halfway through the season right-half Johnny Gilchrist also departed.

All this upheaval meant Celtic were virtually out of contention for the Scottish League. Cassidy was not scoring as freely as he or his fans would have liked. He had suffered a broken jaw in a clash with a Rangers player in late October, but was back three weeks later with his jaw in bandages and a week after his return scored a classic hat-trick against Third Lanark. He was then injured again, but was back to score twice on 30 December at Kirkcaldy when Celtic hanselled Raith Rovers' new stand, a building which still stands to this day. But the defeat at Ibrox on New Year's Day (in which, unlike the glorious occasion of two years previously, Cassidy failed to find the net) meant that, soon after the New Year, it became apparent that Celtic's only real chance of glory that season lay in the Scottish Cup, a trophy they had not won since before the war.

When the Cup began in January 1923, the draw was kind to Celtic. A trip to Fife was their first-round lot, to meet Lochgelly United, who had been relegated to Division Two the previous season. Celtic's many Fife fans were delighted at the sight of Joe Cassidy and the hat trick that he scored in the 3-0 defeat of the locals. He went one better the next round as non-League Hurlford were beaten 4-0 and he contributed all the goals.

The opposition may not have been all that spectacular, but it could hardly escape the notice of Scotland's selectors and others that Celtic had now scored seven goals in two games in the Scottish Cup, and that Joe Cassidy had notched them all. He had not been considered for any of the games in 1922, but now he was being watched again, particularly after he scored both of Celtic's goals in the next game against East Fife.

It was now the quarter-final stage and no-one other than Joe Cassidy had scored for Celtic. Small wonder that the Celts were named the "Cassidy Cavalcade" in the sycophantic Glasgow Observer. It was even less to be wondered at when the Scotland team to face Ireland on 3 March was announced that Joseph (sic) Cassidy was in it.

But there was also a young man called David Morris making his debut in that international team. He was the centre-half and captain of Raith Rovers, Celtic's next opponents in the Scottish Cup. Thus Cassidy faced Morris one week, and played with him the next. The Scottish Cup tie at Parkhead was well attended with more than 30,000 spectators (a huge crowd for an ordinary game in the 1920s). Morris was booed at the start because he had kept Celtic's Willie Cringan out of the Scottish team, but gradually he won the fans over by the way that he, alone of centre-halves that season, kept Cassidy quiet. It was the one round in the Scottish Cup that year that Joe did not score. But he did have the last laugh for, the concentration on Cassidy allowed left winger Adam McLean to score the only goal of the game.

The week after that, Joe travelled to Ireland to play for Scotland. Since his last trip to Belfast two years previously, things had changed totally in that the South was now a free state, but the North had anchored itself in the United Kingdom, proclaiming their loyalty to the Crown and the Protestant succession. In these circumstances, it was hardly surprising that Joe would be singled out for abuse, but he did not mind, for as he said afterwards, it proved that he was worth noticing. In truth, although Scotland won 1-0, it was Andy Wilson who scored and Joe did not have a good game. At least, that is what the selectors thought, because in the remaining two Scotland games of the season, the left-wing pairing was the Rangers duo Tommy Cairns and Alan Morton.

Joe had being playing at inside-left in that Belfast game, and this was out of position, as he was now a centre-forward. Indeed, there were those who felt that he might have been played in the number-nine slot for Scotland, but Andy Wilson could hardly be dropped as he was doing so well for both his club, Middlesbrough, and his country.

In any case, Joe had enough on his plate for Celtic, for next up was the semi-final against a strong Motherwell side. This time supporters dug deep into their pockets and more than 71,000 attended at Ibrox on 10 March. Motherwell had their own cult hero at the time – a fellow called Hugh Ferguson, who in 1927 would score the goal for Cardiff City that won the English Cup final, and thus became "the Scotsman who scored the goal which took the English Cup to Wales". Tragically, during a later spell with Dundee, he would commit suicide by gassing himself in the stand.

To return to the narrative: at this stage both Cassidy and Ferguson were banging in the goals for their respective sides; much was expected of the pair in this epic tie and, sure enough, there was early drama. Barely 40 seconds had elapsed when Joe Cassidy latched on to a through-ball and scored. A good start is often crucial in a semi-final and Celtic remained the better team. Willie Cringan was able to bottle up Ferguson while Andy McAtee scored another goal for the Celts. Cassidy had now scored a record ten goals in this campaign.

TEN WAS ALSO A very significant number in another context of the 1923 Scottish Cup final, for if Celtic were to win it would be their tenth triumph in the competition, equalling the record of Queen's Park, who had done so well in the earlier years, but who had found life so much more difficult after the legalisation of professionalism in 1893.

There were other issues at stake. Celtic had not won the Cup since before the war, and they wished to avoid the sort of complex that Rangers, for example, had about the trophy, which they had not lifted for 20 years. Then there was the case of Hibs, their opponents, who had not won it for 21 years. It had been Hibs who had been the opponents of Celtic in 1914, the last time that Celtic had secured the trophy. The managers were brothers – Willie Maley of Celtic and Alec of Hibs – and there was also the Irish dimension.

The newspapers referred to the game as the "all-green" final, or even the "Irish" final, and it is tempting to assume that the teams had a good relationship with each other. In fact, the relationship was anything but a cosy one, as Hibs had never forgiven Celtic for usurping their status in the game in the early 1890s by offering their good players better terms and conditions.

It would prove to be the greatest occasion of Cassidy's Celtic career, but it was a very poor game. Saturday 31 March 1923 was a dull but mainly dry day, and 80,000 appeared at Hampden to watch the contest. There were a great many more outside, unable to afford the entrance fee and compelled to follow the course of the game by the roars of the crowd. The Celtic crowd wore green rosettes with slogans like "Have A Go, Joe" or "Rumble Them Up, Cassidy" or "Cassidy's Cavalcade". It was clear who the fans expected to deliver the goods. Could he score twice to make it a dozen goals in this competition?

The crowd outside was like a carnival. As was the way in the 1920s, the roads to the ground were lined by beggars and singers with their Scottish and Irish ditties as they held up their placards of "Woonded (sic) in France". A few soapbox orators were ranting at the iniquities of the capitalist system or telling everyone that the Free State Government in Ireland should be ashamed of itself for not attacking the Six Counties of the North. Pickpockets (often Oliver Twist-type gangs working for a Fagin or a Sykes) and prostitutes (most of them appallingly young) plied their trade, while at the same time more respectable tradesmen were selling their fish and chips, chocolate or macaroon bars.

A few artists sold drawings of the players, with Cassidy by far the most popular subject. The handsome features twinkled everywhere, as everyone discussed how he would play. The Celtic charabanc arrived, and people rushed forward to get a glimpse of the man who would make them forget the miseries and the realities of life in industrial Scotland in the aftermath of that dreadful war.

Of course, both sets of supporters wore green and they sang the same songs about Ireland - *The Dear Little Shamrock*, *The Wearing of the Green* and *Erin's Green Valleys*, that prayer to St Patrick to be nice to them:

Hail Glorious St Patrick, dear saint of our isle
On us thy poor children bestow us a smile
For now thou are high in thy mansions above
On Erin's green valleys, look down in thy love"

Half-time came and the game was deadlocked. Then, ten minutes into the second half, Jean MacFarlane punted a hopeful ball into the Hibs penalty box, which international goalkeeper Willie Harper should have dealt with very comfortably. But he came out and fumbled the ball, which fell to Joe's feet, and the Celts' hero did the rest. Some accounts say that he headed the ball into the net, but it matters not a great deal. Celtic were a goal up and Cassidy had scored again.

The rest of the game was a poor one from a Celtic point of view, as attackers had to be brought back to help out the defence, and there were times when Joe was the only forward. But, well marshalled by Alec McNair and Willie Cringan, the Celtic defence held out and the joy of the Celtic supporters knew no bounds. They were as thrilled about the fact that it was Cassidy who scored as they were about the winning of the trophy for the tenth time, thus equalling Queen's Park.

It was one of those great nights to be a Celtic supporter, with dancing in the streets of places like the Garngad, the Gorbals, Croy, Holytown and other Celtic strongholds. It did seem that now the Scottish Cup had been won the team could go on and establish yet again some permanent dominance of Scottish football. A huge crowd had gathered outside Hampden and Cassidy, being the goalscorer, was allowed to hold the trophy as the team climbed on to their charabanc. Life could hardly have been better for the illustrious Joe Cassidy.

But that was as good as it got for Joe at Celtic. An indifferent season followed in 1923/24. Willie Cringan headed a deputation to manager Maley about an increase in salary. This was not only refused but led to Cringan being branded a troublemaker and sent packing. Joe still scored the goals – 25 in the Scottish League – but occasionally hit a drought when he was marked out of the game by defenders. Three goalless draws in October hamstrung any offensive for the Scottish League and the team exited from the Scottish Cup at the first time of asking to Kilmarnock on 26 January. They did win the Glasgow Charity Cup, but by that time damage had been done to team morale.

Cassidy must take his share of the blame for this, and it was probably a mistake for the Scottish Selectors to pick him to play for Scotland against Wales in February 1924. The team lost 0-2 at Wrexham, and Joe, along with several others, never played again. A defeat by Wales always rankled with the Scots, as they were expected to do well against the Leek-eaters, as the Welsh were disparagingly called by the fans.

Cassidy was transferred to Bolton Wanderers at the start of the next season. This move was much criticised by supporters who wondered why their hero was being thus discarded. The answer was probably nothing other than money. Joe would might have been happy to play on for Celtic, but Maley, obsessed with money as always, reckoned that a transfer fee would be better than persevering with his marksman. In addition, there was a talented young man called Jimmy McGrory awaiting the call.

Joe "left home when he left Parkhead" as the Alphabet of the Celts puts it. He settled well enough with Bolton Wanderers and scored some goals, but he was never the same man as he had been with the team that he loved. By now playing more at inside-left than at centre-forward, Joe moved on to Cardiff City, had two years with Dundee, then joined Clyde before dabbling in Irish football with Ballymena and Dundalk, eventually finishing his varied career with Greenock Morton in 1932. His odyssey was not without its success, as he won an Irish Cup medal with Ballymena in 1929, but he never seemed totally happy and settled, and there seems little doubt, had Celtic changed their minds about him, he would have returned like a shot to those supporters who adored him.

It was his old friend Alec McNair who, in his capacity as manager of Dundee, brought Joe back to Scotland in 1926. Both McNair and Cassidy would have loved to put one over their old boss Willie Maley, but this did not prove possible. Cassidy was visibly overwhelmed by the reception that he received from Celtic fans. Normally, ex-players returning to play against their old team can expect a frosty or even a hostile reception. Not in this case, however, as Joe was greeted warmly and clapped and cheered whenever he touched the ball. His cult hero status had not in any way diminished, and how he must have wished that he had stayed with Celtic in 1924.

On 19 February 1927, Celtic were drawn to play Dundee in the Scottish Cup. They won comfortably 4-2, and towards the end of the game, a Negro slave song began to be heard:

"Gone are the days when my heart was young and gay
Gone are my friends from the cotton fields away,
Gone far away to a better place I know
And I hear their gentle voices calling
Poor Old Joe.
I'm coming, I'm coming
Though my head is bending low
And I hear their gentle voices calling
Poor Old Joe".

There was no mockery in all this. Rather it was a spontaneous show of affection for one of their greatest ever heroes, who was apparently nearing the end of his career (actually it still had another five years left to run) and visibly struggling to make any impact on the fine Celtic defence, which was to prove hugely influential in winning that year's Scottish Cup. It was a very poignant indication of the great affection in which Cassidy was still held.

ABOUT HIS LIFE AFTER football, little is known. He did not seem cut out for management. He was far too nice and kindly a character. He was seen now and again at Parkhead to watch the team for whom he played with such distinction, and in 1938 many Celtic supporters would attend the Empire Exhibition at Bellahouston Park because it had been rumoured that Joe was working there as an attendant. He would reward his fans with a smile, a modest handshake and a comment or two on the contemporary football situation. Like most real heroes, he had no problem in talking to fans, even though he was still considered a superman.

Yet his career was curiously incomplete. Only four Scottish caps and one Scottish League Championship and one Scottish Cup (but what a performance in that one!) hardly justified the hero worship and adulation that followed him from the Celtic faithful wherever he went and which even transcended his early death at the age of 52 in 1949. The early 1920s are indelibly associated with the name of Cassidy in the eyes of Celtic supporters.

TOMMY McINALLY

1919-1928

BHOYS CAREER

Games	213
Goals	127
Caps	2

MAGIC MOMENT

The 1927 Scottish Cup final saw the McInally-inspired Celtic team so far ahead that Tommy could afford to entertain his fans by perpetual clowning and also giving an exhibition of his tremendous talent.

'THE BOY WONDER'

TOMMY was one of the bad bhoys. A brilliant football player with magnificent individualist skills and the ability to delight the crowd by his superb play and clowning, Tommy was, nevertheless, a gross under-performer. In character, he would resemble George Best, Jimmy Johnstone or Jim Baxter. He also had a similar amount of footballing ability. The sad fact was that he never came vaguely close to fulfilling his potential.

A key factor in Tommy's life was his relationship with manager Willie Maley. Maley was, of course, strict and stern, at least on the outside. Inside there was a softer side of him. He was a man who had suffered not a few personal disasters in his life, and occasionally his compassion, sometimes his misguided compassion, got the better of him. Sometimes he was far too lenient with McInally. In a similar situation some 40 years later, it would have to be said that Jock Stein handled the wayward Jimmy Johnstone a great deal better.

LITTLE IS KNOWN FOR certain about Tommy's early life. Indeed, there is a mystery about his birth. Legend has it that he was born in Barrhead round about the turn of the century, but diligent research among the records has uncovered no "Thomas McInally" at a suitable date. What seems to have happened is that Tommy was born under another name. Perhaps he was illegitimate, perhaps he was an orphan, but it seems that he was brought up by the mother of another Celtic player called Arthur McInally.

That Tommy had no strong father figure in his life becomes obvious from his subsequent behaviour. But then again, in the 1920s there were many young people who lacked a father figure thanks to the dreadful living conditions of the time, the grossly inadequate medical facilities, the effect of tobacco and the "demon drink" rightly attacked by Christian and Socialist organisations as being the "enemy of the working class". Then, too, there was the horrendous casualty rate of the Great War.

It was during the Great War (when football actually flourished in spite of the authorities' attempt to curtail it) that Tommy cut his teeth in the game. There was a Tom McInally who turned out for Croy Celtic (and that may or not be our Tommy) but certainly our man was playing for the Glasgow junior team St Anthony's in seasons 1917/18 and 1918/19. The "Ants" stadium is close to Ibrox Park, and Rangers' manager William Wilton was sufficiently interested in the precocious youngster to give him a couple of trials.

At this time religion would not have presented a huge barrier to young Tommy signing for Rangers. The sectarian policy was not clearly defined until the 1920s. Nevertheless, there was a tendency for youngsters of a Catholic family with an Irish name to drift towards the then-more-successful club on the other side of the city. Maley's spy network watched St Anthony's, too. Maley himself came to watch one day, and on 22 May 1919, Tommy was offered terms at Parkhead and accepted with alacrity.

The wages for a youngster would not have been a king's ransom, but they were more than adequate and more than average. It is difficult for us to capture any inkling of what

Glasgow's living conditions must have been like in 1919. To the generations of poverty, deprivation and alcoholism had been added other factors brought about by the war. Soldiers were returning, demanding better conditions from a Government cynically indifferent to their plight in spite of all the rhetorical cant about "a land fit for heroes to live in". Violence and revolution had happened in Russia; it was still (poignantly for Celtic's fans) going on in Ireland; and it came very close to happening in Glasgow in the George Square disturbances of 1919.

Yet football was football. Celtic had won the League in 1918/19, and their first game in defence of the title was McInally's debut. It was against Clydebank at Parkhead on 16 August 1919. The attendance given was 12,000 which seems a little on the low side, but then again, the war had affected the Celtic-supporting part of Glasgow badly. In addition, the Scottish League had increased the prices to what many would have considered to be an unacceptable level. The result was that many fans hung around outside the ground listening to the roars of the crowd, then when the exit gates were unlocked to allow the crowd home, would take advantage of the chance to see the last few minutes for nothing.

As he ran out that day, Tommy would have noticed in the enclosure at the front of the Grant Stand on the south side of the ground the large amount of men in the "hospital blue" uniform of the disabled and the badly disfigured, the blinded being brought in, hand upon the shoulder of the man in front to hear a commentary on the action from a stentorian voiced volunteer. The players would also have been aware of the ominously large presence of policemen in case of any disturbance.

Tommy played at centre-forward, Celtic beat the under-strength Clydebank 3-1 and Tommy scored all three. It was as emphatic a debut as anyone could have wished, and little happened in the subsequent autumn to dispel the notion that Celtic had a world-beater in Tommy McInally. "The Boy Wonder" was the phrase used to describe him as the goals rained in. The first trophy of the season came Celtic's way on 4 October in the Glasgow Cup final, when Tommy, having scored a hat-trick in the semi-final, notched the only goal of the game against Partick Thistle on the big day.

Some 45,000 saw this game. It was not so much that the Celtic fans needed a hero in those desperate days. They absolutely craved one. And they found one in this Barrhead boy with the tricks, the speed, the cannonball shot and perhaps, above all, the ability to make them laugh with his gestures and actions, sometimes even bringing a smile to the face of the sternest of referees, and even causing the austere Willie Maley to relax on occasion.

But even at this early stage, the seeds of Tommy's downfall had been sown. Defenders were none too gentle in their treatment of "the boy" and injuries resulted. More insidiously, Tommy began to show signs of an inability to cope with the pressure involved in being talked about incessantly by half of Scotland's population and as Jimmy McGrory would put it later with a certain amount of understatement: "Tommy was not averse to a tipple".

It was not McInally's fault that Celtic failed to land either of the national honours in season 1919/20. He missed the Scottish Cup quarter-final against Rangers, and was sidelined through injury at several key points of the Scottish League season, notably at the end of January when two games were lost. But he did play in the Glasgow Charity Cup at the end of the season, and a haul of the two Glasgow medals was considered to be not bad for his first campaign.

Season 1920/21 was remarkably similar in terms of trophies landed and goals scored (36 in each season in competitive games), and the Tommy McInally cult visibly grew and grew with songs being sung about the new hero. The Sally of Our Alley song clearly lent itself to adaptation to "Tommy, Tommy, Tommy McInally", and Harry Lauder's Roamin' In the Gloamin' found itself becoming:

"Tommy McInally
He's the best player in the land,
Tommy McInally
Is the star of the Celtic Stand,
Even though I got the sack
How I love my Tommy Mack
Yes I love you, Tommy McInally!"

Jokes abounded about Tommy. A billboard near Celtic Park advertised the latest craze for the rich – a motor car. Somebody scrawled on it: "Aye, but is it as fast as Tommy McInally?" Tommy had, in summer 1920, drawn even more attention to himself by entering a few athletic competitions, and in October beat W B Applegarth (generally regarded as Scotland's best athlete) over 100 yards. Tommy himself courted this popularity, frequently being seen talking to fans and, on occasion, to the despair of Maley, entering public houses where he knew that his adoring fans would buy him drinks. Maley once reproved him for this saying: "Tommy, you were seen coming out of a public house last night at ten o'clock". The reply was: "Aye, Boss, I had tae come oot at ten – they were closing!" On another occasion McInally was late for training and Maley said: "Tommy, you should have been here at half-past nine this morning." The riposte: "Why, Boss, what happened?"

Yet season 1920/21 failed to land the Scottish League or the Scottish Cup, and Celtic fans looked at that forward line which absolutely oozed with talent, and scratched their heads. When the team did well, they were absolutely unstoppable, as for example in the New Year's Day game at Ibrox when McInally was instrumental in Joe Cassidy's two goals, or in an encounter with St Mirren at Parkhead in February when the fans lapsed into ecstasies at McInally's hat trick. There was Patsy Gallacher, arguably their greatest ever player, there was the faithful and dedicated Joe Cassidy, fine wingers in Andy McAtee and Adam McLean – and there was Tommy McInally.

A MYTH GREW UP that Tommy McInally and Patsy Gallacher did not like one another and could not play together. Certainly they were two of a kind, and it was no uncommon sight to see them having words with each other on the field when a pass went astray, but McInally was far too light-hearted a youngster to nurture any animosity. Besides, he had his fans to entertain . . .

Perhaps, however, therein lay a great deal of the problem. Entertaining fans and winning games for the team are not always compatible, and several times in the run-in at the end of the 1920/21 season, the team under-performed and lost while McInally appeared less concerned about the team than his own showing. He was marked out of the game at Stark's Park, Kirkcaldy, in April by a brilliant centre-half called Dave Morris, and it was this contest rather than any other which conceded the League title to Rangers.

It was the following season, 1921/22, that McInally began to go to seed. His performances were inconsistent, to put it mildly. The old brilliance was still there, but now apparently kept for special occasions. In addition, he was quite clearly slower, had put on a bit of weight, and looked half fit, often giving the impression of being lazy. In truth, his dissolute lifestyle had already caught up with him at the age of 22.

Sometimes the crowd laughed with him, but more often they turned on him with the viciousness of which a Parkhead crowd is capable, especially when they feel that someone is not pulling his weight. The exit from the Scottish Cup was a dreadful performance from the whole team, and McInally in particular, as Celtic went down 1-3 to Hamilton Accies at home. Maley was seen to remonstrate with his players even before they got to the dressing room for half-time, and McInally was singled out by the crowd. They knew he could do better.

Tommy feigned insouciance, but it was noticeable that the rest of the team made little effort to talk to him. Effectively they were playing a man short, and McInally was dropped at the beginning of March. Immediately after that, the form improved and the team won the League in breathtaking style, but Tommy stayed on the sidelines allegedly injured but in fact dropped.

This was a blow to Maley's pride. He always thought that he could be the father figure for Tommy, that he could talk him round and that Tommy would very soon be a part of the Celtic family. Sadly this would not happen, and indeed Maley's hand was forced by a bizarre incident at the Kilwinnoch Highland Games in the summer when McInally was allowed to guest for Partick Thistle in a five-a-side tournament, but the Celtic quintet refused to take the field unless he was removed.

It was with a heavy heart that Maley decided that McInally had to go. For public consumption, he concocted a story that Tommy had made exorbitant wage demands, but in fact it was for reasons to do with team morale that the player left Celtic Park on 4 September 1922. It might have been better if he had gone to England, but he travelled little more than a mile away to Third Lanark, now managed by ex-Celt Alec Bennett. Even Rangers had renewed their interest, but Maley reckoned that the support could not countenance that!

GLASGOW CONTINUED TO TALK about Tommy McInally, however. He was as famous a character in the city as the Red Clydeside dominie John McLean or the Independent Labour Party MP Jimmy Maxton, who was a friend of Tommy. Tommy remained on good terms with Maley in his temporary exile, and he even made his peace with some of the Celtic players, who were quite content to be friends with him, as long as they did not have to play alongside him.

In truth, he was a difficult man to hate. Perpetually cheery and seldom nasty, Tommy was the perennial Glasgow "keelie" with his patter, his way of talking to children and his general humanity. He may well have had relationships with women (certainly there would be many who would claim in later years to be the illegitimate offspring of Tommy McInally), he certainly drank more that was good for him, but one thing that Tommy did not do was swear. He hated foul language, telling people that they would go to the "big black fire" if they persisted in using bad words, and Bob McPhail, who would in later years play for Rangers, said that than Tommy McInally, there was no more gentle or sociable character.

Tommy was with Third Lanark for three years. His play was the same as it had been for Celtic, inconsistent with the occasional piece of brilliance, and his application was suspect. He was in trouble with referees – he was, for example, sent off in a game against Celtic in January 1925 – and it was not one of the happiest times of Tommy's life. He was also out of sorts because he really did want to return to his first and only love, the Celtic. Aware that he had messed up badly, he would frequently seek out Willie Maley in the same way as he would seek out his parish priest, and confess.

At this point in spring 1925, Maley took a gamble. He knew that McInally was "pining for home", but how would the Celtic players and fans react if they got more of the nonsense that had befouled season 1921/22? Celtic had won the Scottish Cup in 1925, but Maley knew that the hero of that particular hour, Patsy Gallacher, was now 34 and increasingly injury prone. The three years without McInally had not been great ones. Perhaps Tommy had at last grown up. On 12 May 1925, everyone was happy. Third Lanark got a transfer fee for the under-performing McInally, and Tommy was returning to his spiritual home. The Celtic fans, already on a high after their Cup success, welcomed him back with rapture. It was, indeed, almost an exact parallel with the biblical story of the prodigal son. The fatted calf was delivered to Tommy in the shape of fanatical devotion once again.

And everything must be forgiven in the context of that brilliant 1925/26 season. Tommy was now no longer centre-forward – that position had gone to a youngster called McGrory – but was now an inside-forward of talent, application and flair. Celtic were fortunate to be fairly clear of injuries that season, and thus it was that a fine forward line of Connolly, Thomson, McGrory, McInally and McLean brought home the bacon in spectacular style.

The Glasgow Cup in October was lost thanks in part to Maley's strange decision to bring back the blatantly half-fit Patsy Gallacher, but then during the winter months the team buckled to, and lost only two League games between then and the end of the season. McInally was superb. "His control and nerve was such that he could still cause bewilderment among defenders and amusement on the terracings with his patented mannerism of stopping suddenly, in order to look around with casual insolence, before re-directing the flow of the game" (The Glory and The Dream, Woods and Campbell). In addition, Tommy was able to bring out the best in young McGrory.

It was the time when Tommy's attitude was right. He trained hard, he worked hard, he played hard and he was very recognisably a cog in a very well-oiled Celtic machine. In short, he toed the line. It was as if he realised that he had done wrong in the past, that Maley had given him a second chance. Now he was saying to Maley and his vast following: "I'm sorry". Crowds rolled back to Celtic Park, and the away following often caused safety problems, such was its extent and boisterous nature.

Although he was now a purveyor rather than a predator, Tommy still managed to contribute 24 competitive goals that season, a frequent ploy of his being to get the ball on the edge of the penalty box, feint a pass to the ever lurking McGrory, and then when McGrory had taken two defenders with him, Tommy would run through and score himself.

The Scottish League was thus won for the first time since 1921/22 (an indication, perhaps, of what life might have been like if Tommy had not gone to Third Lanark) and the Scottish Cup final was reached. Tommy did not have a great game in that disappointing encounter with St Mirren, partly because of the absence through injury of his left-wing partner, the prodigious Adam McLean. St Mirren scored early on, Celtic were not wearing their green-and-white jerseys, and all in all it was one of the club's less happy Hampden appearances.

But if Tommy was disappointed, as well he might have been, there was a certain compensation in the winning of the Glasgow Charity Cup. This competition was played at the same time as the 1926 General Strike, and the final against Queen's Park took place at Hampden on 15 May, the day after the strike had collapsed. For a change, the issue was not religion in Glasgow. If anything, it was social class, with Celtic clearly representing the workers against the fat-cat, capitalist Queen's Park. The workers may have lost the General Strike, but Tommy spearheaded Celtic to victory that day with a goal he scored himself and another feed to Jimmy McGrory.

TOMMY ALSO MADE HIS international debut that season. The Celtic left wing of McInally and McLean was chosen for the game against Ireland at Ibrox on 27 February. It was a fine Scottish win, 4-0, with the great Hughie Gallacher of Newcastle United scoring a hat-trick. Tommy played well, and possibly felt that he was good enough to keep his place for the "big" International against England at Old Trafford. Sadly, both he and Adam McLean were passed over in favour of Rangers' Andy Cunningham and Everton's Alec Troup.

Not for the first time did Celtic fans see an element of bias in this. Cunningham was a fine player, but McInally was having a superb season, and on any rational basis, it was difficult to see why he was not playing for Scotland. But Scotland teams in those days were picked by a bunch of selectors who did not always know much about the game. It may be that McInally's character counted against him, rather than his footballing ability. In any case the edge was taken off McInally's objections when Scotland won 1-0.

His only other international cap came the following autumn, once again at Ibrox, but this time against Wales, whom Scotland beat 3-0, a good performance against a nation whom they didn't always beat. But by the time of the England game, McInally was once again passed over. In truth, McInally hadn't had such a successful season in 1926/27. Although the Glasgow Cup was secured by a fine win over Rangers, League form was inconsistent, mirroring the performances of McInally, who was sometimes brilliant, at other times lethargic and uninterested. A series of weak defeats away from home in the spring effectively killed any challenge.

But there was the Scottish Cup, the final of which has been called not without cause "The McInally Cup Final". The final had been reached by disposing of strong teams like Dundee and Patsy Gallacher's Falkirk, and the opponents on the big day were Second Division East Fife, a part-time team from the mining town of Methil, who had earned everyone's admiration for coming back from the horrors of the General Strike and its aftermath, to reach the final. But no-one really expected them to win.

Tommy was back in the centre-forward position that day because of an injury to McGrory, and although the Fifers scored first, they were never really in it, as McInally took charge. When the score had reached 3-1, Tommy had no real desire to hammer the Fifers. Celtic might have made it double figures if he had taken all the chances that came his way that day, but he decided to clown instead. "McInally delighted the now happy Celtic choristers with a few of the balloon variety" was the way one newspaper put it to describe his deliberate attempts to put the ball as high into the terracing as he could. The Celtic fans loved this, and even the Fife fans realised that he was doing this to keep them out of the record books.

He also did impersonations of Charlie Chaplin with his famous walk, talked incessantly to the referee Tom Dougray about horse racing, politics and even religion, clapped any good move from East Fife and at full time presented every single East Fife man to the crowd. The 1927 Scottish Cup final was indeed the Tommy McInally show. It was also the first Scottish Cup final to be broadcast on the radio (enterprising ice-cream parlours and restaurants in Methil, the home of East Fife, rigged up primitive wirelesses with loudspeakers for their customers). Sadly no recording of the game seems to exist. It would be interesting to hear what the radio commentator made of all this.

IT MIGHT HAVE BEEN better if Tommy's Celtic career had finished there, for his last season 1927/28 was a disaster. Tommy was back to his slothful, profligate ways, earning several unhappy nicknames as a result. The storm petrel was a bird that was seen when trouble was imminent, and such was Tommy's ability to fall out with Maley and his team-mates that he was named after it. Even less pleasant was "the Glaxo Baby". Glaxo produced baby food, and their advertisement contained a picture of a healthy, chubby faced, fat baby – something which struck a chord with the undernourished of Scotland in the 1920s, when emaciation and "failure to thrive" were common. Tommy McInally put on so much weight in the summer of 1927 that the fans were visibly shocked to see him take the field. In spite of that, he played well in the side which won the Glasgow Cup in October.

But, following one or two indifferent performances, the crowd turned on him in a big way on 3 December 1927 in a miserable home defeat by Motherwell. Celtic fans are very unforgiving when someone doesn't try, and when they feel that he can do better. This was clearly the case with Tommy. The press turned on him with quotes like "McInally was deficient in every phase", "One despairs of the wasted talent of Tommy McInally", "McInally seems to think that the ball should come to him as of right, wrapped up like a Christmas present". Maley, who should have taken action earlier, had a word with him before the following game.

It was to be played at Perth, and McInally turned up at Buchanan Street station in no fit condition to play football or do much else. In addition, he became abusive and told Maley and the rest of the team a few home truths. Naturally he had to be suspended for this – in this case for the rest of 1927.

He recanted, apologised and was allowed back into the team for the New Year's fixture against Rangers. Once again, with McInally toeing the line, the form of the team picked up, with Tommy feeding McGrory to score his record eight goals against Dunfermline in late January. But the team then went up to Keith on Scottish Cup business. Both McInally and McGrory scored hat-tricks, but McInally then went AWOL and pleaded unconvincingly that he had "fallen asleep" somewhere. Whether this was Tommy on a bender or whether there was a Highland lady involved was never established, but he was allowed back on sufferance.

But the next time this happened, things were far more serious. It was before, not after a Scottish Cup game. Celtic were based at the Seamill Hydro hotel before a quarter-final game against Motherwell, and his team-mates played a trick on him. One of them phoned up and in a disguised voice pretended to be a reporter for a newspaper wishing to interview Tommy. He accepted and talked at length about how good a player he was etc, until giggles gave the game away. Tommy, himself a great prankster, could not take this, and disappeared for about a month, presumably finding solace in the liquid refreshment not available at Hydro hotels.

In his absence the team prospered, and looked set to win the League and the Cup without him. But Maley once again fell for the pleadings of the apparently repentant Tommy McInally, who had seen his priest, who was seeking help for his problem, who was now training hard etc, and allowed him back. The team immediately lost the next two games (effectively handing the championship to Rangers) and then catastrophically went down 0-4 in the Scottish Cup final.

Much has been written about how Rangers broke their 25-year hoodoo when Davie Meiklejohn sank the penalty kick; not enough has been said about the culpability of McInally, whose poisonous attitude soured the Celtic dressing room and led to a heavy defeat by a team who were their inferiors. The League thrown away, the Cup lost, Maley now realised that his wayward genius would have to go. "I must confess I always had a soft spot for the boy" said Maley. But this soft spot had led Celtic to disaster in 1928.

When Sunderland came in with a bid for Tommy and his left-wing partner Adam McLean, it was with heavy heart but nonetheless a feeling of relief that McInally said "Goodbye". The fans were devastated, but the wiser of them realised to what extent Tommy had been responsible for the 1928 disasters, and were reconciled to his going. Celtic would take a long time to recover.

Tommy's subsequent life was a peripatetic one at Sunderland, Bournemouth, Morton, Derry City, Armadale and Nithsdale Wanderers. He never stayed long at any of these places, as his heart was still with Celtic. Yet he'd had his opportunity to be the greatest of them all, and had thrown it away. He was hardly the first or last Scottish footballer to press the self-destruct button, but few have done it so many times after being given opportunities, and few have done it so comprehensively, killing the faith of all those who adored him, like the man whose house was on fire and who urged the fireman to "save Tommy McInally", the picture that he kept of him. It was a pity that Tommy did not do more to save himself.

Yet Tommy was not a man who bore any sort of grudge. Very happily in early January 1932, he turned up to be a linesman at Patsy Gallacher's testimonial game. Looking now like a house end and walking like a barrel being rolled down a hill, Tommy joked and clowned continuously. At Celtic's Golden Jubilee dinner in 1938, Tommy was joking with Maley and generally being the life and soul of the party.

For money, he turned to other entertainment, trying stand-up comedy and singing, impressing everyone with his wide repertoire of Scottish and Irish songs. During the Second World War, he did his bit in the munitions industry, the only job he ever had outside football and then only because wartime regulations compelled him to do something. People would nudge each other in the street, pointing at the overweight roué and say: "That's Tommy McInally". Occasionally he would write columns for newspapers on the contemporary football scene. Like many footballers he died young, only in his mid-fifties, in 1955.

THE CULT STATUS OF Tommy McInally was due to the fact that in his day so many of the supporters were like him. He was, indeed, one of them. It was a very rare working-class man in Glasgow in the 1920s and 1930s who did not have some sort of problem with alcohol, either indulging himself or experiencing the effects on others. Many other people might have starred in other walks of life as well, had it not been for that fatal flaw. Yet it was particularly galling when a Glaswegian footballer lacked the discipline to make the most of his superb talent. Celtic under-performed in the 1920s and 1930s, allowing Rangers to win far too much. Had Tommy McInally been able to harness his own talents, to believe in himself, this need not have been the case.

The story goes that Maley, in his late eighties, was asked one day who was his greatest ever footballer. He talked at length about Doyle, Quinn, McMahon, Delaney, McGrory and Gallacher before being pressed on who was actually the greatest. Maley paused, looked reflectively into the fire, turned to his interlocutor and said: "The greatest? Why, that was Tom McInally!"

JIMMY McGRORY

1921-1937

BHOYS CAREER

Games	501
Goals	522
Caps	7

MAGIC MOMENT

In March 1936 Jimmy McGrory scored a hat-trick in three minutes against Motherwell as he led Celtic to their first Scottish League triumph for ten long barren years.

'THE GOLDEN CRUST'

SO sang the Celtic fans throughout the 1920s and 1930s. There may have been unemployment and depression, there may have been the dismal sight of the war wounded and the fear of another conflict as the funny man with the moustache rose to power in Germany, there may have been some dreadful performances on the field from Celtic . . . but there was always Jimmy McGrory.

McGrory gave the Celtic fans what they wanted _ the scoring of goals. The song which begins "They gave us James McGrory and Paul McStay" ends up with "to play football in the good old Celtic way." He was what Celtic fans needed. He was the icon of the team. He was the man who scored the goals that sent the crowd home happy and helped them to forget the miseries of what might have been a fairly pointless existence.

He was from the Celtic stronghold of the old Garngad, and he cut his teeth playing for St Rochs. Maley, always on the lookout for new talent, was told of him and watched him. McGrory himself would say that he didn't want to go to Celtic because of the pressure that would be put on him, but when the call came, he did not hesitate. "I grabbed my cap and ran all the way" he was reputed to have said.

It was Maley who looked after the youngster. McGrory's own father had died in a freak accident in the autumn of 1924, and the manager, whose own family life had been far from happy, tried to be a surrogate father to the earnest young McGrory. Jimmy had attended his father's funeral in the morning, and Maley suggested he play for Celtic in the afternoon. He did so, and scored a goal. Maley had already tried this paternal approach with Tommy McInally, but Tommy had been a bad boy and had let him down. McGrory, a decent lad from the traditional poor but honest home background, would not.

THE 1924/25 CAMPAIGN was McGrory's first at Parkhead following a year in which he had been farmed out to Clydebank. It was not a great League season for Celtic, with results being inconsistent and disappointing, and it was now becoming clear that the great Patsy Gallacher was ageing. In addition, the young McGrory picked up a few injuries as he was beginning to learn some unpleasant truths about brutal defenders in the top flight of Scottish football.

But he had recovered as Celtic had reached the final of the Scottish Cup. They had done so by astonishing the world and showing their fans what they were capable of, beating Rangers 5-0 in the semi-final. McGrory had scored twice that day, but the fans really craved something more tangible. Were they to win the Scottish Cup that year, it would mean that they would have won it 11 times, once more than the record of Queen's Park.

The opponents were Dundee, who were 1-0 up at half-time. This was the day that Patsy Gallacher scored his remarkable goal. A spectator at that game has little great recollection of that goal, as it followed a melee with loads of players involved. It all happened quickly and very few of the fans got a great view. He did, however, have a clear recollection of the young McGrory's winner. "It was a free-kick to be te'en by "Jean" McFarlane on the left. Jean pu'ed up his stockings afore he took the kick. The ba' cam ower and hovered ower the tap o' the line o' defenders and forrits. Suddenly a green-and-white figure catapulted forrit and heided the ba awae inti far corner. It was a lang time afor the crowd realised that he had scored. It happened that quick". McGrory himself claimed that he was stunned as he hit the ground and he thought he heard thunder. It was, in fact, the roar of the crowd, greeting a monumental Celtic goal.

The full-time whistle saw great scenes of Celtic rejoicing. Not only had they won the Scottish Cup, but they had also seen the emergence of a new Celtic cult hero, in this young, shy but courageous figure. He was still trembling long after the game when Maley came in with the Scottish Cup. In those days, the Cup was presented in private to the manager and directors of the club in the board room of Hampden and the best that the fans could hope for was the sight of some of their heroes with the trophy on the team bus.

They lined the streets about eight deep that night, and great was the joy at the sight of the young McGrory holding the trophy. Maley had insisted on this. His young protégé had won the Cup for the club. It was therefore right that he should be the man who carried it. "Give young McGrory the Cup" he had said.

Glory had thus begun for James Edward McGrory. Celtic fans do love a personality goalscorer, and they had clearly enjoyed this 20 years earlier in Jimmy Quinn, who had similarly marked his Celtic career with a triumph in a Scottish Cup final, namely the hat-trick scored against Rangers in 1904. There were remarkable similarities between the two Jimmies. Broad shoulders, speed, ability to jump and head, courage, wholeheartedness and, importantly, an irrepressible love of the Celtic and their supporters. "Once a Celt, always a Celt" it was said.

Jimmy Quinn had now been retired for about a decade, but was still very much part of the Parkhead scene, always there to help (unpaid) and attending every game. Like McGrory, he was modest and shy – characteristics which belied their enthusiastic and aggressive performance on the field. The elder Jimmy sought out the younger one, and offered advice, guidance and support. McGrory was possibly overwhelmed by all this. Here was this demigod seeking him out to talk to him. McGrory was delighted to discover that the man from Croy was just as shy as he was, but the two of them struck up an immediate rapport, and now McGrory had the greatest advice going.

He was also very quickly a Glasgow personality. Walking down the street was now a difficult operation as supporters sought him out to talk to him. Less pleasant ones would beg tickets or even money from him, and there would always be the odd abusive comment from a supporter of the other side. The kind-hearted Jimmy always found it difficult to deal with unpleasant people, and it would perhaps explain why he was never the greatest of managers in later years.

The year after the momentous Scottish Cup triumph saw the winning of the Scottish League. Patsy Gallacher had now gone, but in his place had returned the great Tommy McInally. The football played in that year was absolutely superb, McGrory scored 52 goals and the supporters were perpetually in raptures. The creative among the support made up songs for every member of the side, but the chorus was always:

"McGrory, McGrory, Hallelujah!
The Celts go marching on."

But things would not stay as good as that forever. Rangers had a fine side as well, and although McGrory seldom fell short of the mark, several other departments of the team did not do so well. McGrory was injured in the latter part of the 1926/27 season and thus missed another Scottish Cup final, but there had been compensation in the winning of a couple of caps for the Scottish League. Speculation was rife about the possibility of a full international cap for Scotland.

The problem was a man called Hughie Gallagher, a superb centre-forward for Airdrie and Newcastle United. It was difficult to unseat him, as he was such a prolific scorer, but McGrory's chance came on 25 February 1928 when he was chosen to play for Scotland against Northern Ireland at Firhill. It was felt that he could hardly be ignored, as six weeks previously he had set up a record by scoring eight goals in a single game against Dunfermline Athletic.

Playing for Scotland was a great honour, but Celtic fans were often very cynical about the lack of caps for their own players. Sunny Jim Young, for example, had only played once for his country, and although the great Jimmy Quinn had won the day for Scotland against England at Hampden in 1910, in both 1908 and 1912 he had been played on the left wing out of position to accommodate someone who was not quite so good. In any case, many Celtic supporters made it clear that they were Irish rather than Scottish.

Jimmy's first big day for Scotland was a disaster. Scotland lost 0-1 to Northern Ireland, and that was considered a disgrace for a country that, not without cause, considered itself the best in the world. Scapegoats had to be found, and although Jimmy was not the only failure, he was not invited to play again for the national side for some time, the centre-forward's spot returning to Hughie Gallacher for Scotland's most famous International of all, the 5-1 Wembley Wizards' beating of England on 31 March 1928.

It would be less easy to explain some of his other omissions from the Scotland squad, in particular why he never played for Scotland against England at Wembley. In 1930, 1932, 1934 and 1936, Scotland travelled to London without McGrory. Apart from the last mentioned which was an honourable draw, these games ended in dreadful defeats in which England took full revenge for the Wembley Wizards game of 1928 which hurt them so much. Celtic fans could not understand it, and did little to hide their glee as Scotland were defeated time and time again while the solution to the goalscoring problem was ignored. In 1930 Jimmy Fleming of Rangers got the nod, in 1932 it was Neil Dewar of Third Lanark, 1934 saw the surprising recall of Hughie Gallacher and in 1936 came the astonishing choice of David McCulloch of Brentford. With all due respect to these men, they were not a patch on James McGrory.

Such was the paranoia of Celtic fans that the non-selection of McGrory was seen in terms of anti-Celtic prejudice. There may have been something in that in the minds of certain selectors, but it is more likely that incompetence rather than bigotry was responsible. McGrory did play twice for Scotland against England at Hampden. On both occasions Scotland won and McGrory scored. In 1931, in front of Labour Prime Minister Ramsay MacDonald, McGrory netted in the 2-0 victory, and in 1933 he scored twice, the second the late winner when he picked up a pass from his friend Bob McPhail of Rangers and hammered home the goal which created the Hampden Roar and was heard clearly on the other side of the city. These two great McGrory occasions, which raised his cult status to all of Scotland rather than just among Celtic fans, did little, however, to answer the question of why he was never given a chance to play for Scotland at Wembley.

Apart from the games already mentioned, he played twice each against Wales and Ireland. On the three of these four occasions he scored, which makes it even harder to explain why the great Jimmy McGrory played only seven times for Scotland.

BUT THERE WAS NEVER the slightest doubt that he could produce the goods for Celtic, and the affinity he had with Celtic and their fans was proved in the incident when the despicable Maley tried to sell him. It was despicable because there was a slight feeling of underhandedness and subterfuge about it all. Maley and McGrory, good Catholics both, were going on a pilgrimage to Lourdes in the summer of 1928. As if by chance en route in London, they met Herbert Chapman, the newly appointed manager of Arsenal, a man with unlimited funds at his disposal to awaken the sleeping and grossly wealthy giant that was Arsenal. The sum of £8,000 (huge in 1928) was offered on the way down. The two managers were in agreement, but McGrory, the home-loving Celt, refused. On the way back from Lourdes, they all met again and this time the offer had been raised to £10,000, then more or less a blank cheque, with McGrory virtually asked to name his own terms. He still said 'no'.

The background to all this was the need for Celtic to build their new stand at the London Road side of the ground. Celtic required money, and the transfer of their most priceless asset was required to pay for it all. Celtic without McGrory would have been completely unthinkable, but no more so than McGrory without Celtic. As he said himself: "McGrory of the Arsenal would not have sounded anything like McGrory of the Celtic." When this story became known, McGrory was loved even more, if that were possible.

The goals continued to rain in. A grand total of 550, with 410 of them in the Scottish League, sounds impressive, but even that does not take into account the quality of the goals scored. As with so many strikers, a large percentage were simply tap-ins because of his ability to be in the right place at the right time, but so many were far more aesthetic than that. A high proportion were headers, as McGrory possessed the ability to time a jump, and he had powerful neck muscles, propelling it netwards as if it had been kicked. A goal scored at Arbroath in 1936 is much remembered. The ball was bobbing about on the edge of the penalty area about knee height, when McGrory hurled himself forward to head the ball home from about 18 yards.

One curses those who were far too late in inventing videos and DVDs, for very few, if any, of McGrory's great goals are available for us to see. Ironically, one that is visible is the only goal of the 1933 Scottish Cup final against Motherwell, and it was a simple tap-in, a goal which he himself would dub in later years "the saftest o' the faimilie" after the famous Harry Lauder song of the time.

In addition to his other attributes, Jimmy was also fearless. Not all the defenders in Scottish football were as sporting as he was, and he was not infrequently the object of brutal tackles from those who knew of no other way to stop him. There were some fair players as well, not least his great adversary Davie Meiklejohn of Rangers, with whom he retained a good relationship until Davie's untimely death in 1959. Then there was the legendary goalkeeper of Queen's Park and Hearts, whose very name is a byword for fair play. This was Jack Harkness.

There was the famous occasion at Parkhead when McGrory dived to head home, but the ball flew over the bar. Harkness momentarily relaxed, but then saw that McGrory's head was about to collide with the upright. He dived and diverted McGrory's head to one side of the post, thus preventing a serious injury. To the Celtic crowd, however, it looked bad and McGrory's words of "Thank You, Jack" looked from a distance like a threat. Everytime thereafter that Harkness touched the ball, he was booed for his apparent violent assault on Parkhead's darling Jimmy McGrory. The following week, McGrory made sure that the true version of events was printed in the programme, and every subsequent visit to Parkhead after that saw Jack Harkness cheered to the echo.

Harkness himself always told the tale of how one day he was walking down Buchanan Street in Glasgow when he saw McGrory on the other side of the street. McGrory nodded to him, and such were Harkness's reactions that he dived into the gutter hoping to save the imaginary ball. This story, one presumes, was not entirely true, but the fact that it was repeated on many occasions at functions and dinners did give some indication of how popular and well known a figure Jimmy McGrory was.

The year of 1931 was momentous. Not only did Jimmy get married, and tour the United States and Canada, but also he was involved in one of Celtic's most famous Scottish Cup finals, the epic struggle against Motherwell and its replay. Celtic were two goals down to a great Motherwell side, and supporters looked up at the huge clock which used to hang from the South Stand at Hampden and watched the minutes ticking away. McGrory had been subdued, but then a Napier free-kick was lofted over the heads of the defence and Jimmy was there to give a lifeline. McGrory disdained all congratulations and celebrations and ran back up the field pointing to the clock and telling everyone that eight minutes remained to be played.

Once again, Motherwell dug in and looked to have weathered the storm until the very last minute, when a cross came over from the right. Everyone rose for the ball, as the Motherwell defence could not take the risk of leaving it for the peerless McGrory. But it was not McGrory who scored. It was his marker, Motherwell's centre-half Alan Craig. "McGrory's peal of delight was heard in the stand", but he was also the first to comfort the luckless and distraught Alan Craig. In the replay, McGrory scored twice as Celtic ran out 4-2 winners.

There were bad times as well. The deaths of John Thomson and Peter Scarff cast a huge shadow over Celtic Park for several years, as indeed did the Depression and its consequent unemployment which seemed to hit Celtic supporters particularly hard. McGrory could usually be relied upon for a goal, but he was now getting older and increasingly injury prone as Celtic failed to make any impact on Rangers' supremacy.

Far too often we read in accounts of dismal performance before poor crowds in 1934 and 1935 that "McGrory ploughed a lonely furrow", "McGrory waited for the ball that never came",

"Celtic's one-man forward line ran aground again". The crowds dropped to alarming levels, with Maley berating publicly both the players for not living up to what they could be, and the crowd for not turning up in sufficiently large numbers to support them. Nostalgia for the great days of Jimmy McMenemy, Patsy Gallacher and Jimmy Quinn was the order of the day.

BUT THE TIDE TURNED as it was always likely to with McGrory around, and by season 1935/36, Jimmy's 13th in professional football, another superb Celtic team had emerged. McGrory at last had the support that his talents deserved, and the forward line of Delaney, Buchan, McGrory, Crum and Murphy was a truly phenomenal one. Buchan and Crum were superbly tireless inside-forwards, and the wing play of Delaney and Murphy was excellent. McGrory himself would later claim that all he had to do was to be there and the goals would come.

In this, Jimmy does himself less than justice, as a feature of that forward line was their ability to interchange, and that included McGrory, who would frequently appear on the left wing, in the inside-right position or even drop further back to change places with centre-half Willie Lyon for a spell. But he would never stray for long far from the centre-forward position where all the action was.

He scored 50 goals that season, as the Celtic fans rejoiced in the rebirth of their team. The crowds were now flocking back, for indeed the worst of the recession was over, and the standard of play was scintillating. McGrory's admirers ran out of nicknames for him - "King James", "The Golden Crust", "The Goal-Scoring Machine" - as the goals kept coming. The team had a few stutters, notably when they crashed shockingly out of the Scottish Cup in February to St Johnstone, but League form remained impressively consistent. McGrory's greatest day that year would be on 14 March when in a game against Motherwell he scored three times in three minutes in the middle of the second half, one of the quickest hat-tricks of all times.

> "But, wait a bit, don't be so fast,
> We've left the star turn till the last,
> There in the midst o' a'his glory
> Goal a minute James McGrory!"

This was the season in which McGrory beat the goalscoring record. In fact, he did it twice, as a mistake had been made by those who totted up the scores for records. On 19 October 1935, he overtook Steve Bloomer's record of 352, and everyone congratulated him until someone discovered that Hugh Ferguson had scored 364 goals. It mattered little, as on midwinter's day, 21 December 1935, Celtic beat Aberdeen 5-3 and McGrory's hat-trick was enough to bring him up to 366, one of them being the goal that was Jimmy's own favourite.

This time a seemingly irresistible tide swelled up for the inclusion of McGrory at Wembley. Now, as he approached his 32nd birthday, it did not take a genius to work out that he would not have many more chances of representing his country at Wembley, and no-one could say that he was not at the top of his game. "I can confidently predict that McGrory has already been pen-cilled in and will be in the team to-night, along with young Delaney" said a journalist the day that the team was to be announced. But the confident predictions proved false.

Still, McGrory continued to score his goals for Celtic, and the League was won for the first time in ten years, with Jimmy the only man to bridge those two momentous years of 1926 and

1936. It is often said that McGrory was the man who made the Celtic fans forget. Forget, that is, the horrible reality that existed in the world away from Parkhead. He had been with Celtic through the labour problems associated with the General Strike and its revengeful, vindictive aftermath, through the unemployment of the early 1930s, and now his role was surely to help them forget about the international situation. The strident bullies of Nazism were spoiling for another war, oblivious, perhaps, or little heeding, the potentially awful consequences and presumably little aware of the crowds of war-blinded or those in wheelchairs who attended Celtic's home matches at Parkhead and whose only real joy in life was the sight of another goal for Jimmy McGrory.

Nightmare scenarios abounded of aerial devastation, of appalling casualties, of the famines and plagues predicted by the Four Horsemen of The Apocalypse as the football season for 1936/37 began. War was already under way in Spain, and it was difficult not to believe that it was coming to the rest of us soon. This would be Jimmy's last full season for the club. Celtic were unlucky not to retain the Scottish League, but there was ample recompense in the shape of the Scottish Cup, won in an epic final before a record crowd against the black-and-golds of Aberdeen in April 1937. It had been hoped that McGrory might score in the final as he had done in 1925, 1931 and 1933, or even score a hat-trick which would put him in the same bracket as Jimmy Quinn, but it was not to be. He may have been disappointed, but he needn't have been. He had now collected four Scottish Cup winners medals, and his popularity remained untarnished.

He did not play many games for the club in 1937/38 as injuries were now taking a longer time to heal. On the other hand, Maley felt that even a half-fit McGrory at the age of 33 was better than anyone else and felt that another year could be eked out of him. No-one realised it at the time, but Jimmy's last game for the club was against Queen's Park in October 1937. He was yet again injured in that game, and disappeared from the team. In December Kilmarnock approached him to become their manager.

There is a certain amount of circumstantial evidence to indicate that Willie Maley was not best pleased with McGrory's departure, even though the amount of injuries that he was sustaining would make one think that the decision was the right one. Luck would have it that his first game as manager of Kilmarnock was at Celtic Park on Christmas Day 1937. He received a tremendous cheer from the Parkhead faithful as he took his seat in the directors' box (where managers sat in those days), but Celtic them proceeded to thump Kilmarnock 8-0, with Maley clearly revelling in the discomfiture of his old protégé who had dared to disobey him.

It being McGrory's first game in charge, he could hardly be blamed for it all, and very soon revenge came McGrory's way. Having by now learned a little about his own Kilmarnock players and also knowing that some of his old team-mates would take the game too lightly in the wake of the Christmas Day result, he was able to mastermind a Scottish Cup upset by beating Celtic 2-1 at Parkhead.

It was the reaction of his old boss that astounded him. Although men like Jimmy Delaney and Willie Lyon shook his hand in sporting congratulation in spite of their disappointment, Maley ignored him even when Jimmy went upstairs to his room to talk to him. Yet Maley was the man who repeatedly said: "It is our proud boast that we can taste the fruits of victory in the same spirit as the bitterness of defeat". In fact, he never had any huge problem in admitting that, on occasion, Rangers or Motherwell had been the better team. It was the fact that McGrory was an old Celt, a cult hero, that hurt. It was noticeable, too, that when Jimmy Quinn died in 1945, Maley went out of his way to stress that Quinn was the "best" and the "greatest" in circumstances that seemed to be a point being made to McGrory.

IN TRUTH, JIMMY MCGRORY was no manager. He took Kilmarnock to the Scottish Cup final in 1938, but they lost a replay to East Fife, and when, after the war, he took over at Celtic Park, his record over the next 20 years was a poor one for a team of Celtic's standing. His triumphs were as spectacular as some of the goals he scored – the all-British Coronation Cup of 1953, the 7-1 beating of Rangers in the 1957 Scottish League Cup final and a glorious League and Cup double in 1954 – but they were not nearly as many.

He was, of course, in some ways a glorified office boy for the dictatorial and ineffective regime of Bob Kelly, whose say over everything including team selection and team tactics was almost total. McGrory was far too nice a man to cause trouble, and went along with all that Mr Kelly said. It would be a different matter from 1965, after Jock Stein took over.

It was the fact that McGrory had been and remained a cult hero for Celtic that allowed Kelly and his henchmen to exploit this situation so cynically. It was very difficult for supporters to get angry at the saintly Jimmy, whose presence in the directors' box, smiling benignly at all concerned as he puffed away at his pipe, or on a train journey to Aberdeen as he was seen in the restaurant car of the train enjoying his lunch, seemed to sum up all that was old and beautiful and almost sacrosanct about Celtic. A verbal broadside on McGrory would almost be like shouting at one's granny. It was simply one of those things that was not done.

Yet results continued to be poor and disappointments intense. The inability to win the Scottish Cup in 1961 and 1963 (both finals went to heart-rending replays) led to massive street disturbances in August 1963 after a feckless game against Queen of the South. After it became known, however, that chairman Bob Kelly was away having attended the reserve game at Dumfries, the heat was taken out of the situation, as no-one felt like shouting at Jimmy McGrory. It was like the way that a garage proprietor, when he is aware that he has not done a job adequately and sees the irate customer approaching, will send out a sweet-faced 17-year-old girl to deal with the situation, knowing that it will be very difficult for the customer to rant, rave and swear at her.

It was arrant cowardice on the part of the Celtic board to hide behind their great hero. But the remarkable thing was that the hero status of McGrory did not diminish. Even after Stein took over in 1965, McGrory, by now in his early sixties, was not put out to graze, but given the loosely defined job of public relations officer, a move that was way ahead of its time and a job for which the kindly McGrory was eminently suited.

He continued, although plagued with ill health, to work until 1979 when he retired officially. He died in October 1982, an event which provoked an orgy of mourning among football fans everywhere, even among those far too young to have seen him play. Such was the cult status that he achieved – and it is no accident that in the Willie Maley song, much loved by the Celtic fans, that it is the name of Jimmy McGrory which comes first:

"Oh, they gave us Jimmy McGrory and Paul McStay…"

PETER WILSON

1923-1934

BHOYS CAREER

Games	395
Goals	15
Caps	4

MAGIC MOMENT

The day after the General Strike finished, in a tense game between working-class Celtic and middle-class Queen's Park in the Glasgow Charity Cup final, Wilson excelled as Celtic lifted the trophy 2-1.

'PETER THE GREAT'

IT is a sad fact that since the urbanisation of society there has been a certain contempt expressed of "rustics", i.e. people who live in the country. They are perceived as slow, backward and ever so slightly uncivilised. In football terms this means that supporters of Aberdeen, Inverness or Forfar, for example, are accused of doing unlikely things to sheep, and even fans of teams like Dunfermline are asked if they remembered to milk their cows.

Footballers tend not to come from a rustic background. Their haunts tend to be the teeming slums of the large cities (or at least industrial villages like Cleland or Croy) where their families have to scrape a living in order to provide them with football boots, and this life stands them in good stead for the rough treatment they will receive from brutal defenders and villainous and bigoted officials.

Peter Wilson was an exception. He came from Beith in Ayrshire, and did not know very much about Glasgow or any other city when he joined Celtic in 1923, having impressed Maley's scouts at junior level. In 1923 the move from country village to the second city of the Empire (as Glasgow was called) was an enormous step. It was not, geographically speaking, all that far, but culturally and in other ways it was light years away.

The *Third Statistical Account of Scotland*, published in 1951, describes Beith as a "wonderfully self contained" village in that people lived and worked in the village without too many commuters to Glasgow. No doubt that has changed now, but the Statistical Account also says that rather too many of the houses are "working class" and that there is a variety of employment available, from net-making for the fishing industry to glove-making, and in particular furniture-making, which was to be Peter's trade once he retired from football.

The first half of season 1923/24 saw Wilson on the fringes of the Celtic team and once or twice farmed out to Ayr United for the occasional game, but more often still playing for Beith Juniors, even though he was technically a Celtic player and paid as such to the amazement and delight of his family. He was a youth of unprepossessing appearance, with a red face, large ears (about which he would joke in later years but not at this vulnerable stage of his life), wearing on his first appearance at Celtic Park short knickerbocker trousers and a cap which was several sizes too large for him. He was shy and gauche, and there must have been times when he wondered whether he had made the right decision in joining Celtic among so many apparently worldly-wise players like Patsy Gallacher.

But there were supportive influences as well. Maley himself was kind and polite, if a little distant now and again, and there were older players like the kindly Alec McNair, now clearly past his best but still with enough football knowledge in him to benefit a youngster. In addition there were others in the same boat as himself, like Alec Thomson from a similar background in Fife, also learning the trade. Nevertheless he was always glad to get home to his native Beith after a day's training for there he was with his own folk.

He once famously got lost in Woolworth's, the popular department store, a huge shop in the 1920s. Peter was so involved in looking at the goods on display that he wandered away from his team-mates before someone realised that he was no longer with them, and a rescue operation had to be launched. In addition, special care had to be taken when crossing roads and dealing with other hazards of urban life in Glasgow.

But he never really got lost on the football field. All this time in training and in practice matches, he was impressing everyone by his footballing ability. His position was right-half, and he was particularly good at ball distribution, with many inch-perfect passes which impressed Joe Cassidy, Andy McAtee and even (eventually) that hardest of taskmasters, the quixotic and waspish Patsy Gallacher. He was tall and well built, and worked hard at his training, enjoying the physical challenges and the building up of stamina.

BUT ALL WAS NOT well at Celtic Park. Players like Johnny Gilchrist and Willie Cringan, good players both, but who had fallen out of favour, were very soon shown the door. Consequently the team were making little impact on the Scottish League. In January 1924, Celtic departed the Scottish Cup after a defeat at Kilmarnock, and after another defeat to Morton the following week, Wilson was given his chance in the first team.

It was, however, only in a friendly, and a strange friendly at that. It was 9 February, Scottish Cup day, and as both Celtic and Third Lanark had been knocked out, they were asked to stage an experimental game in which there would be two referees! That experiment was soon abandoned, but Peter Wilson played well enough to be retained at right-half, a position that would be his own, barring injury, for the next decade and more.

His first real game was the following midweek at Fir Park. Wilson had no idea where Fir Park was but merely turned up at Maley's restaurant – The Bank in Queen Street – at the given time and was taken to Motherwell. He was not even sure whether he was getting a game or not, but eventually Maley approached him and told him with a tremendous degree of understatement that his direct opponents Stevenson and Ferrier were not bad players. "Watch them!" said Maley, in what was as near to a team talk as there was likely to be. Wilson did indeed keep them quiet, the team earned a somewhat fortuitous 1-0 win through an own goal, and Peter's Celtic career had begun.

From then on he never really looked back, and very soon earned a place in the hearts of the Celtic faithful. Celtic fans began to like his funny walk, his face which always seemed to be smiling and his 100-per-cent effort. By the middle of the following year, inch-perfect passes were his trademark as well. Wing-half was a position which was vital in the 1920s. The wing-halves were the engine house of the team, the men who turned defence into attack and the men who, nine times out of ten, determined the success of the team. Peter enjoyed consistently good reports in the press with only one man, Alex James of Raith Rovers, able to claim that he had got the better of him.

It is always hard to break into a team, particularly an established team. Anyone who starts any job will know that, and will be appreciative of any help that can be given. It is even more true in the tough, competitive world of professional football, where so many players are performing under pressure, proving that old maxim: "You are only as good as your last game". When the team contains acerbic characters like Patsy Gallacher, regarded by some as having been the best player in the world but now beginning to struggle with fitness and anno domini, it is even more difficult.

It may be that Patsy did not like Peter, at least in the early stages. Certainly there was one occasion when Wilson scored one of his rare goals and the crowd applauded, most of his team-mates joined in the congratulations, Maley in the stand beamed his pleasure, but Patsy snarled and growled, because Wilson was meant to be a midfield player, not a goalscorer. Patsy had been expecting a pass, so that he, and not Peter, could have scored the goal.

Peter, however unworldly and naïve in the big city of Glasgow which contrasted so vividly with the Ayrshire countryside, could understand human nature. He knew that there were hierarchies and pecking orders, and that the only way to gain entrance to inner circles was to persevere, keeping one's head down if necessary, and then discover that gradually one could be accepted. One or two beautifully accurate passes for Patsy would do the trick, as, indeed, could a simulated deferential attitude towards the great man. Very soon Patsy saw that there was something in the boy, and Peter became in every sense a member of the club.

Other onlookers were beginning to appreciate Peter as well. His apparently laid-back and lackadaisical approach to the game hid the fact that he was a deep thinker. All this added to the impression that the country boy was just a little slow on the uptake. Appearances however were very deceptive. A contemporary chronicler in the Glasgow Observer wrote: "I like the way that Wilson surveys the position before he makes a pass. He is cool, quick-thinking and a shrewd constructor. The crisp, inch-accurate passes to a well placed colleague stamp him as a half-back who knows just what is required . . . no flurry or hurry . . . just cool and calculating . . . he will be a top-notcher yet."

Season 1924/25 was the third poor League season in a row for Celtic, but Peter, not as yet the finished article, learned the game and visibly grew in confidence. His reputation as being ice cool and Mr Dependable was not harmed in a game against Hearts at Parkhead in October 1924. Celtic were on a downer having lost the final of the Glasgow Cup to Rangers the week before. They were as yet undefeated in the League but this game looked like fizzling out into a miserable goalless draw.

The supporters were on the backs of the team, but then ten minutes from time Celtic were awarded a softish penalty. Patsy Gallacher took it, but the goalkeeper saved. However, there had been encroachment from some of the Hearts players, still upset about the award of the penalty, and the referee awarded a retake. At this point Patsy turned awkward, not happy at the jeering of the crowd. He refused to take the retake, and this time it was Adam McLean who earned the raspberries as he blazed it over the bar.

Incredibly, the referee ordered yet another retake. Hearts players and supporters would remark that the referee was called Quinn and would draw dark and damaging inferences from that name, but Celtic now had nobody who wanted to make himself the third Celt in a row to miss the same penalty. Cometh the hour, cometh the man, and forward stepped the young Peter Wilson, looking for all the world as if he were about to load a cart with hay. Calmly, with the crowd in an uproar, he placed the ball, stepped back, then ran up and kicked. To his horror, he saw the ball hit the bar, for he had leaned too far back, but then his horror turned to joy as the leather bounced into the net. Parkhead then erupted in relief rather than bedlam, and a few drinks were drunk that night to Peter Wilson.

The League that season was lost after more than a few inconsistencies over the winter and the undeniable fact that Rangers probably were the better team that year, but there was ample compensation in the shape of the Scottish Cup campaign. In 1925 Celtic landed the trophy for the 11th time in their existence, beating the record of Queen's Park. Three games were required to dispose of St Mirren in the quarter-final, and then Celtic found themselves up against Rangers in the semi. They were not given very much of a chance as this was a great Rangers team, but that equinoctial day of 21 March 1925 was one of the most famous in the history of the Parkhead club.

This Celtic side, which had not performed very well hitherto, suddenly turned it on, and beat Rangers 5-0. Legend has it that Patsy Gallacher masterminded the victory and young McGrory earned his spurs that day as well, but there were other stars as well, notably Peter Wilson, who controlled the midfield, nullifying any Rangers threat, breaking up attacks before they even started and passing the ball with stunning accuracy. "Peter Wilson didn't pass the ball. He stroked it, caressing it lovingly as he delivered it to a good home".

The Celtic fans were in raptures about all this. They had had little cause to be happy for a few years, but they would never forget this day. It is often said that the song Hello, Hello is a Rangers ditty, borrowed from an American Civil War song called *Marching Through Georgia*. Not so, for Celtic fans would sing their version from this day in 1925 until a good 40 years later:

"Hello, hello, we are the Celtic boys!
Hello, hello you'll know us by the noise!
We beat the Rangers in the Cup, twas great to be alive
Not one, not two, not three, not four but five."

And then there was the final on April 11, arguably the most famous in Celtic history, immortalised by Patsy's great individual goal – he somersaulted into the back of the net with the ball wedged between his feet – and Jimmy McGrory's glorious header which won the Cup. But there is a danger that not enough is said about the other players in that team. Standing 0-1 down to a stuffy Dundee outfit, many a team might have buckled when the breaks did not come. But this Celtic team had the young Peter Wilson earning his first Scottish Cup medal. Notice was here given that Celtic had an outstanding pair of wing-halves in Peter and left-half John "Jean" McFarlane.

It got even better the following year. Patsy Gallacher was now more or less finished at Parkhead, but it hardly mattered as in his place came Tommy McInally, returning like the prodigal son from Third Lanark and setting the support alight by his exploits. But he would never have done so well if it had not been for the promptings of Peter Wilson, a man who quite clearly had now arrived as a top-class footballer. Playing at right-half, Peter was now part of a triangle on the right hand side of the field with the two forwards Paddy Connolly and Alec Thomson. Connolly has been curiously neglected by historians, but he was a fine right winger, and beside him was "Mr Reliable", the "Ever Ready" Alec Thomson, whom Maley correctly credits for bringing out the best in the young McGrory.

With Tommy McInally in the side, there was no place for another clown, so Peter tended to play everything straight. This did not prevent him, however, from deliberately cultivating his rustic gait and bucolic look, and from responding appropriately to the cries of "Farmer George" or "Celtic's Country Bumpkin". Now and again, he would pretend to chew on straw, or scratch his head, and it was rumoured that in the dressing room he would say things like "Aar". This was a mark of the confidence in himself and in his role that he had developed over the last year.

He was particularly good at passing a ball, knowing exactly the right amount of weight to put on it. He could also tell who would be in the best position to receive it – the moody but brilliant McInally, the reliable Thomson or the eager young McGrory. McGrory simply could not help but score goals that year, as he was fed by four sources, Wilson, McFarlane, Thomson and McInally, but he would always claim that it was Peter who provided the best service.

Fifty years later when Jimmy McGrory was writing his book, A Lifetime in Paradise along with Gerry McNee, he was picking his best ever team. He agonised for a long time about the right-half position and could not make up his mind whether to plump for Peter Wilson, whom he had played alongside, or Bobby Murdoch, whom he had managed and watched. Murdoch eventually got the nod, but only because he was a better finisher than Wilson. They were both as good at passing the ball and in general midfield play. Anyone who ever watched Bobby Murdoch in his prime will thus get some sort of idea about how good Peter Wilson was.

Another example will point at Peter's greatness as well. It was Dens Park on 4 November 1961 in a thrilling match between Dundee and Celtic. Dundee would eventually win this game and the 1962 Scottish League Championship, but today Celtic were possibly the better team. It was in the good old days when Dundee had a team, and when fans of both sides could mingle together in friendly good-natured banter and express mutual respect and appreciation of each other's fine players.

Pat Crerand was at right-half, and at one point with Celtic pressing for an equaliser, he sent a 40-yard pass across the field right to the feet of Bobby Carroll. A veteran Celtic sympathiser in the stand purred his admiration and said: "Peter Wilson!" The young Dundee fans in his hearing were amazed, and had to be told who Peter Wilson had been. A few minutes later, almost on the final whistle, Bobby Seith of Dundee won the ball on the edge of his own penalty area and sent another brilliant 40-yard pass to Alan Gilzean. A Dundee supporter turned to the veteran Celt and said: "What did you say that guy's name was?"

THE SCOTTISH LEAGUE WAS won by some considerable distance in 1925/26, clinched with a goalless draw against Kilmarnock in early April. Form had been consistent, and the team had been lucky enough to have avoided injury to any large extent. Also they all knew each other, and could cope with each other having a bad day without falling into recriminations and self-pity. "The team played as if they were comfortable with each other" acknowledged the Fife Free Press after a competent win over Raith Rovers in November. Maley and the rest of the supporters enthused about their performances, and it was widely expected that with the Scottish League in the bag, the Scottish Cup would follow it for the first Double since 1914. The confidence was hardly misplaced in view of the League form, and there had been some excellent results in the Cup itself to defeat Hearts at a dangerously overcrowded Tynecastle and then Aberdeen in the semi-final at the same venue.

Sadly, the team chose to put on one of their worst performances of the season to lose the Scottish Cup final to a St Mirren team who raised their game sufficiently. Wilson was at a loss to explain why. He himself was shut down, and when he did get the ball through, nothing happened up front. Celtic were without the injured Adam McLean on the left wing, but that hardly explained why so many other players were off form. It was a salutary lesson for a team which had come far, but perhaps not as far as they thought they had.

But Peter's career had now come on by leaps and bounds. He was clearly a hero with the Celtic fans, earning all sorts of nicknames like "Peter the Great" after the famous Russian Czar, "Peter the Painter", curiously enough after an anarchist involved in the Siege of Sydney Street of 1911, and even, incredibly considering the religious affiliations of most of the support, "Saint Peter".

He had by this time won himself an international cap. This had come in February 1926 at Ibrox when Scotland had defeated Northern Ireland 4-0. In the same way as he was supplying the ammunition for McGrory when playing for Celtic, so on this occasion he did the same for Hughie Gallacher for Scotland. It was, therefore, all the more of a disappointment when he did not make it for the team to play England at Old Trafford the week after the disappointing Scottish Cup final. It would be some time before he played again for Scotland, and Jimmy McGrory is surely not the only one who considered that Wilson was ludicrously under-capped.

TO A CERTAIN EXTENT, Celtic made up for their disappointment in losing the Scottish Cup by winning the Glasgow Charity Cup. This is one of the more interesting tournaments in Scottish football history, for it was played at the same time as the General Strike. The final against Queen's Park was played in a poisonous atmosphere for reasons other than football, but for a change in Glasgow football politics, the issue was not religion or Irish infiltration as much as social class. Queen's Park were identified with the ruling classes and the bosses, whereas Celtic had many players and supporters from a mining background. The boy from the village ignored this, got on with his job and Celtic won the Charity Cup.

In season 1926/27, Peter helped to win the Glasgow Cup with a 1-0 defeat of Rangers, and then his second Scottish Cup medal. The team failed to retain the Scottish League championship, losing a few important games in the run-in as Rangers strengthened their challenge. But once again Peter was one of the consistent stars of the team, something that made it all the more surprising that he failed to win another Scottish cap that season. The Glasgow Observer, lavishly pro-Celtic as always, took up his cause. But other periodicals, such as the Weekly News, asked the pertinent question: "Wilson plays once for Scotland, and the team wins 4-0, then it is down the plughole with him! Where is the justice in all this?"

It was the Scottish Cup that Wilson enjoyed the most that year. The semi-final at Ibrox did not seem likely to cause too many problems as Falkirk were the opponents. But the Bairns now had Patsy Gallacher playing for them, and Patsy had been instrumental in putting Rangers out in a previous round. This was the remarkable semi-final at which the Celtic crowd hijacked the community singing and chorused: "Will ye no'come back again?" for their beloved Patsy. But Patsy did not have a good game that day, being outplayed by Peter Wilson.

Wilson was even prepared to compromise on his normal game on this occasion. Normally an attacking wing-half, this time he was prepared to do his bit to nullify the potential menace of Gallacher, as everyone in that Celtic team knew how dangerous he could be, even at the age of 36. Patsy hardly got a kick of the ball, and Celtic ran out 1-0 winners thanks to an Adam McLean goal.

The final was Wilson's, and Celtic's, third in a row and it was against the Second Division part-timers from East Fife. This game was frankly a mismatch, as East Fife were still struggling to recover losses of support and finance in the wake of the General Strike and the miners' strike, which went on a lot longer. The game finished with Celtic toying with their opponents, Tommy McInally clowning and Peter Wilson barely breaking sweat on the halfway line.

The next few years, however, were bad ones for Celtic. Rangers beat them 4-0 in the 1928 Scottish Cup final, and by 1929 the recession began to bite very hard at Parkhead. Celtic supporters often feel, rightly or wrongly, that they suffer more from unemployment that anyone else, but in truth there was little to attract them to Parkhead, as Maley, needing to pay for the construction of a new stand, sold McInally and McLean and tried to sell McGrory and the prodigious young goalkeeper John Thomson.

Peter plodded along, obviously frustrated with the lack of success and suffering, on a personal level, from being passed over for another Scottish cap, thanks mainly to the poor performances of the rest of the Celtic team. But he was at last chosen in summer 1930 to go to France to play for Scotland. It was Scotland's first game against France, and only the second time that they had ever gone to Europe to play full internationals, foreign football having been considered "infra dig" for Scotland up to that point.

Thus it was that the boy from Beith found himself in Paris, an exotic and distant place in 1930. His Celtic colleague, goalkeeper John Thomson, was making his international debut that day, and both Celts played well as Scotland beat France 2-0. As remarkable as anything for Peter would have been that the game was played on a Sunday, something that was most unusual at that time and certainly would not have happened in Scotland itself. Be that as it may, Hughie Gallacher scored the two goals which defeated the French.

Wilson would have been disappointed that an injury prevented another Scottish cap against Wales in October 1930 (although he did win a Scottish League cap against the English League in November) but 1931 was a remarkable year for both he and Celtic. In the first place, Peter was chosen to play for Scotland in the goalless draw against Northern Ireland in Belfast, but was unfortunate enough to pick up another injury. He had generally been very lucky with injuries in his life, but now he had sustained two in the one season, this one in Belfast serious enough to keep him out of the game that everyone wanted to play in, against England at Hampden. His time would come, though.

He recovered in time for the month of April and thus he took part in the extraordinary rollercoaster that was 1931 for Celtic. The Scottish Cup was won in a replayed final against Motherwell (Wilson was outstanding in both games, urging Celtic on in the first encounter, when they were 0-2 down and only ten minutes remained), the League was only narrowly lost, and the team then went on a groundbreaking and very successful tour of the USA and Canada. The country boy from Beith had thus travelled far, thanks to his football, but he remained a Beith boy at heart and was glad to get home. Then in September came the tragedy of the death of goalkeeper John Thomson in a game against Rangers at Ibrox. Wilson was involved on that occasion, which dwarfed everything else that had gone before in terms of tragedy. Naturally Peter was upset about the death of his friend, and his play, like that of everyone else at Parkhead, suffered accordingly.

But time heals, and Peter was to have a glorious swansong to his Celtic career in 1933. On 1 April, he was at last given his chance to play for Scotland against England at Hampden, in a game rightly considered in the 1930s to be the most important in the world. Even though 1933 saw Great Britain not yet entirely out of the depths of the Depression, and more than a little concerned about the funny little man who had recently become Chancellor of Germany, more than 134,000 were at Hampden to see what was possibly the best ever game between the two countries.

It was the day of the birth of the Hampden Roar, the noise that startled and alarmed all Glasgow until everyone realised that it meant that Scotland had scored a goal. Scotland were leading 1-0 late in the game and the strong England team were pressing hard until Peter cleared a ball which found Doc Marshall. He released Bob McPhail, who passed to McGrory and the lethal marksman unleashed a magnificent drive into the roof of the net. The noise around the stadium was immense and lasted until long after the final whistle. Peter, who had played well throughout, was treated as one of the heroes of the hour, and as if that wasn't enough, he was back at Hampden a fortnight later to collect his fourth Scottish Cup winner's medal as Celtic beat Motherwell 1-0.

WILSON HAD ONE FINAL season at Parkhead, but 1933/34 was a very bad one for all concerned. Wilson, now approaching his 30th birthday, began to slow down and to pick up more injuries. With Peter out of touch and several others clearly past their best, the team suffered, and Maley turned on his players, moaning in the Celtic programme about "players not possessing pride" and "teamwork being a lost art". In addition, money was still not in great supply, and after a dispute about terms, Peter felt that he had done ten years at Parkhead and that was enough. Duly he was put on the transfer list in May 1934.

He moved to Hibs at the start of the 1934/35 season, and spent four years in the grossly under-performing Easter Road. He was always given a great reception from Celtic fans whenever they played Hibs, but he probably realised that his best days were behind him. Nevertheless he did well enough for Hibs, playing his part in keeping them away from the icy finger of relegation, which had beckoned once or twice.

In 1938 Hibs released him and he became player-manager of Dunfermline for a year, but war then intervened and Peter joined the Royal Navy. He returned to Beith to resume his career as a cabinet-maker, and although he did a little scouting and coaching for various clubs, it was on a part-time basis. He died in Beith in 1983.

Those who saw Peter in his heyday were often surprised that more was not made of him, because he was as good as any player who wore the green-and-white during that decade. The reason probably lies in his character, as Peter Wilson was not a show-off, a headline-seeker or an attention-grabber. He was merely a shy country boy who loved his football, and was proud to wear the green-and-white. Like many an Ayrshire man, he was an expert on Robbie Burns and in the long tradition of Celtic players from that county (Sunny Jim Young, James Hay, Jamie Weir) he would always do his bit of Burns when Celtic were staying away overnight and Maley had organised one of his soirees. He would never have survived a big-money move to an English club; he was what he always wanted to be – Peter Wilson of Celtic.

BERTIE THOMSON

1929-1933

'BERTIE'

BHOYS CAREER

Games	131
Goals	30
Caps	1

MAGIC MOMENT

In his second game for the club at Muirton Park, Perth on 23 November 1929, Bertie scored and played brilliantly in the rampaging 6-1 victory.

IT is the custom in the best of Celtic families when grandparents are playing with their grand-children for the patriarch to take the tiny fingers of the young scion and say – not "This little piggie went to market" etc, but something along the lines of "Bennett, McMenemy, Quinn, Somers and Hamilton", or "Johnstone, Wallace, Chalmers, Auld and Lennox" or perhaps "R Thomson, A Thomson, McGrory, Scarff and Napier".

The last of these three quintets was the forward line of 1931 – one of Maley's most famous attacks, although by no means his most successful. It was the team that had three Thomsons – John was in goal, Alec was the inside-right and Bertie was the right winger. Everyone knows the tragic circumstances of the great John Thomson, killed at Ibrox on 5 September 1931. Fewer are aware of the equally tragic life and death of Robert "Bertie" Thomson.

Robert Austin Thomson was born in Johnstone on 12 July (of all days!) in 1907, the year in which Celtic had become the first team to win both the Scottish League and the Scottish Cup in the same year. He was small but sturdy – clearly he was never likely to be a defender, but he was also fast and tricky, with a great deal of ball control. He had played for juvenile teams such as Broomfield Juveniles and Possil Hawthorn, before joining the famous junior team Glasgow Perthshire in 1927.

It was in autumn 1929 that he was invited to join Celtic, who were struggling at the time. It was, of course, the beginning of the Depression, but there had been another kind of depres-sion hanging over Parkhead for some time. Celtic's followers, being mainly of a dispossessed ethnic minority, had suffered throughout the 1920s, thanks to the institutionalised discrimina-tion sanctioned by such august bodies as the Church of Scotland. As a result the support at home games was not always what it could have been, because Celtic fans suffered a dispro-portionate share of unemployment. In addition, Rangers had a really excellent side at the time, and although Celtic had the odd success against them, they had not managed to win the Scottish League since 1926.

There was, in addition, a certain problem with the Celtic directors and manager. Far too often the impression was given that making money was more important that winning football matches. Tommy McInally and Adam McLean had been sold to Sunderland, and there had even been a disgraceful attempt to sell Jimmy McGrory to Arsenal – something that had been stopped in its tracks when the saintly Jimmy refused to go! This, naturally enough, had an effect on the team's performances. Bertie, for example, signed for Celtic on 17 October 1929, the day after a shocking 0-4 collapse to Rangers in the final of the Glasgow Cup.

BERTIE THOMSON WAS PICKED up by Celtic from the juniors because he was cheap. A minimal signing-on fee for the player and a small lump sum to Glasgow Perthshire were all that was really required to land an outside-right to replace the worthy but ageing Paddy Connolly. Yet Paddy still had enough left in him, and for a while he was tried on the left wing while the young Bertie Thomson was brought in on the right.

The day of Bertie's debut was 16 November 1929, against Cowdenbeath at Parkhead. It was a dull, typical Glasgow November sort of day with a mediocre crowd, and the performance of Celtic was in tune with the uninspiring form they had shown all season. But the young Bertie, slight and slender, had a few runs down the wing and some worthwhile crosses, and this was enough to keep him in the team. The following week at Muirton Park in Perth, Bertie impressed as Celtic won 6-1. He scored himself and played a part in at least two of McGrory's three goals. He was thus established in the Celtic team.

But that team continued to be unpredictable and disappointing, and four successive defeats around New Year 1930 killed what chance there might have been of any challenge for the Scottish League, fated predictably to be won by Rangers again that year. The Scottish Cup also disappeared when Celtic went down 1-3 to St Mirren at Parkhead in mid-February.

This was a significant day in Bertie Thomson's Celtic career, because he was dropped or "not considered to have recovered sufficiently from injury" for this game, and Paddy Connolly played in his place. Fans always need someone to blame, and poor Connolly suffered the fate of the scapegoat. As a result, in a perverse sort of a way the stock of Bertie Thomson rose.

There were other reasons for this, of course. Bertie was emerging as a great player in his own right. He was a curious little man with a funny walk and a strange style of running, and noticeable for his "custard bowl" haircut. This was a style of coiffure employed in most working-class families in the 1920s and 1930s when a visit to the barber's was frankly outwith the financial reach of quite a lot of people. The young man was placed in a chair, a bowl was placed over his head and the rest was clipped or shaved, not always too skilfully, by the mother or the father. Long hair, of course, was shunned, such was the fear of lice and beasties, and a "bowl" cut often sufficed. Pictures of Bertie Thomson show this phenomenon to perfection.

Thus it was that the Celtic fans recognised him as one of them. He was the traditional "little man" so beloved by people in those days because the audiences could identify with them. Charlie Chaplin was by now long past his peak, of course, but the feelings associated with a "little man facing a big bully" was a leitmotif of the age. The underfed identified with Charlie Chaplin being pushed around by the bullying overseer. In the same way, wee Bertie Thomson running at a big bruiser of a Rangers defender would excite similar emotions.

But none of this would have worked if Thomson had been a poor player. Throughout the early months of 1930, in spite of the continuing inconsistent performances of the team, discerning pundits began to realise that there was something in this frail, insignificant looking youngster. He had speed, and he could use the ball at speed; he had the ability to turn a man, to charge for the byline and to cross. Not only that, but he could dribble and tease as well, and in addition could score the occasional goal himself.

Celtic fans, at the end of season 1929/30, were in their annual state of despair. But there was a suspicion that better days might be forthcoming. They did, after all, have the magnificent Jimmy McGrory, whose goalscoring feats continued to bemuse everyone as to why he was not regularly selected for the Scotland team. On 5 April 1930, when Celtic were playing Partick Thistle at Parkhead, the loudspeaker announced at half-time the score at

Wembley – England 4 Scotland 0 – and this was greeted with a huge acclaim by the Celtic fans, something which shocked the press. It was because they felt their striking hero was overlooked.

But any great goalscorer needs service. This had been sporadic. Certainly there was Bertie's namesake, the quiet, unassuming "frail lad who wore the green" in Alec Thomson from Buckhaven in Fife, and the "country bumpkin" in Peter Wilson from Beith in Ayrshire, but there were glaring deficiencies. Celtic fans were now beginning to hope that in Bertie Thomson on the right wing, they might just have plugged at least one of the gaps.

But Glasgow being the place that it was, a rival for any village in gossip, stories circulated about Bertie's lifestyle. His association with publicans and bookmakers was well known. Bertie was a youngster who saw life for the enjoyment. As a professional football player, he recognised the need to keep himself fit and to train regularly. This did not prevent him enjoying life to the full when he was off duty, and the pleasures that he pursued were not always the most salubrious. There would, of course, be a tragic pay-back for his dissolute lifestyle.

CELTIC WERE FORTUNATE IN 1930/31 in having a steady team, comparatively free of injuries and playing some fine football to cheer up their fans who had suffered for so long. Bertie Thomson fitted into this team perfectly with his right-wing partner Alec Thomson, and with Peter Wilson, that tremendous passer of a ball, at right-half, the "right side triangle", as it was called, was a mighty one. In the centre was Jimmy McGrory, centre-half and captain was Jimmy McStay and in the goal was John Thomson. There was little wrong with that team, and it was often said in newspaper reports that "the Thomsons all played well".

Celtic had an important early success when they beat Rangers 2-0 at Parkhead in September 1930. The great Alan Morton of Rangers missed a penalty early on, then immediately afterwards Celtic broke down the right, with Bertie Thomson feeding Alec to put them ahead. Then, as time ticked away with Celtic growing more and more confident, it was Bertie himself who settled the issue. Celtic had set down an early marker.

The first big event of the season was the Glasgow Cup final on 11 October 1930. Unemployment or no unemployment, 71,806 were at Hampden that autumn day to see the Old Firm. It turned out to be a bitter-sweet occasion for Bertie, as Celtic won the Cup with goals from Charlie Napier and Jimmy McGrory, but Bertie Thomson was sent off for retaliation.

Realising that Bertie was a major threat, Rangers employed a disagreeable character called Jock Buchanan to deal with him in any way he could. Buchanan had already created history of a dubious kind by being the first player to be sent off in a Scottish Cup final. This had happened in 1929, when Rangers went down to Kilmarnock, and yet Buchanan was looked upon as a sort of hero for Rangers.

This day he fouled Bertie repeatedly, in the same way as foreign thugs would in later years go for Jimmy Johnstone. On the other wing Charlie Napier was similarly assailed by Dougie Gray, and indeed twice was taken off for attention. Bertie took Buchanan's abuse (physical and verbal) for long enough until he suddenly snapped and lashed out at Buchanan. The referee saw this and Bertie was sent off, but he would have the last laugh as Celtic won 2-1.

It was noticeable that Thomson received no major disapproval from Willie Maley. Indeed, Celtic would protest about the deplorably lax refereeing, but it mattered little for the Glasgow

Cup was now back at Celtic Park, and Celtic had beaten Rangers again. The team's form between October and the New Year was first-class, and Bertie Thomson received consistently good reports. On 25 October, for example, in a classic 3-3 draw at Fir Park against the strong-going Motherwell, the Glasgow Observer reported: "Every time Bertie Thomson got the ball, the crowd rose on its toes expecting something special and they were seldom disappointed". "Robert (sic) Thomson played a great part in the destruction of Ayr United" on November 22nd and the dreadful year of 1930 ended with Celtic, having defeated Leith Athletic, Kilmarnock and Falkirk in December, one point ahead of Rangers and with a game in hand.

Bertie had also won himself an honour in being chosen to play for the Scottish League against the English League at White Hart Lane on 5 November. Unfortunately the result was by no means favourable – 7-3 for the English League, and Thomson's chances of winning a full international cap took a setback. His time would come, however.

THOMSON'S PRIVATE FAN CLUB within the Celtic support grew. He could go anywhere in Glasgow and be recognised by those who adored him. Like many Glaswegians, he was gener-ous, sometimes too generous, handing out money to anyone who was able to turn on a little emotional blackmail about "hungry weans". He also (it was well known even to Maley) was more than a little fond of a drink, often being seen drinking with supporters after a game. He was, indeed, a supporter himself, and often said that if he were not on the field at Parkhead, he would be on the terracing.

Celtic's chances of winning the League championship took a blow when they lost at Ibrox on New Year's Day. It was only a 0-1 defeat, but it led to a few other mishaps including 0-1 defeats to two other Glasgow clubs, Clyde and Partick Thistle. Yet they pushed Rangers to the very end and finished only two points behind them. It was to be Bertie's best season with con-sistently good press reports along the lines of "fine aggressive play from Bertie Thomson", "Bertie Thomson made the goals easy for McGrory" and "discerning fans would note with approbation and later with acclaim the fine wing play of R Thomson"

But if the League championship in 1931 was a disappointment, there was more than ample compensation in the Scottish Cup. The progress to the final was difficult with East Fife, then Dundee United (on a snow-covered pitch on a Wednesday afternoon) and Morton all putting up a fine show. But then Bertie Thomson scored a hat-trick to the delight of 64,699 fans when Aberdeen came to town in the quarter-final, and although he did not score in the semi-final against Kilmarnock when Celtic won 3-0, most of the 53,973 crowd left Hampden convinced that Bertie was the man of the match.

He was certainly unfortunate not to be picked for Scotland against England, but the selectors thought that Sandy Archibald of Rangers was the better player, and few could argue with their judgement when Scotland won 2-0. But Bertie Thomson's finest hour would come in the two epic Cup finals against Motherwell, which remain, 75 years later, so much a part of Celtic history and folklore.

Yet he almost did not make it. On the Monday before the Scottish Cup final, Celtic played a League game against Clyde at Shawfield. "Bertie Thomson gave the opposition a terrible roasting and kept lively to the last despite heavy treatment" said one newspaper report. Some felt that "heavy treatment" did not quite cover it, as he was felled several times. Fortunately he had learned from his indiscretion with Jock Buchanan earlier in the season, and did not retaliate, contenting himself with a glower at his attacker. He was seen, however, to limp off at the end, and on the Tuesday and Wednesday was listed as "doubtful" before more optimistic bulletins began to emerge. Things might have been different if Bertie Thomson had not been playing.

The facts of the Celtic v Motherwell Scottish Cup final of 11 April 1931 are well known for their sheer drama. Celtic down to two unlucky goals, and the time wearing away. The Celtic fans, raucous and pervasive before the game, were now strangely silent as the Motherwell supporters, sadly bolstered by some wearing blue favours and brandishing Union Jacks, were growing in confidence. The Well had never won the Scottish Cup before, although their manager, John "Sailor" Hunter, had won it as a player with Dundee 21 years previously. Dundee had been down to Clyde, and had come back in the first game. Poor Sailor – the same was about to happen, but in reverse!

In truth, Celtic had been more than a little disjointed as desperation began to creep into their play as they swept forward to the King's Park end of the ground, where their fans were congregated. Bertie Thomson was always a danger, and Motherwell were aware of that, but the other forwards were less productive, with the inside men Peter Scarff and Alec Thomson both looking out of sorts and McGrory lacking his usual sharpness. Yet they kept pressing, compelling Motherwell to concede free-kicks, and on one occasion Celtic claimed a penalty kick, which referee Peter Craigmyle turned down. When confronted by the irate Bertie Thomson and Peter Scarff, Craigmyle, ever the extrovert, ran away from them, round the back of the goalposts before appearing on the other side. Even the angry Celtic fans had to laugh at that.

A few of the weaker elements among the Celtic support were now traipsing disconsolately to the exits. The majority, however, still clung on, obdurately but not without some self-doubts, to some sort of hope that Bertie Thomson could conjure something up or that Jimmy McGrory would again turn up trumps. Everyone stared at the famous huge Hampden clock which hung suspended from the South Stand, and the minutes ticked away.

Twenty minutes, fifteen, ten – those of us in the modern age who watch the digital clock on the TV screen will identify with that. More and more fans began to disappear, as the Motherwell supporters at the Mount Florida end began to grow ever more appreciative of their heroes. "Give us an M". Someone would hold up a letter M. "Give us an O" . . . and so on until the world "M-O-T-H-E-R-W-E-L-L" was spelt out. But then, well within the last ten minutes, Celtic struck. It was McGrory from a Napier free-kick, lofted over the heads of the Motherwell defence.

Immediately the atmosphere changed. McGrory shrugged off any congratulations and charged back up the field, pointing to the clock. There was still time, and now Celtic were only one goal down. Bertie felt a charge of electricity. Like everyone else, he had been lethargic and almost resigned to defeat, but the roar of the crowd acted as a spur. Peter Wilson took charge of the midfield, spraying passes to right and left, and Bertie began a few runs past his marker, Hunter, down the right wing – the one that was in front of the main South Stand and Celtic's enemy, that clock!

But no further goal came and Bertie had looked at the clock to confirm his impression that the game was over, as he found himself out on the right wing with the ball. Rumour has it that Bertie had no intention of saving the game but was merely holding on to the ball so that he could keep it as a souvenir. This is scarcely credible, as he would surely not have wanted a souvenir of a defeat, and in any case, a medal would have been a far better keepsake. Bertie may himself have started this story as a joke, but it is hard to take it seriously.

Having left Hunter for dead, Bertie crossed, "hard and high" as Jimmy McGrory put it, hoping the find the Golden Crust of the immortal Jimmy. He could hardly have believed what happened next. As Alan Craig, the Motherwell centre-half, rose to nod clear, crucially at the vital time he took his eye off the ball (literally) and the leather hit his head at the wrong angle and went into the net.

Hampden exploded. McGrory and Thomson ran to greet and hug each other. The final whistle came immediately. Thomson was lauded by all the support (he had had a fine game up until then, in any case) and the occasion was looked upon as a Celtic victory, so close had they come to defeat. Motherwell lay shattered, Glasgow belonged to Celtic, even though a replay remained.

No-one really believed that the broken Motherwell team could ever win the replay, and that was the way it turned out the following Wednesday evening. Bertie Thomson collected two goals in the 4-2 victory – one a tap-in from a goalmouth scramble, the other a fine drive from a very tight angle. He also sent over an inch-perfect cross for McGrory to score the decisive fourth goal at a time when Motherwell were threatening to make a comeback.

Glasgow had seldom seen anything like that Wednesday night. The team bus was mobbed and stopped several times in the Celtic heartlands of the Gorbals as young children were held up to see their heroes with the Scottish Cup, and Bertie, sentimental as ever, would have been affected by all that. Eightsome reels, Highland flings and impromptu waltzes were taking place all over Glasgow as the bus, a blue one apparently, eventually made its way to Maley's restaurant, The Bank, in the centre of the city. It was one of those occasions when it becomes apparent how much Celtic means to so many people, and such feelings do not exclude the players, no matter how professional, cynical or hard-bitten they might be on the outside.

No doubt Bertie had a drink that night. Maley would have looked the other way, for this was a great Celtic night. Maley said: "You boys rose to the occasion and read to the world another lesson that when Celtic want to do it, they will do it." Captain Jimmy McStay was less effusive, adding with more than a touch of under-statement: "I captained a team of triers"!

ALL THIS WAS GOOD enough for the young Bertie Thomson, but even better was to come that summer in the shape of the tour of North America. It is, perhaps, difficult for us some three-quarters of a century later, to comprehend what this would have meant for a youngster from Thomson's background. America was the land of wealth and opportunity, the place where the brave or the desperate went for a new and better life. Thomson had been lucky in that football had given him a hint of what a better life could be. Now he was to have the opportunity of seeing something even better.

Even the crossing itself (which would normally take the best part of a week) was an adventure. There would be captains and cabins and lifeboats and cinemas in which to watch films. There would also be the opportunity for the less salubrious of pleasures in drink and women. Even the ever-vigilant Willie Maley, who in any case was a bad sailor and suffered dreadfully from seasickness, could not keep an eye on him all the time!

The tour itself consisted of games against the locals, who were still learning the arts of this British game. Maley always tried to portray this as some sort of missionary exercise, as grateful second-generation Americans, (usually of Scottish or Irish origin) came to watch the mighty Glasgow Celtic, who had brought with them the Scottish Cup.

It was not always like this. Some of the teams they played against were perhaps short of football skills, but had no lack of aggression or violence. More than once Bertie Thomson, targeted because of his small stature, had to look after himself. He was, however, more than capable of doing that. One did not grow up in Glasgow in the 1910s and 1920s without acquiring a certain repertoire of self-defence techniques. Survival would have been impossible without them.

However, also there some very fine games of football and opportunities for Celtic to show the American world the way in which football should be played. Indeed, in retrospect, that summer tour of 1931 was probably the high point of Bertie Thomson's life. After this, things were not so good.

Bertie was badly affected by the terrible event of 5 September 1931, when John Thomson, the goalkeeper, met his death in a collision with Rangers' Sam English. It was, of course, a total accident, and no-one ever really thought anything else, but concentration on playing the game became very difficult for a long time after that. Celtic probably did well to maintain some kind of a challenge, but the honours in 1931/32 would go to Motherwell, who won the Scottish League, and gained revenge for their Scottish Cup final defeat by removing Celtic from that competition in February.

At Parkhead the collective depression over John Thomson refused to go away. It was a case of depression in every sense, as there was still the economic depression to endure. Poverty lowered attendances, and particularly affected Celtic supporters, in contrast to the Rangers supporters in Govan. Rangers fans in the 1930s tended to work in the shipyards, where the depression had considerably less effect.

But the 1931/32 season was not without its moments for Bertie Thomson. Deservedly he won his one and only full Scottish cap when he was chosen for the match against Wales in Wrexham on 31 October. The Wrexham crowd were impressed by his performance, cheering him again and again as he beat their own man Arthur Lumberg, who had played for Wrexham before his transfer to Wolverhampton Wanderers, and it was Bertie who scored Scotland's second goal in a 3-2 win. The following week he played for the Scottish League against the English League at Parkhead and again he was on the winning side.

IT WAS BEGINNING TO look as if Bertie was about to have a great career in international football, but on 23 January 1932, in a 0-1 defeat at Hamilton Accies, he was taken off with a broken bone in his right foot, putting him out of action for the foreseeable future (although he did manage to return before the end of the season) and certainly depriving him of the chance to play for Scotland at Wembley.

It was probably this long lay-off that finished Bertie's career. Footballers find it hard to cope with a long spell on the sidelines, and it is in these circumstances that the siren voices of alcohol and other blandishments are hard to resist. By the time that the 1932/33 season began, Bertie was not as fit nor as sharp as he might have been. The skill was still there, and he was as yet only 25, but the rot had sadly set in.

Yet his rapport with the fans remained undimmed. His name was always cheered when announced over the loudspeaker, and with every touch of the ball, there was the hiss of expectation that something might happen, but even his greatest fans sensed a certain lack of enthusiasm, an apparent reluctance to get going.

The team went to Hampden on 17 September 1932 to play Queen's Park. It was a shocker, and the team went down 1-4. Defeats by Queen's Park were always hard for manager Maley to take, and he blasted all and sundry, but singled out Bertie Thomson in particular. Presumably he did this because he knew that Bertie could do better, but the winger was in no mood to take this. Maley ordered him to train on Monday morning with the rest of the players and to come back on Monday afternoon for an extra spell.

Both sides in the dispute then over-reacted. Thomson refused and Maley suspended him sine die. Thomson asked for a transfer, then recanted and wrote a letter of apology, which was ignored until the middle of November, when he was allowed back to train.

This piece of petulance did no-one any good, and the team suffered as a result. Once Bertie returned (and he had made an effort with his fitness) the team's form slowly improved, and Celtic restored a little self-respect when they won the Scottish Cup in April. The finalists were again Motherwell, but the 1933 Final was a dull game played on a dull day with only one goal between the teams. That was when Bertie made space on the wing and crossed to give McGrory a simple tap-in. Maley was gracious enough to shake Bertie's hand and to congratulate him, but the damage to the relationship had been done.

After only two games of the next season, Blackpool approached Maley for Bertie Thomson. A fee of £5,000 was handed over and Bertie possibly felt that, much as he loved Celtic, a change might do him and his health some good. His departure allowed the arrival of Johnny Crum to that position and later Jimmy Delaney, but Bertie never adapted to life in Lancashire. He always would be Bertie Thomson of Celtic – and really of nobody else. Illness, injury and unhappiness pursued him, and little more than a year later he returned to Scotland to play for Motherwell, a team, like Bertie, well past their best.

There was one touch of nostalgia when Motherwell came to Parkhead in December 1934. A supporter presented him with a green horseshoe decked in Motherwell's colours of claret and amber. This was given a great cheer by those who still loved Bertie Thomson for his brief but brilliant Celtic career, but Thomson had a poor game that day, with neither his mind nor his body in tune with the demands of a professional footballer.

THOMSON'S CAREER FIZZLED out at Motherwell, then he had some games as an amateur for a Dublin side called Bridewell in 1936, but little is known of what was left of his short life. The Celtic fans had not exactly forgotten about him, but he was no longer the topic of conversation that he once was simply because Celtic, come 1936 and 1937, had a tremendous new side to enthuse over. It came, therefore, as a shock to read in the death notices of the newspapers that Robert Thomson had died on 17 September 1937 at the house of his mother, 327 Argyle Street, Glasgow. He was only 30.

Hardly anyone had even known that he was ill, suffering from heart problems. He was buried at the Abbey Cemetery, Elderslie, and the tombstone sums him up when he is described as "Bertie of Celtic". He would not wish to be known any other way. Thus little more than six years after the epic events of 1931 with which he was so identified, Bertie became the third man of that team to die. John Thomson died on 5 September 1931, Peter Scarff died of tuberculosis, that scourge of the 1930s, in December 1933, and now Bertie Thomson had died as well. Those who saw him play enthuse about him. What a pity that his career and his life were so short.

MALCOLM MACDONALD

'CALUM'

1932-1945

BHOYS CAREER

Games	118
Goals	8
Caps	0

MAGIC MOMENT

In September 1938, as the world held its breath fearing war over Czechoslovakia, Celtic beat Rangers 6-2 at Parkhead before 74,500 spectators thanks to an inspirational Malky hat-trick.

SUPPORTERS of Newcastle United will tell you that there has been only one Malcolm MacDonald. This was, of course, "Supermac", who thrilled Newcastle's Gallowgate and Leazes Park Ends in the first half of the 1970s – and a fine player he was. But Celtic fans will tell you that there was another player of this name.

The name of Malky MacDonald has been curiously neglected by Celtic historians, yet there were and are those who claim that he was the greatest of them all. Even the legendary Jimmy Delaney, who played in the same glorious team in 1938, when someone said that he (Jimmy) was the best player in that line-up, protested: "Hoo could I be wi' Malky MacDonald in the side?" Delaney and MacDonald were, of course, great friends, sitting beside each other in the Parkhead stand in their later years to cheer the team that they both still loved.

Delaney's opinion was echoed with a surprising unanimity by those who saw him play. The forward line in the Empire Exhibition Trophy side – Delaney, MacDonald, Crum, Divers and Murphy – was without peer in world football at the time and their memory soothed many an aching heart in the painful war years which came so soon afterwards. The countless strident English voices extolling the virtues of Tommy Lawton or Stanley Matthews could be stilled by the mention of that great forward line, and the inside-right who was the jewel in the crown.

MALKY MACDONALD MUST BE one of the very few Celtic footballers to have come from South Uist. Most reference books claim that he was born in Glasgow, but he was, in fact, a Hebridean by birth, although he moved to Glasgow at a fairly early age, and lived during his Celtic career in Alison Street, Govanhill, before moving to Ardrossan.

It comes as a surprise to discover that Malky, or "Calum" as he became known, originally joined Celtic as a centre-half. At 5 feet 9 inches, he was on the small side for that job, yet he was a good stopper, a ball winner and breaker-up of attacks, being particularly effective on the ground rather than in the air. It was while he was playing in that position that a few of his admirers began to wonder whether he might not be of more value to the side in another role. Certainly, what no-one could deny was that, although he was doing well enough himself, the team were definitely lacking in some respects while Malky was centre-half and his talents could be better deployed elsewhere. Centre-halves were ten-a-penny, but the exceptional ability of Malky was wasted there.

Malky had joined Celtic from St Anthony's, the famous junior team whose ground is merely a stone's throw away from Ibrox Stadium, and he was given his first game at outside-left, a position with which he had little acquaintance, in the last game of the 1931/32 season. Nothing was at stake in the encounter with Partick Thistle at Firhill, and manager Willie Maley felt it was a good time to try out this boy who had had many impressive performances for the reserves in the Alliance League, and had seemed so versatile.

Maley's judgement proved to be spot-on, as MacDonald scored both goals (within five minutes of each other in the second half) in a dull game. He was rewarded with another appearance – same time, same place, the following Wednesday in the Glasgow Charity Cup. This time the final score was 2-1, but it was once again the young and very impressive Malcolm MacDonald who scored both the Celtic goals. This was the sort of stuff that made everyone sit up and take notice, and he was retained in the team for the semi-final of the Glasgow Charity Cup against Third Lanark at Parkhead. On this occasion, although he played well, he did not score and Third Lanark won the tie in extra time, thereby bringing to a close a poor Celtic season.

IT WAS A SHAME for young Malky that the season ended when it did, as his star was definitely in the ascendancy at that point. By the start of the next term, however, things had changed, and MacDonald played only played 11 games in that campaign, usually as a cover for injury. The 1933/34 season was little better, but MacDonald knew that his time would come if he were patient. He kept learning his craft, and he probably did well to avoid that dark period in the club's history, as attendances dropped and nothing was won.

The press reports of MacDonald in the games that he did play were consistently favourable. On one occasion, playing at centre-half, he tamed Third Lanark's Neil Dewar, who had once been given the nod to play for Scotland at Wembley instead of Jimmy McGrory. "It was as if Dewar was not on the field. MacDonald was no mere third back. He came up with the ball and his passes were as good as you would wish. When it came to recovery, MacDonald was there". On another occasion: "If MacDonald is given time, he will be a real good one".

All this begs the question of why MacDonald was not given more of a run in seasons 1932/33 and 1933/34. He seemed able to impress the newspaper reporters, and equally importantly, the fans, but he was still being kept as merely a cover for injuries. The answer must lie in the broodingly despotic management of Willie Maley, who was growing increasingly stubborn and remote, drifting in and out of depressive moods, and who gave every indication of not liking Malcolm MacDonald for some irrational reason.

But in season 1934/35, the patient MacDonald was given his opportunity. Veteran captain and centre-half Jimmy McStay was now on his way out, and there was a vacancy at the heart of the rearguard. Following a few games with Chick Geatons at centre-half and MacDonald in the forward line, Malky was given a run in the middle of their defence. It was a better season as a result, and the feeling that Celtic had acquired a good defender began to gain ground.

But the perspicacious writer of the *Glasgow Observer* said in early September 1934: "MacDonald is a born footballer with wonderful ball control, but surely Celtic don't hope to start a revolution against the three-back game by playing him at centre-half? If they do, they may spoil a player who might be a star in any of the positions alongside or in front . . ."

The writer obviously did not like the three-back game employed by most teams at the time, and equally obviously he was saying what all the fans were saying – that MacDonald was too good a player to be a centre-half. Centre-halves in the 1930s tended to have the word "rugged" applied to them. Meiklejohn of Rangers and McStay of Celtic were certainly that – hard tackling and never disdaining the punt up the field, but MacDonald was simply a better player than that.

In 1934/35 the wheel slowly began to turn for Celtic. Delaney's prodigious talent began to appear on the right wing, and in an inspirational decision, Jimmy McMenemy was appointed trainer and gradually began to make the tactical changes that Maley wouldn't. But MacDonald stayed at centre-half, earning this rave notice in a game which Celtic had lost 0-2 to Clyde. "For sheer genius, scheming, manoeuvering, purveying, MacDonald was in a class by himself", the clear implication being that although Malky was lining up as centre-half, he was actually playing a different game.

Monday 6 May 1935 was a significant day in MacDonald's life. It was the day of a Glasgow Charity Cup game against Queen's Park at Parkhead. The team appalled their fans by going down 1-4 and Malky was sent off for kicking a Queen's Park player. MacDonald would always claim that it was a case of mistaken identity while loyally refusing to incriminate the real culprit, but the real significance of the game was that Celtic were sufficiently impressed by Queen's Park's centre-half Willie Lyon to sign him on for the next season.

Buying a player from another club was something that Celtic seldom did in the 1930s and it sent out a clear signal to Malky that in spite of his fine season, his position at centre-half was now under threat. Perhaps MacDonald felt that his job hung in the balance, for Maley was a strict disciplinarian and would have roundly disapproved of the sending-off in the Queen's Park game, but he need not have worried. The first game of 1935/36 saw Lyon at centre-half and MacDonald at inside-left.

It proved to be an outstanding, but short-lived success. It turned out to be one of the best seasons in the history of the club, but poor Malky participated in only 11 games before serious cartilage problems hit him in a Glasgow Cup game against Third Lanark at the end of September. Cartilage problems were serious in the 1930s, and he needed an operation, which effectively ruled him out of the game for the rest of the season. But for the 11 games that he played, press reports were consistently positive about how well he fitted in at inside-left. Alec McNair, for example, a Celtic star of 20 and 30 years previously would purr to the press: "I have not seen such a clever young Celtic team in action for years", a clear reference to the fine side in which he had played during the early part of the century.

The whole team merited rave reports, as after a defeat in the first game, at Pittodrie, Celtic went on an unbeaten run in the Scottish League, with MacDonald making it all happen. In particular, he had played a brilliant game at Ibrox on 21 September, when it was his through-ball that allowed Johnny Crum to score the winner.

But for Malky it was the agony of being in hospital with the problem that all footballers dread – serious injury – that would characterise the winter of 1935/36. By the turn of the year, however, he was on the mend, and by March he was able to resume some light training. He might have hoped to be able to play a game or two by the end of the season, but it was not to be. But MacDonald, committed to the cause, was seen sitting in the stand and clapping and cheering with the rest of the supporters as Celtic won the Scottish League for the first time in a decade.

The League won, Malky might well have hoped for an opportunity in the Glasgow Charity Cup, especially when he was included in the party for a quick tour of Ireland. Indeed, he was given a game against Waterford on 29 April. Alas, it was too soon. His knee gave way under him on the heavy pitch and he had to be taken off. Yet he felt that he had made some progress, and by the start of the season in August he was back in contention for a place, enjoying the training sessions so well organised by Jimmy McMenemy.

The problem for MacDonald was that there was already an excellent forward line in place. This was Delaney, Buchan, McGrory, Crum and Murphy – none of whom could he realistically expect to be dropped, as they were all fine players – and the goals kept coming, particularly from the great McGrory, of whom it was said that they dare not send him to the music shop to buy any record, because he would just break them! Indeed "he already had more records than Harry Lauder" (the great Scottish music hall performer of the 1930s).

Had this been 30 years later, there would have been no problem for Malky, as he (and John Divers) could have been used as substitutes, but in 1936 only 11 men were allowed, and usually the team selection was rigid, in that a side which won one Saturday would be called upon (barring injuries) to do the same the following week. It was only when the team hit a losing streak that changes were made. But this Celtic team seldom lost.

MacDonald's role in the 1936/37 season, therefore, was simply to cover for injuries, something for which his versatility made him an ideal candidate. Indeed, he played only 14 games that season, but made an appearance in every attacking position except centre-forward. The highlight of his season was the last game, in which he played at outside-right (Jimmy Delaney being in Europe with Scotland) as Celtic beat Queen's Park to win the Glasgow Charity Cup.

There must have been times in the summer of 1937 when MacDonald questioned his future at Celtic Park. He must surely have yearned for a permanent first-team place. But he was still young, not yet 24, and as it turned out his turn was just around the corner. It all centred on an event which was roundly condemned, both at the time and by subsequent Celtic historians, but in fact can be regarded as a fairly nifty piece of business.

This was the transfer of Willie Buchan to Blackpool on 15 November 1937. A reported £10,000 changed hands – it was an enormous sum in 1937 – and Celtic were accused of money-grubbing and the old accusations of the "Catholic Jews" were trotted out again, along the lines of Celtic being only interested in money even at the expense of having a good football team.

This accusation at other times, before and since, in Celtic history has more than a little validity. In November 1937 it was the suddenness of it all that caught everyone by surprise, and the fact that there was no apparent need for it, as attendances were high. But this one was different in that Celtic had a ready-made replacement, who was possibly even better than Willie Buchan, in the reserves. This man was Malky MacDonald, and no-one could possibly argue that the team suffered because of the transfer of Buchan. Six months later, Celtic were the champions of Scotland. A couple of months after that, very few people could dispute the contention that they were the best in Britain.

It may have been a game in the middle of October 1937 that decided Celtic on the transfer of Willie Buchan. Injuries compelled the selection of MacDonald for a meeting with Queen's Park. It was a thrilling game, won 4-3 by Celtic, and the press unanimously enthused about the performance of MacDonald at inside-right, "MacDonald's jugglery (sic) , cunning passes and quickness on the draw were an object lesson to all". Maley may well have thought that, given the interest of Blackpool in Buchan and their willingness and ability to cough up a very large transfer fee, this would be a fine time to earn money without impoverishing the performance of the team.

Be that as it may, MacDonald, who had been playing (versatile as always) at right-half, was moved forward to the inside-right position, Johnny Crum moved to centre-forward (McGrory having now retired and become the manager of Kilmarnock) and Johnny Divers came in at inside-left. There was no stopping this forward line of Delaney, MacDonald, Crum, Divers and Murphy, who interchanged at will, understood each other, played at speed and could all score goals.

THERE WAS ONE BLEMISH, and it was a bad one, namely a defeat by Kilmarnock in the Scottish Cup, but the Scottish League was won, and in the summer came the great triumph of the Empire Exhibition Trophy. MacDonald had aggravated his knee injury and had missed the last few games of the League campaign and the Glasgow Charity Cup, but was fit again for the Empire Exhibition Trophy games against Sunderland, Hearts and Everton in which he played a glorious part.

He would have been embarrassed if anyone had tried to claim that he was the star of the team. The truth was that this was an all-star team, one of the marks of which is an ability to weld together without over-reliance on any one individual. Nevertheless, most of those who saw this mighty side were of the opinion that Malky's contribution was a tad more influential than most in that fine outfit.

MacDonald must have felt good about himself as he sat at the dinner held at the Grosvenor Hotel a few days after the lifting of the Empire Exhibition Trophy. It was to celebrate 50 years of the club, and how appropriate it was that Celtic were, in 1938, the unofficial champions of Great Britain. MacDonald was modest enough to admit that he was only part of that great team, but a vital part he had been, and as he listened to Maley making his eloquent and emotional speech, he was proud to have been a part in this success. Maley, the skinflint, the "Catholic Jew" as he was unfairly called, had had his judgement vindicated by the selling of Buchan and the immediate introduction of MacDonald. Maley was undeniably proud of young Malcolm MacDonald

Yet Malky had ambivalent feelings about Willie Maley. No-one could deny (or would want to) the contribution of the man who made Celtic, but there was no doubt that his methods and his manner were by no means agreeable to a young player. He was aloof, cold and austere, and insofar as he talked to a player at all, it was to bring him down a peg or two, in some cases unnecessarily. MacDonald, for example, was told to cut out the dribbling, when, in fact, dribbling was only part of his game. He was also a visionary passer of the ball, but Maley never complimented him on that. MacDonald was by no means the only player who would tell stories of how, if he happened to be on the same tram as his illustrious manager, he would always try to be on the lower deck if Maley was on the upper one, and vice versa, or how he would get off at a different stop rather than have to share his company. Yet Malky felt happy that he had vindicated the trust and belief of this demigod, and he was also profoundly grateful to Maley for having kept him at Celtic Park, through all his injury problems, for this glory season.

It would have been as well for Malcolm if time had stopped in June 1938. It was as well that he did not know what was coming. He would, of course, have had to be very naïve not to realise that another dreadful war was looming on the horizon, however hard Mr Chamberlain, the British Prime Minister, tried to avoid it. What he could not have foreseen, however, were the problems that were lurking in the shadows both for Celtic and for MacDonald himself.

THE SUMMER OF 1938 WAS passed in euphoric, gay abandon, in a spirit not dissimilar to that of 1967, with everyone talking about the great Celtic team, unable to wait for the start of the season, and with grandparents now picking up their baby grandchildren and counting their toes along the lines of "Delaney, MacDonald, Crum, Divers and Murphy". Life was good for those who loved the green-and-white.

The new season started with MacDonald in such blistering form that newspapers were beginning to predict confidently that he would win a Scottish cap in the near future. Sadly, this did not happen, not even a cap for the Scottish League, and Celtic supporters, paranoid as always about Scottish team selection, began to wonder whether there was a "quota" system in operation, so that Scotland did not have too many Celtic players playing for them.

Indeed the way that Malky was playing, it was hard to explain his omission from the international team. On 10 September 1938, for example, he scored a hat-trick in a 6-2 defeat of Rangers, his third goal being a cracker from well outside the penalty box, and on 15 October he won his first Glasgow Cup medal as Celtic beat Clyde 3-0 at Hampden. The Glasgow Cup was much prized in those days, as witnessed by the 43,000 crowd which attended to see Crum, Geatons and Delaney score the goals while "Malky, like an expert puppeteer, pulled the strings". Director Tom White was moved to say: "This was the best Celtic side of my experience."

By this time, the world was breathing a temporary sigh of relief, as a couple of weeks previously Mr Chamberlain had returned from a meeting with Herr Hitler in Munich, brandishing a bit of paper which seemed to guarantee "peace in our time". This had involved letting the Germans have a slice of Czechoslovakia, but there was not a huge amount of criticism for this at the time, with the exception of a few "war-mongers" like Winston Churchill. Those who looked around the crowd at any football match and saw the amount of men with only one leg or one arm or blinded or (more commonly) suffering from nervous disorders would not have wished another conflict.

Nor would Celtic and Malky MacDonald, for whom life was exceptionally sweet. He was now at the peak of his form, delighting his fans with his visionary passing, his speed, his ball control and his ability to take a goal. But as winter approached, the form of the team shaded a little and Malky became increasingly aware of some apparently muscular discomfort in his abdomen. The discomfort changed to occasional sharp pain and began to affect his performances on the field. He played very badly in the 1-3 defeat by Motherwell on 19 November, even though he scored the only goal, but then by the following midweek the abdominal pain intensified and medical opinion had to be consulted.

It was what everyone suspected and feared – appendicitis. One of the medical improvements of the first half of the 20th century was the ability to remove surgically an inflamed or burst appendix. Since the operation on King Edward VII on the eve of his coronation in 1902, appendicitis had ceased to be a killer, and Celtic players such as James Hay had lost an appendix and returned to play football. Nevertheless it did require an operation and it knocked Malky out of action until after the New Year.

By the time that Malky returned in January, the damage had been done to the season. Celtic did now need him to be at the top of his form, but the appendicitis operation was a serious one and it would be a few months before he returned to the sort of form that he was showing the year before. That and other factors meant that Celtic finished the 1938/39 season trophyless, the only plus point for MacDonald being his inclusion in the SFA team to tour North America in the summer.

This was Malky's first international recognition. It was a tour that the SFA would organize from time to time to bring on young players and to spread the game to other parts of the world. They were not full internationals, however, as evidenced by the fact that the only other Celtic player to take part in the tour was Willie Lyon, the centre-half and an Englishman! Fourteen games were played, most of them mismatches against teams such as Ontario, Saskatchewan and the American Soccer League, and MacDonald played in most of them, scoring goals and impressing the Scottish selectors with a view to the next season.

Yet everyone must have known that there might not be a next season. Hitler had taken over all of Czechoslovakia in March, and by the time that the team sailed in early May, he was already making noises about Poland. It was a bizarre voyage, sailing away to the land of plenty and from the troubled continent. There were severe worries that war might break out while they were away, and that the return voyage might be a dangerous one, with U-Boats and other threats. As it happened, Hitler waited until the Scottish football season had started again before making his move.

Life would never be the same again. After a hysterical two weeks in which the authorities tried to ban football altogether, a wiser counsel prevailed and some football was allowed. The Scottish Cup, the Scottish League and internationals were all suspended, and only part-time football was sanctioned, with players obliged to work in some war-related industry before they were allowed to turn out for their club on the Saturday.

Malky never joined the forces, but worked long shifts in the munitions industry. He played for Celtic all through the war, his career more or less finishing as the conflict ended. The war years for Celtic were terrible ones. Maley fell out with the directorate in the first winter of hostilities, and retired or was sacked, according to whatever spin one believed. He was replaced by Jimmy McStay, a man who might have done better in more normal times.

McStay had played briefly with MacDonald (in fact, one could say that it was MacDonald who replaced him as centre-half) and he used him steadily throughout the war years, though mainly at right-half rather than inside-right. But there is little to enthuse about in Celtic's performances during the war. In general, they were dismally inadequate and took place in odd circumstances, with balls that were well past their sell-by date, strips that were faded and motheaten, and referees who were too old and occasionally lacking in the basic competence required for the job.

It was Malky's misfortune to be involved in the dark hour of Celtic's history that was the Second World War, and the darkest day of all was New Year's Day 1943 when Celtic went down 1-8 to Rangers at Ibrox. MacDonald was the captain of that dysfunctional shambles that masqueraded as a Celtic team. Although far more exciting things were happening in Africa and Stalingrad and the Pacific, the defeat still hurt the Celtic faithful, more so when captain and hero Malky MacDonald was sent off for arguing with referee Willie Davidson about one of the Rangers goals, which was clearly offside. This was bad enough, but then the SFA suspended him for the rest of the season. It was one of many draconian decisions against Celtic at that time which made the fans wonder about the so-called impartiality of the SFA.

But Malky kept plugging away, and was chosen for Scotland on three occasions to play in war-time international matches against England. While such fixtures must be considered unofficial, and rightly so because the best players were not necessarily available, this is not to say that the games were not taken seriously. Certainly the results were eagerly anticipated by everyone at home and overseas. Sadly, Scotland did very badly, but Malky's versatility was once again proved by the fact that he played in three different positions – right-half, left-half and right-back. It would be his misfortune never to win a full international cap for Scotland, because by the time that the first official season arrived in 1946/47, MacDonald was well past his prime.

He had also left Parkhead on loan and then through a permanent transfer to Kilmarnock in autumn 1945. Indeed, he spent the rest of his football career alternating between Kilmarnock and Brentford, both as player and manager. But he would never deny that his heart lay at Celtic Park, and the love was a mutual one, as was evidenced any time he appeared with Kilmarnock at Parkhead. He became manager at Kilmarnock in place of Willie Waddell in July 1965, but after he was dismissed in 1968, he returned to Celtic Park as a season-ticket holder and supporter.

While boss of Kilmarnock, he was also given the privilege of being manager of Scotland for a couple of games between the resignation of John Prentice in October 1966 and the arrival of Bobby Brown in early 1967. The two games were against Wales at Cardiff, a drawn contest which should not have taken place as it was on the day after the horrendous Aberfan disaster, and a 2-1 win over Northern Ireland.

The love and esteem in which he was held was shown when the Celtic Supporters Association in January 1947 invited him to receive a testimonial gift, even though he had by now left Celtic Park. To resounding cheers, he told his audience that he did not want to be remembered as anything other than Malky MacDonald of Celtic, even though he could also claim an allegiance for Brentford and Kilmarnock. Years after that, long after his retiral, he declared: "I look back with great affection on the 14 years I spent with the club and the wonderful colleagues I had there. We were only temporary custodians of Celtic's greatness and they were happy days. I wouldn't change them for anything".

The curious thing about Malcolm MacDonald was how few games he played for the club. Fewer than 150 appearances in official Scottish League and Cup matches is not a large amount, but he suffered badly from injury, illness and the outbreak of World War Two. Yet he played so well in that 1937/38 season that he was quite rightly recognised as one of the greatest of all time by Celtic supporters. What a pity that his star was in the ascendancy for such a short time.

CHARLIE TULLY

1948-1959

'CHEEKY CHARLIE'

BHOYS CAREER

Games	319
Goals	47
Caps	10

MAGIC MOMENT

At Falkirk Tully scored direct from a corner, but was ordered to retake it by an officious linesman. Tully took the corner a second time - and scored again as Brockville erupted.

CHARLES Patrick Tully was born in Belfast on 11 July 1924 and died in the same city on 27 July 1971, a couple of weeks after celebrating his 47th birthday. Like many great Celts, it was Charlie's fate to die young, but those who saw him on the football field would always consider him to be an immortal. Indeed, there was the famous quote on the occasion of his funeral when someone said to Jock Stein: "Charlie was immortal. And noo he's deid!"

He was a hero for Celtic at a time when a hero was badly needed. The immediate post-Second World War years were in Great Britain the years of the establishment and consolidation of the Welfare State. Probably in material terms, the supporters were better off than they had ever been before, even though it would be several years in the future before Prime Minister Harold Macmillan could honestly claim: "We've never had it so good". But in terms of the performances on the field, Celtic were in a trough from which it seemed hard to emerge.

In 1938 the club had experienced a high point with the winning of the all-Britain Empire Exhibition Trophy, but Celtic had a bad war and immediate aftermath, including a joust with relegation in spring 1948. There is little doubt that other teams, spearheaded by Rangers, would have launched all sorts of initiatives to prevent Celtic joining a lower division, and the team, as it happened, did save itself. But it had been a humiliating process for all concerned and questions were being asked about whether Celtic would ever rise again.

In addition, the ground itself, "that dear old Paradise", was anything but what it claimed to be. It was large and spacious, with a well-appointed grandstand, but no-one seemed willing or prepared to do anything about the weeds on the terracing. Worse still were the holes in the roof of the only covered enclosure, an ugly barn-shaped construction which had earned the nickname of "The Jungle", presumably because those ex-Servicemen from the Far East theatre saw certain resemblances.

Enter Tully stage right. He joined Celtic from another Celtic, the Belfast variety. Belfast Celtic were doomed to extinction the following year, but Tully had done enough for them to convince the Glasgow version that he could play. He was a dribbler, a teaser, a fast runner, a ball-player and very definitely a crowd-pleaser. He was well worth the enormous fee of £8,000 which manager Jimmy McGrory convinced the reluctant and traditionally parsimonious board that he was worth.

It was possibly a crowd-pleaser that Celtic lacked most of all. Celtic's team in 1948 mirrored the drab austerity of the times. There were utility players, committed players and hard-working players, but flair players were lacking. The Celtic crowd would sigh for someone like Gordon Smith of Hibs to entertain the fans. More poignantly, they would search their recent memories and come up with Jimmy Delaney, one of Celtic's greatest ever entertainers but now plying his trade with Manchester United.

TULLY'S CELTIC CAREER BEGAN miserably with a laboured 0-0 draw with Morton, then came defeats by Aberdeen and Rangers. The *Glasgow Herald* was forceful when it said: "The wearin' o' the green (and white) is still a tale of toil and tribulation", "Celtic plumbed the depth of inefficiency", although it does hint at future possibilities when it says that "Tully, from Belfast, was the most attractive ball player on the field but I cannot recall his delivering a single shot".

It was a different matter when Rangers came to Parkhead in the League Cup on 25 September 1948. Tully had by now grown in confidence and under a headline of "Tully Bewilders Rangers", Cyril Horne of the *Glasgow Herald* declares emphatically that Tully is "undoubtedly the cleverest forward in the last ten years of Scottish football". In the 3-1 rout (it should have been a great deal more) Tully scored and the hitherto under-performing Gallachers, Willie and Jackie (sons of the peerless Patsy and the incomparable Hughie respectively) also found the net as the famous "Iron Curtain" Rangers defence was torn to shreds.

"Jackie, Willie, Weir and Tully
The lads that ran the Rangers sully".

Hyperbole has always been a facet of Scottish football fans, and on this occasion, Glasgow's East End absolutely exploded with paeans of praise for Charlie Tully. Almost overnight on Saturday 25 September 1948, Charlie became a cult hero. He was the one who would restore Celtic to greatness. He was Patsy Gallacher, Jimmy Delaney, Jimmy McMenemy and Malcolm MacDonald all rolled into one. "The" Celtic, as they were called, were on the way back.

Such euphoria and rapture was hardly dispelled on the Monday afternoon, the Glasgow autumn holiday, when 87,000 were at Hampden to see Celtic win the Glasgow Cup by beating Third Lanark 3-1. The Glasgow Cup was a much valued trophy in those days and Celtic had not won it since 1940. Little wonder that the streets from Hampden Park back to Celtic Park were thronged with thousands of fans, treating the inspired genius Charlie Tully in the way that pre-war dictators had been feted in Germany and Italy. Chanting was not a regular feature of football fans' repertoires in 1948. Nevertheless, the beat of "Tull-ee, Tull-ee" resounded all through the streets of Glasgow that Monday night, and there was (as there had been the previous Saturday) dancing in the streets of the Celtic heartlands, the Gorbals and the Garngad.

Songs were made and became current with rapidity. On the template of the song about the American millionaire wishing to buy the lakes of Killarney in Ireland and being rebuffed, came an imaginary reply to the manager of Arsenal enquiring about Charlie Tully:

"How can you buy all the Cups that we've won?
How can you buy old Ma Tully's son?
How can you purchase that son of a gun?
How can you buy our Charlie?"

Then The Wild Colonial Boy was adapted to Charlie Tully, who was "Celtic's Belfast Bhoy:"

"There is a great football player
Charlie Tully is his name

He plays for Glasgow Celtic
And wins them all their fame.
He crosses and he scores a goal
To give the fans their joy
And that is why we all love him
He's Celtic's Belfast Bhoy"

In Scottish football, of course, as in the rest of life, there is "nothing easier gotten than a shitey drop", as the vulgar put it, or as the more elegant might say "pride comes before a fall". Indeed, the higher one climbs, the harder one falls, and the rest of the 1948/49 season was a grievous and heart-breaking disappointment for the huge Celtic support. This was not all the fault of Tully. Indeed, on many occasions he was the only bright light in the all-pervasive Stygian gloom that was Celtic Park.

But he did lack support, as the rest of the forwards were Celtic players in name only, and would never have made the reserve team in previous or subsequent eras. Some 30 years later, Jock Stein would say: "The Celt shirt does not shrink to accommodate lesser players". Had Jock not still been playing for Albion Rovers in 1949, and had he seen Celtic oftener, he might have had to suggest to the outfitters that a smaller size might have been appropriate in exchange for the ration coupons that were still required for clothing.

Tully must share some of the blame. He was never a great team man and not infrequently the Celtic crowd (which, hard times or not, seldom fell to below 40,000) was treated to the somewhat unedifying spectacle of the Irishman exercising his debating skills with his team-mates about how the game should be played. He also had a particularly annoying habit of beating a man, thus earning the acclaim of the denizens of the Jungle, then beating him again to earn even more acclaim, when a wiser option might have been to pass to a better placed colleague.

Yet the crowd loved his antics. "Cheeky Charlie's capers" became the talk of Glasgow, and even Rangers fans, accustomed to their more direct and efficient, but less talented players, gave him on occasion some reluctant respect. He would take a throw-in and aim the ball at an opponent's back to get the rebound; he would go down on his hand and knees before a linesman to beg for a corner rather than a goal kick for the opposition, and he would hold play up as he was about to take a corner to go to the crowd and shake hands with a ragged, ill-fed-looking wee boy whom the Welfare State had not yet reached.

Stories abounded about him, like the time when his car broke down outside a lunatic asylum and he asked for help saying: "I'm Tully". One of the inmates with a speech impediment said: "But we're all tully (sully, i.e. silly) in here!". On another occasion the Celtic team bus broke down on the way to Ibrox, but Tully, who had made his own way there, took on Rangers himself and at half-time was beating them 1-0. But the team bus arrived at half-time – and then Celtic lost 1-2! And the most famous one, (which would have been considered blasphemous in the eyes of the Celtic support if it had featured anyone else) was the time that he met His Holiness the Pope on the Vatican balcony. The massive crowd of pilgrims all started to cheer as the two figures appeared on the balcony, but soon asked the question: "Who's that chap with the funny hat up there beside Charlie Tully?"

A more elevated note was struck in educational circles concerning the famous Latin author Marcus Tullius Cicero. He had been known by 19th century scholars as "Tully" but that nomenclature had faded in the 20th century and the man who defeated Verres and Catiline was known as Cicero. Suddenly, from about 1950 onwards, Latin teachers, particularly in Roman Catholic schools, began to talk once again about "Tully"!

BUT ALL THIS COULD not disguise the fact that Celtic were going nowhere with a poor team. Indeed it was often said of the story about the Pope that when the two heroes were on the Vatican balcony, His Holiness was asking Charlie: "When are we going to win something again?" Indeed, the halfway point of the century was reached with nothing to show apart from the slightly irrelevant Glasgow Charity Cup, won thanks to two Rangers own goals.

Prior to this, there had been serious doubts about the continuation of Old Firm games. Nastiness and violence had reached a serious pitch. The Glasgow slums were still the disgrace of Western Europe, and no sociologist would be surprised to discover that young men from such provenance could turn aggressive. There was to be added to the cocktail Glasgow's traditional sectarian background, a legacy to Scotland from the bad old days of John Knox and Mary Queen of Scots, and a feature of industrial Glasgow for the past 100 years since the victims of the Irish potato famine first began to arrive seeking jobs. Also the 1950s represented the heyday of the Glasgow razor gangs, and there were still a large amount of young men who had learned rather too much violence in the khaki of the British army.

Tully had been the innocent victim in the first major incident. In a surreal and unbelievable moment at Ibrox on 27 August 1949, Rangers' Sammy Cox had suddenly turned from chasing a ball and kicked Tully so high that he even missed his private parts! A kick in the stomach has no place in any kind of football, and astonishingly, the referee, Mr Gebbie, failed to send Cox off the field. This did little to dispel the notion that referees would condone any sort of Rangers thuggery against Celtic, and the Celtic crowd responded with a hail of bottles. The authorities later told Tully that he had to behave and not incite the crowd!

Less than three weeks later, Tully was not so innocent. After a few questionable decisions by the referee, a free-kick was wrongly awarded to Rangers, who were allowed to take it while Celtic players were mildly protesting to the referee, and before the official, Mr Davidson, had signalled for the kick to be taken. Rangers ran upfield and scored against a disorientated Celtic defence, and all hell erupted, with Tully quite clearly urging the Celtic players to leave the field in protest.

Yet another game against Rangers was played nine days later. Celtic fans boycotted this fixture, and Tully was not playing. He was not even in Scotland, as he had gone back home to Belfast. Celtic tried to claim that Tully was injured, but few were convinced by this, and when he missed the next game as well, it was widely believed and never officially denied that he was serving a club suspension. Indeed, his whole Parkhead future teetered on the brink for some considerable time, but Tully was far too valuable a player in the eyes of the support to be allowed to slip away lightly.

The miserable form and the lack of success of the team continued until the bright spring day of 21 April 1951, when the Scottish Cup returned to Celtic Park. Tully's finest hour in this campaign had come in the semi-final against the strong-going Raith Rovers, when before

84,237 fans he "played some delightful football throughout" and scored the winning goal immediately after Raith had equalised. In the final itself, against Motherwell (who were probably the better football team), the glory belonged to the captain, John McPhail, who scored the only goal of the game. But no-one would underestimate the role played by the all-Irish left wing of Bertie Peacock and Charlie Tully in the recapture of the old Celtic glory.

A tour of North America followed. Hysteria was the order of the day in Glasgow as Celtic departed and came back, and this atmosphere was in no way diminished as the Celts, with the Scottish Cup carried famously in a shopping bag (and once almost left behind), toured various American cities where folk of Irish or Scottish descent flocked to see this great man called Charlie Tully.

Now that Celtic were back among the honours, it was felt that with Tully approaching his best, Celtic could dominate Scottish football for the next decade. That this did not happen was due to several reasons. One was that there were so many other good teams around. Rangers were always able to present a robust challenge, but there was also the fine play of Hibs, for whom the "Famous Five" forward line were in their heyday, Hearts were also developing fast, and Motherwell, Aberdeen and Dundee would all have their moments of success.

The main problem as far as Celtic were concerned was the lack of good or even clear management. Jimmy McGrory, the hero of the Celtic support of the 1930s, was the manager, but a manager in name only, as the real power was wielded by Robert Kelly, the chairman. No-one could ever doubt his sincerity and love for the Celtic. What was in question was his knowledge of the game, and his inflexible obstinacy, particularly when it involved spending money.

Yet money was not really a problem. Celtic's support stayed loyal. Indeed, it was vast, and huge crowds crossed the length and breadth of Scotland wherever Celtic were playing. The behaviour was often less than perfect, and more than once pictures appeared in Sunday newspapers of men like Charlie Tully, Bertie Peacock and Bobby Evans appealing to the Celtic fans to desist from throwing beer bottles. But the root cause was frustration – frustration at having a team, full of talented players like Tully, but which consistently failed to deliver trophies

The man who would eventually change all that was Jock Stein, who arrived anonymously at the club, as an afterthought in an injury crisis in December 1951. For a long time it was rumoured that he and Tully did not get on. Whether Tully did not trust Stein because of his non-Catholic background has never been proved, but it took a long time before a good relationship was established.

They were each what the other wasn't. Stein was a reliable (but no more than that) centre-half; Tully was, on his day, the best forward in the world. Tully was cheeky, played to the gallery and showed off to an extent that wiser elements in the team like Bobby Evans and Jock Stein found unacceptable. But Stein also could bring out the best in players, and when he was appointed captain (to the initial dismay of Tully), he soon set about creating a businesslike atmosphere on the field.

Tully took a long time to adapt to that, but eventually grew to respect and appreciate Stein to such an extent that on the eve of the 1954 Scottish Cup final, Charlie was so besieged by fans importunately demanding tickets that he asked if he could stay with Mr and Mrs Stein. This request was granted and in later years, when Stein became the manager, he had no greater fan and supporter than Charlie Tully.

Tully played ten times for Northern Ireland between 1948 and 1959. On one occasion against England he scored direct from a corner, and on other occasions made life miserable for luminaries like Alf Ramsey and Billy Wright. Against Scotland he was less lucky, never being on the winning side. As has happened with other Celtic players, notably Anton Rogan and Neil Lennon in more recent times, Charlie was on the wrong side of the sectarian fence for large sections of the Ulster crowd and was often given a disproportionate share of the obloquy when things went wrong. Yet many Irish fans were ashamed of this treatment given to a star player, and it would be wrong to say that he was ever deterred from playing for Northern Ireland for that reason. In any case the bigots were well and truly silenced when Bertie Peacock, a Northern Ireland Protestant and a fine player, became captain of Celtic – and Northern Ireland!

THE YEAR 1953 SAW the great Tully incident, the story of which has been retold from one generation to another, clearly losing nothing in its telling, but in some ways a suitable metaphor for the Tully career. Charlie frequently disappointed in his attitude and his commitment, but just occasionally something happened which betokened brilliance. It was at Brockville, Falkirk on 21 February. It was a Scottish Cup tie and Celtic were deservedly 0-2 down. Early in the second half, Tully took a corner on the left and scored direct. The small ground erupted and the pitch was invaded, several youngsters being injured. The celebrations were premature, as the linesman had his flag up because Tully had not put the ball properly inside the arc.

Waiting patiently for the crowd to get back on the field, Tully prepared to take the kick again, this time handing the ball very politely to the linesman to place it for him. The linesman obliged, the referee blew his whistle, Tully took the kick and scored again. If Brockville had erupted the first time, it exploded this time, and indeed some crush barriers collapsed, causing mainly minor injuries. This time the goal was given, Charlie performed a little sand dance before disappearing under adoring team-mates and fans, and Celtic, now only 1-2 down, went on to win the tie 3-2.

That same year saw the Coronation of Queen Elizabeth II. In honour of this event, a football tournament was held in Glasgow to which were invited the best eight teams of Great Britain. Celtic could not really have claimed in 1953 to have been among the best 20 teams in Great Britain, after their piteous performances in that year, but they could hardly not have been invited, given their huge support and financial drawing power, especially as all the games were to be played in Glasgow.

History tells that Celtic upset all the odds and won this tournament, and that the fans had a song which had a refrain: "Tully-ee-Tully-aye-oh-Tully-ee-aye-oh-ee". Unfortunately, Charlie was injured and did not play in the final against Hibs, but it was as much Tully as anyone else who put them there through fine wins against Arsenal and Manchester United.

And then there was the wonderful season of 1953/54, in which Celtic at long last realised their potential and won the Scottish League and Cup double, for which their fans had been craving since before the First World War. Unfortunately, Tully was carried off with a nasty leg injury in a 1-1 draw against Hibs on 7 November, and did not reappear until the beginning of February. But he was there when it mattered, and took part in that epic Scottish Cup final victory over Aberdeen in 1954, an encounter often regarded as the best final of them all.

But for fans who expected now the "promised land" of sustained Celtic success, this proved illusory. Two Scottish Cup finals were lost, one in 1955 through a goalkeeping error and another in 1956 through a static Celtic performance which had the fans puzzled and which leaves the uncomfortable feeling more than 50 years later that the whole truth has not yet been told. The prickly Tully was certainly out of sorts that day, as were several other players, and it was on a day like that that some Tully magic might have been expected. Sadly none was forthcoming.

All through this time, nothing had happened to diminish the cult following of Charlie Tully, even though little was happening on the field to justify its continuation. Tully had certainly slowed down as a result of general old age, loads of injuries (many of which were caused by cynical defenders) and the undeniable fact that Charlie was none too energetic in his training. He would frequently find excuses for not lapping the track, saying things like "you don't learn to play snooker by walking round the table", and the impression of ageing was encouraged by the fact that he was prematurely bald. This did, of course, happen to men in the 1950s, thanks to overuse of hair oils like Brylcreem and the permanent wearing of bonnets, but in the case of Charlie Tully, he seemed to have been old for a very long time, even though in 1956 he was still only 32.

He was also no innocent on the field. He was seldom a dirty player in the blatant sense, but he did know how to niggle, to chat, to undermine an opponent's confidence by remarks about his wife and other things. He did get off with a great deal from referees who possibly sensed that a riot might follow if Tully disappeared up the tunnel, and in any case Charlie, with his natural Irish blarney and disarming smile, was often able to talk himself out of it. Naturally, jokes circulated about how Jack Mowat, a famous referee, had threatened to send Tully to the pavilion. There was in Glasgow a famous theatre called the Pavilion, so Charlie said to Mowat: "Can you no' make it the Empire or the Regal, instead, Mr.Mowat? There is a better show on there this week!"

Yet there was at least one occasion when a sending-off might have been called for. It was in his best ever game, namely the one already referred to involving the twice-taken corner at Brockville in 1953. Just at the start of the second half, a cynical body-check on a Falkirk player left the man on the ground, aroused the Falkirk fans to justifiable anger and hushed the Celtic fans into embarrassed silence. The Falkirk player, you see, was one Jimmy Delaney, who had been one of Celtic's greatest ever players in the years before the Second World War.

Tully's last three seasons for Celtic between 1956 and 1959 were even more injury-plagued than the previous ones, and although he was still loved by the fans, it was clear to everyone that Celtic's future interests might be better served without the Belfast Bhoy. Not that he didn't have his moments, of course. In October 1956, when the whole world was holding its breath fearing World War Three in the wake of the Suez crisis, Celtic at last won the Scottish League Cup, after ten years of constant disappointment. Heavy weather was made of it in the final against Partick Thistle. Tully looked out of sorts in a 0-0 draw in which Thistle were the better side, but then in the replay the following Wednesday afternoon, in front of a miniscule crowd, Tully took charge and although he did not score, he was instrumental in helping Collins and McPhail to do so.

Then came the most famous game of the 1950s, very much involving Charlie Tully. It was the Scottish League Cup of 1957/58 when, for the first time ever, the Old Firm met in the final. The run-up to this game contained an incident in the Parkhead dressing room at training which everyone tried to hush up, but this being Glasgow (the biggest gossipy village in the world), everyone got to hear about it.

Two weeks before the final, Scotland had played Northern Ireland in Belfast and had been lucky to get away with a 1-1 draw following a feckless performance. Tully was not playing for Northern Ireland, but was writing a column for the *Glasgow Evening Citizen*. Whether or not the column was ghosted by a journalist (as often happened) was irrelevant, it was Tully's name at the top of it. Tully saw fit to criticise the Scottish team, and said that despite having a few fine players (whom he named and exonerated) the chances of Scotland making the World Cup finals of 1958 with that team were slim. The "exonerated" list failed to contain Bobby Evans or Bobby Collins.

Collins, a feisty wee character, did not seem to be too upset about this sneer, but Evans saw a personal attack in this (as well he might have) and relations between himself and Tully (which had never been great in the first place) took a dip, culminating in a bout of fisticuffs at training on the Thursday before the final. Such things are not unknown in football teams, but this did seem to be a problem before a major final against Rangers.

Fortunately Celtic had a fine diplomat in captain Bertie Peacock. Peacock had himself played in that international match, and once everything had calmed down had a word with the two men individually, then together, then in front of the rest of the team. Handshakes were exchanged, and although the incident was not exactly forgotten, it was put on the back burner until the final was over.

The League Cup final of 1957 was a famous, yet galling and frustrating occasion. Celtic, as any fan will tell you, won 7-1 and it was a brilliant exhibition of that team at its best. It showed the world what that side containing such fine players as Fernie, Collins, Evans, Peacock, McPhail and Tully could have been. Sadly, there was only that brief October encounter which showed Celtic at their best – then the team dissolved soon after. But it was a glorious sunset.

INJURY MEANT THAT TULLY played only another seven games that season, and by 1958/59, clearly one of the worst in the history of the club, the emphasis was very much on a youth policy so the veteran played only 15 games. His last was a 4-0 win over Albion Rovers in the Scottish Cup on 31 January 1959, and he was given a free transfer in the following summer. He had played 11 seasons for the club, made 319 appearances and scored 47 goals.

His subsequent career saw him as a boss with Cork Hibs, Portadown and Bangor (twice), but he was never really cut out for the serious side of football management. He did return once to play at Parkhead and that was for the Irish League against the Scottish League in season 1960/61. He was given a great reception by the Parkhead crowd, who clearly retained their love for their "cheeky Charlie," singing songs about "Bonnie Prince Charlie", the likes of *Will ye no'come back again?* and *Clap hands, here comes Charlie*.

It is, indeed, a shame that Tully left Celtic with a fairly miserable total of one Scottish League medal, two Scottish Cup gongss and two Scottish League Cup medals. Other lesser players have won more, but Tully came at a bad time in Celtic history, with a weak manager and a dictatorial and pig-headed chairman. Events after the departure of Tully would prove how bad things were. Perhaps for this reason a little credit must be given to Charlie for his ability to hold the line and arrest this decline.

Tully was very much a man of the 1950s. Things were changing fast, with new team formations and more tactics coming into the game. Tully would have found it very hard to adapt to the new ideas, and certainly would not really have fitted into Jock Stein's great Celtic team of the mid-1960s. He was, of course, delighted with the team's triumph, and when asked where would he have fitted into that side, he said (perhaps only half as a joke): "I could have taken the corners".

He continued to take a great interest in the team and in football, writing a column for various newspapers, like the *Daily Record*, talking about "Tullyvision" and saying things like "You've seen it on television, now hear comes Tullyvision!" "If you don't like it, then turn your Tully off!" "My son wants to come to Britain and to play for two teams – Manchester United are the other one!"

He died suddenly in his sleep in the summer of 1971. The Falls Road area of Belfast, with the British Army looking on, saw scenes of grief and mourning which presaged, in some tragic way, the funerals in subsequent years for victims of paramilitary terror or British Army repression. As the cortege made its way to Milltown Cemetery, goalkeeper Johnny Bonnar looked at all the huge crowds and said to Jock Stein: "Charlie would have loved all this, Jock". "Aye, he would that" came the reply.

JOCK STEIN

1951-1956
1965-1978

BHOYS CAREER

as player

Games   148

Goals   2

as manager

1 European Cup

10 League titles

8 Scottish Cups

6 League Cups

MAGIC MOMENT

It could only be lifting the European Cup in Lisbon in 1967.

'BIG JOCK'

THE jealous Cassius speaks thus of Julius Caesar in one of Shakespeare's greatest works. Had he lived in Scotland between the years 1960 and 1985, there would have been little doubt who the Colossus was.

Jock Stein was a big man in every sense of the word. His bulky frame was ever present, towering over everyone else and the atmosphere changed whenever he was around. More than one newspaper reporter would say that it was obvious whenever Jock Stein had entered the room, even when you had your back to him. Such was the immediate change in deportment and body language from those who were facing him.

Although not without his moments of glory on the playing field, he was not a great player. As a centre-half, he would describe himself in a rare outburst of humour and with deliberate ambiguity as "passable". He never won a cap for Scotland, and in the one game that he played for the Scottish League, his team was heavily defeated. His best game for Celtic was probably the Coronation Cup final against Hibs in 1953, when he and goalkeeper John Bonnar managed to keep out the great "Famous Five" forward line to bring off an unlikely victory for Celtic.

But it was as a captain and leader that he made his mark, guiding Celtic to a League and Cup double in 1954. When an ankle injury ended his career a couple of years after that, he was appointed coach to the youngsters, as chairman Bob Kelly realised that there was leadership potential there. In that capacity he discovered and brought on great young players like Billy McNeill, Pat Crerand and John Clark, and in other circumstances he might well have moved up to being the manager.

But there were several factors that counted against it. One was that Celtic did not, as a rule, change their manager. Jimmy McGrory was only the third in 70 years of the club. Another factor was that Jock Stein was a Protestant. This would not have mattered anywhere in Scotland or England other than in west central Scotland, and the irony was that being a Protestant, in Stein's case, did not mean that he attended a Church of Scotland service every Sunday. It meant simply that he had been brought up on the other side of the divide, a factor that weighed heavily with Bob Kelly, but not, as we shall see, with the supporters.

The major factor, however, with Kelly was that Stein would have challenged the chairman's authority. Kelly was a bully who could always persuade the kindly and gentle Jimmy McGrory to choose the team that he, Kelly, wanted. The chairman, in fact, hid behind McGrory, a man with whom the Celtic fans would find it very difficult to get angry, as his playing career had been such a legend. Stein would not have consented to be the glorified office boy that Jimmy was.

So, for the moment, Stein was allowed to leave Parkhead. This he did in 1960 to go to unfashionable Dunfermline Athletic, at that time struggling to avoid relegation. How Stein made Kelly pay for his decision to let him go! Not only did Dunfermline beat Celtic in Stein's first game, but a year later in a Cup final that is still painful for Celtic supporters to recall, Dunfermline overcame the Bhoys in a replay to prolong the trophy famine that had haunted Celtic Park for several years.

In the meantime, Dunfermline had saved themselves from relegation, had established themselves as a force in Scotland and had even made their mark in Europe, beating teams like Everton, for example. Celtic were going from bad to worse with a massive inferiority complex about Rangers, a self-destruct button and an inability to win important games. Their massive support occasionally turned violent and nasty, organised boycotts, stopped going to games, and on one spectacular, memorable and painful occasion, 60,000 embittered and stunned supporters turned their backs on Celtic en masse and walked out of the 1963 Scottish Cup final replay against Rangers.

STEIN HIMSELF, MEANWHILE, left Dunfermline in 1964, hoping presumably for the call from Celtic, and when that did not come, went to Hibs instead. He was on the point of bringing back the glory days to Easter Road when things got so bad at Celtic Park that changes had to be made. The midwinter of 1964/65 was the nadir of Celtic, and even the thick-skinned Bob Kelly realised that things could not be ignored. Stein was the obvious choice, but there still remained the issue of his religion.

This problem only really existed in the mind of Bob Kelly and a very small bunch of bigots. Celtic supporters, frankly, do not care about anyone's religion. From the earliest of days men like Sunny Jim Young, Dun Hay, John Thomson and Willie Lyon had been accepted as foot-ballers. As Willie Maley said: "It's not a man's creed or his nationality that counts – it's the man himself." Ten years previously the mighty half-back line of Bobby Evans, Jock Stein and Bertie Peacock had all been Protestants, Peacock coming from Northern Ireland and loosely even described as an "Orangeman".

The support had accepted all of them without a murmur, even when Bertie Peacock was made captain in 1957. Celtic supporters' concerns about Ireland were political rather than reli-gious. Supporters songs did include anthems of Ireland's struggle for independence over the centuries and there was a desire to see a united Ireland, but religious bigotry never played any great part. Indeed, a sizeable section of the support, particularly from the East of Scotland, were themselves Protestants.

So if Kelly fretted about Stein's religion, he was doing so needlessly. His hand was, in any case, forced by the dreadful results and his appointment of Jock Stein was, in fact, an abdica-tion. Stein insisted on full powers to pick the team, putting his foot down admirably in the choice of Bobby Murdoch as a right-half rather than a forward (an opinion shared by many of the supporters). Kelly now retired to the business side of the club, doing well enough, however, in the reflected glory brought to Celtic by Stein to earn for himself a knighthood on New Year's Day 1969.

From 31 January 1965, when Stein's appointment was announced, Celtic were born again. The Scottish Cup was won in 1965, the other two domestic honours likewise in 1966 and the support returned to fill Celtic Park in a way that had never been seen before.

Celtic's first Cult Hero - Dan Doyle. Seen (on the left) with one of his eight Scottish caps and (on the right) in the 1896 Celtic line-up next to the legendary 'Man Who Made Celtic' Willie Maley (who sits on the right end of the middle row). Maley was on the verge of retiring as a player when this photograph was taken, leaving Doyle as the unquestionable number one in the public's affections.

This rare photograph was taken shortly before Celtic's infamous Cup defeat at Arthurlie in January 1897 for which Doyle, not for the first time in his career, went AWOL.
Doyle sits in the middle of the second row, behind the man with the ball.

All smiles for the camera, but this was the other game before which Dan went 'missing'. This time it was against England at Goodison Park in 1895 and Scotland lost 0-3 after Dan turned up an hour before kick off. He is second from the right in the middle row.

Sandy McMahon - elegant, late-Victorian gentleman and Celtic hero. On the right he is wearing the cap in the front row, before he grew his famous moustache.

'Sunny Jim' Young was the captain and heartbeat of the Celtic teams which swept all before them from 1903-1917, winning ten league titles. (Right) A rare photograph of Young in action, on this occasion in a friendly against Aston Villa in 1912.

Celtic's great team of 1913/14, the year of their third league and Cup double under manager Willie Maley. The second back row contains Cult Heroes Jimmy Young (third from left) and Jimmy Quinn (second from right).
(Right) The handsome face of Joe Cassidy who scored two famous goals in the 1921 New Year's Day victory at Ibrox and the only goal of the 1923 Scottish Cup final.

Joe Cassidy is kneeling (third from left in the second row) before this game in 1922 between the British Army on the Rhine and Celtic.

(Left) Tommy McInally became known as the Boy Wonder due to his dazzling ball skills.
(Right) McInally hooks the ball over his head during a game against Rangers at Celtic Park.

Celtic's 1925/26 team, including Tommy McInally (back row, second from left) and Jimmy McGrory (front row, second from left).

(Left) Jimmy McGrory; scorer of a club record 522 goals in 501 games for Celtic.
(Right) McGrory shows off the Scottish Cup on the team's summer tour of America in 1931.

Two famous goals of Jimmy McGrory. On the left at Celtic Park on 19 October 1935 against Airdrie, McGrory beats Steve Bloomer's English league record tally of 352. Then (right) on 21 December 1935 a diving header against Aberdeen beats Hughie Ferguson's tally of 364 to establish a British league record.

(Right) The Scottish Cup Winners of 1925 featuring Peter Wilson and Jimmy McGrory.

(Below) The huge crowd at Hampden to see that Cup final between Celtic and Dundee.

(Above left) Peter Wilson; the rustic hero, who once got lost in a Glasgow department store.
(Above right) Bertie Thomson (seated in centre); a more urban, working-class hero, who scrapped and partied with the best of them.
(Below) A revealing picture of Malky MacDonald (back row, extreme right). Malky is as far away from the brooding presence of Willie Maley as possible and looking askance at him, even when Celtic are clearly in holiday mode.

(Above left) MacDonald the Cult Hero member of the famous 1938 forward line of Delaney, MacDonald, Crum, Divers and Murphy.
(Above right) Charlie Tully; loved by Celtic fans for his cheeky, impish ball skills.

(Below) Celtic's 1953 Coronation Cup-winning side, featuring centre-half Jock Stein (seated in front row, third from let)

Little is spoken of Stein's playing career because of his legendary status as a manager, but he was a tough centre-half. Here he clears from Rangers' Derek Grierson.

1954; outside Hampden Park and Celtic have just won the Scottish Cup. In the picture are Charlie Tully, Mrs Stein, Jock Stein and trainer Alec Dowdalls.

(Above) Stein addresses his players on his first day as manager at Celtic. He proved an instant inspiration as the team won the Scottish Cup within months of him taking the reins. (Below) Stein was deified by fans young and old after Celtic became European Champions on an incredible night in Lisbon in 1967.

Stevie Chalmers' goal hits the back of the Inter Milan net and Celtic are now 2-1 up in Stein and the club's greatest triumph, the 1967 European Cup final.
(Below) The night after the Lisbon triumph as the team return to Parkhead. Stein carries the trophy amidst the gleeful throng.

Jock Stein's record as manager of Celtic included ten Scottish League Championships, eight Scottish Cups, six Scottish League Cups and the European Cup.

Adored by his players as much as his fans, Stein (top) is chaired onto the pitch before the final match of the season after the 1967 League Championship was wrapped up in the penultimate game against Rangers. The Celtic players are (left to right) John Clark, Jim Craig, Bobby Lennox, Bertie Auld, Bobby Murdoch, Billy McNeill, Tommy Gemmell, Jimmy Johnstone and John Fallon.

Celtic's 1997 vintage observe a minute's silence for Stein before a UEFA Cup tie at Ninian Park, Cardiff where Stein had collapsed and died whilst managing Scotland in 1985.

(Above left) Pat Crerand; the blue-eyed Bhoy of the early 1960s.
(Above right, from left clockwise) Bertie Peacock, Bobby Evans (hidden), Pat Crerand, Bertie Auld and Charlie Tully (in hat) welcome Italian trialist Santessori (no. 3) to Celtic Park.

Crerand (left) breaks the hearts of all Celtic fans by signing for Matt Busby (seated right) and Manchester United in early 1963.

John Hughes' achievements became the stuff of legend as shown by this contemporary magazine clipping. What it doesn't mention is that this feat arrived with the club at the lowest point in its history in an 8-0 win over Aberdeen.

(Above) Hughes gets in a shot against Rangers despite Doug Baillie's attentions.
(Below) Hughes could score goals with both feet and his head. Here he nets against
Airdrieonians in the 1961 Scottish Cup semi-final.

Hughes smashes the ball into the roof of Airdrie's net. This goal was disallowed for offside, but Hughes became one of the highest goalscorers in Celtic history, with a grand total of 189 goals.

The wing wizard; 'Jinky' Jimmy Johnstone weaves some magic with the ball at his feet.

Johnstone was loved as much for his fiery, passionate nature as his dribbling skills and pace, which could destroy opposition defences.

Trainer Neil Mochan pours some bubbly for Johnstone after Celtic's 1966 league title victory... the first since 1954 and the first of the 'nine-in-a-row'.

John 'Dixie' Deans in action during the 1974 Scottish Cup final victory over Dundee United. Dixie scored the third goal in a 3-0 win.

Deans was all about scoring goals. (Above) He nets one of his legendary treble against Hibs in May 1972 and (below left) celebrates in style. (Below right) Deans is embraced by manager Jock Stein after his hat-trick in this 6-1 Scottish Cup final victory.

Roy Aitken heads for goal against Rangers in May 1979. Only two men, Billy McNeill and Paul McStay, have made more appearances for the Bhoys.

Aitken celebrates winning the 1988 Scottish Cup against Dundee United in traditional style.

Captain Aitken exchanges pleasantries with his opposite number Terry Butcher and introduces the England defender to his first Old Firm derby in August 1986.

One of Aitken's greatest assets was his strength. Here he holds Rangers' Ian Ferguson off the ball with typical grit and determination.

Three fine shots of 'Champagne' Charlie Nicholas; the darling of Celtic's feverish support for the first half of the 1980s (above), and in the early 1990s (below).

Nicholas turns on some of that Champagne style which captivated the hearts of
Celtic fans as much as his phenomenal goal return.

Super Swede Henrik Larsson complete with his famous, distinctive dreadlocks, and (below) in celebratory mood after winning the League championship in 1998 - not only Celtic's first for a decade, but the victory which prevented Rangers winning ten titles in a row.

The trappings of the modern footballing cult hero; masks, flags and even the famous 'tongue out' goal celebration adorn a wide variety of Celtic fans.

(Above) Bedlam in Seville after, for the second time, Larsson brings Celtic back into the ultimately unsuccessful 2003 UEFA Cup final against Porto.

(Below) Parkhead bids a tearful farewell to the greatest Cult Hero of Cetic's modern history.

Perhaps the most unlikely Cult Hero of the twenty featured in this book, Shunsuke Nakamura stole Celts' hearts with his effervescence and incredible ability from free-kicks.

Nakamura is mobbed by his team-mates after scoring the the vital free-kick which secured a 2-1 victory at Kilmarnock and won Celtic the SPL in April 2007.

(Above left) Celtic fans turn Japanese in salutation of their hero, while (above right) the shy Nakamura lifts the 2007 League Championship trophy.

(Below) Wall art in Nakamura's hometown of Yokohama captures traditional Japanese culture in a green and white jersey.

After winning six successive league titles, with Jimmy Quinn leading scorer in four of those seasons, Celtic won the Scottish Cup in 1912 (above) thanks to goals by Jimmy McMenemy and mercurial Irishman Patsy Gallacher. Quinn is fourth from right in the middle row, and two to the right is 'Sunny Jim' Young, next to manager Willie Maley.

Below are the 1923 Scottish Cup winners who beat Hibs 1-0 with a goal from Joe Cassidy (second from left in the front row).

Celtic pose with the three Cups which they won in 1907/08 (the Charity Cup, the Scottish Cup and the Glasgow Cup): (middle row, left to right) manager Willie Maley, Jim Young, Peter Somers, Jimmy McMenemy, Davy Adams, John Mitchell, Jamie Weir, R Davis; (front row, left to right) Davy Hamilton, Donnie McLeod, Willie Loney, James Hay, Jimmy Quinn and Alec McNair.

(Left) Jimmy Quinn, who scored an incredible 216 goals in 331 games for Celtic; the first man to pass the double hundred mark for the club. (Right) An array of Celtic legends; (from left) Jimmy Quinn, Willie Maley, Jimmy McGrory & Patsy Gallacher.

Enthusiasm and young, modern, progressive ideas now took over in a way that was somehow in tune with mid-1960s. This was to be the new world, and the future was going to be Celtic and green-and-white, as pop tunes of the Beatles and others were given Celtic lyrics and the chant of "Jock Stein" was frequently heard. So much for Kelly's fears of the support being unable to accept a Protestant as a manager.

Stein was not unaware of what the religious situation in Scotland was, and he was shrewd enough to exploit his advantages. Knowing full well that Rangers were reluctant to employ a Roman Catholic for fear of antagonising their support, he would frequently target young Protestant players with a view to persuading them to join Celtic. His thinking was that this would deprive Rangers of a potential recruit – young men like Kenny Dalglish and Danny McGrain joined the club on this basis – whereas young Roman Catholic players would, in any case, wish to join Celtic.

In this respect, his greatest coup came late in his career in 1977. After Rangers had stated publicly that they would now sign Roman Catholics following yet more trouble from their alleged supporters, but had as yet failed to do so, Jock signed Alfie Conn from Tottenham Hotspur – the same Alfie Conn who had played for Rangers a few years previously. The Celtic support accepted Alfie immediately, and Jock then gilded the lily by stating that he was sure that they would. In fact, he had consulted Kenny Dalglish and Danny McGrain about it. There was a subliminal message in all this for those with an eye to see, and that was that the triumvirate of McGrain, Dalglish and Stein, who made this decision, all had one thing in common, and that was that they were Protestants.

Stein, ironically perhaps, was not a practising Protestant, but neither was he a godless man, either. The story is told about the Sunday in Bermuda on a tour in 1966 when the Roman Catholic players went off to Mass, leaving Stein with men like Tommy Gemmell, Ronnie Simpson, Bertie Auld and Ian Young kicking their heels at the hotel. Stein then found out that there was a Church of Scotland on the island, hired a taxi and took his men to it. They sat near the front, sang the hymns lustily, introduced themselves to the overawed minister at the end of the service. They then joined the rest of the congregation in the church hall, drank tea, were polite to all the ladies of the choir and held court about football and life back in Scotland.

IN 1967 CELTIC WON the European Cup, a feat totally incomprehensible in the context of their recent history, yet somehow it was as if destiny had beckoned. Anyone who had witnessed or experienced the horrors of the early 1960s would have appreciated any kind of success brought to the club and might, indeed, have settled for the Scottish League Cup once every three years or some such, but this was riches and joy on a scale completely unimagined. Even the oldest of supporters, who could recall graphically the exploits of Jimmy Quinn and Patsy Gallacher, were now convinced that this was the greatest Celtic side of them all. Another hugely successful Scottish manager, who would lay the foundation for Liverpool's domination of Europe, but not quite manage the feat himself, was certain of where this placed Stein in the pecking order of manager. "John, John (sic) you're immortal now," exclaimed one Bill Shankly.

Other achievements were winning the Scottish League nine years in a row and once after that, eight Scottish Cups and six League Cups, including five in a row from 1965/66 until 1969/70. He also had many near misses in the shape of Cup final defeats, including the tragic year of 1970, when over-confidence after defeating Leeds United in the semi-final led inexorably to Celtic's downfall in the European Cup final. He also reached the semi-final of that great tournament on another two occasions, losing heartbreakingly on a penalty shoot-out in 1972 and being kicked off the park by a set of hooligans masquerading as Atletico Madrid in 1974. These reverses, however heartbreaking at the time, nevertheless represented great success and respectability for Scotland, a point of which the patriotic Stein was very proud.

Stein's great strength was in his assessment of players. He knew all about Billy McNeill, as he had helped to discover him. He found Bobby Murdoch's true position; he appreciated the talents of the midfield general Bertie Auld, and he rescued Jimmy Johnstone from a life of under-achievement which might well have led to alcoholism. When he bought a player (something that he did not do very often and never without a considerable amount of thought) it was usually a winner – Joe McBride, Willie Wallace, Tommy Callaghan, Harry Hood, Dixie Deans, Alfie Conn and Pat Stanton, for example, all played glorious parts in the sustained success of Celtic.

It was his relationship with fans that earned Stein a great deal of love and respect from the Scottish public. He always said that the fans were the lifeblood of the game, that "football without fans is nothing" and, unlike some others who said that, he actually lived it. He would always attend supporters' functions and insisted that his players did likewise. He visited sick supporters in hospital in an age before mobile phones and text messaging, on one occasion he personally flagged down buses en route to Dundee to tell the fans on board that the game was off, and once, when a mother wrote to him to tell about her son having rheumatic fever, a football was sent to the boy in hospital, signed by himself and all the team.

Nor did he lack courage in dealing with the hooligan element. On several occasions when bottles were thrown, it was Stein himself who was seen appealing for calm. One or two mind-less idiots who invaded the field were physically thrown off by his mighty bulk, and on one occasion at Stirling Albion, with an almost reckless disregard for his own personal safety, he plunged into the middle of the crowd to stop offensive chants.

But his greatest achievement was the permanent change that he brought about in Rangers' role in Scottish football. Before the arrival of Stein at Celtic Park, Rangers had been the establishment team of Scotland. "We are the people" cried their fans. Boys' Christmas books were full of laudatory paeans about "Glasgow's football palace" that was Ibrox. The BBC in Scotland did not disguise their love for the club, newspapers lauded them and the talk on a Monday in Glasgow's tearooms included discussion on how the Gers had done.

Jock Stein had, in fact, driven a horse and cart through Rangers, and he had done it by playing football which was both successful and popular. The 1967 victory in the European Cup had perhaps not gone down well with everyone in Scotland, but it could not be denied that many supporters of other teams were delighted to join in the triumph of Celtic. It was in a very real sense a victory for Scotland, as every single man in the squad was Scottish, while Irishman Sean Fallon, the assistant manager, was the solitary exception among the staff. This had come at a time when Scotland needed a triumph, just a year after England had won the World Cup.

Newspapers now talked about little other than Celtic. To a large extent, Stein engineered this, realising that there is no such thing as bad publicity. He would always be prepared to give newspapers a story for a dull November Tuesday, and he had the unfailing ability to knock

Rangers off the back pages. The Ibrox men would perhaps have had a good win on the Saturday and therefore expect maximum publicity on the Monday – but the back page would have a story about how, for example, Celtic were thinking of arranging a friendly with a crack Brazilian outfit. This story might or not have substance, but it mattered not. All that really mattered was that the word "Celtic" was there on the back page of the Scottish Daily Express in larger letters than that of "Rangers".

Stein himself was a frequent and welcome participant in TV programmes, and it was often said that he was the only Scotsman who could be instantly recognised in England when he was seen on the screen. This was most obvious after the defeat of Leeds United in the European Cup semi-final of 1970. There is a myth about this game that everyone in England resented the Scottish upstarts beating their darlings. Not so! Leeds, with their somewhat robust approach to the game, were by no means popular with fans of other clubs, and the victory by a Scottish club was much welcomed. Stein became as well known and loved a Scotsman as Robbie Burns, as he did seem to represent Scotland.

He differed from the Ayrshire bard of two centuries previously in his attitude to alcohol. He had possibly seen rather too much alcohol abuse in his early life in the mining communities, and he was a committed and even obsessive teetotaller. He did try to make his players the same, but in some cases failed miserably. It was not for the want of trying. European trips and foreign tours would see Jock prowling hotel corridors and foyers, getting chambermaids and bellboys to spy on the prime suspects and even listening outside bedroom doors for the tell-tale sound of bottles being clinked.

He was, as we said, not entirely successful, but his efforts did make sure that his players were usually as fit as they could possibly be. In this he was backed by trainer Neil Mochan (himself by no means a teetotaller) and he would frequently say that there was no excuse for a professional footballer not being 100 per-cent fit. Bobby Murdoch, arguably his best player for Celtic, presented a special problem in that he was prone to putting on weight. On two occasions when this seemed to be a problem, Murdoch was whipped off to a health farm in England to lose a few pounds. Stein had identified him as a key man and well worth going the extra mile for. There was a sequel years later when Stein and his wife met Mr and Mrs Bobby Murdoch on holiday. Bobby was by this time playing for Middlesbrough and was enjoying a pint of beer in the Mediterranean sunshine. This did not prevent Stein berating him about what it could do to him. "You're far too good a player for that" thundered Jock, forgetting that Bobby was now playing for another club.

But if he went the extra mile for Bobby, he had to go several more for Jimmy Johnstone. The relationship between Stein and Johnstone was complex. Both were, in their own way, in awe of the other, in total admiration for what the other could do. But Jimmy enjoyed life as well. "He was not daft, was Jimmy – he just did daft things" was the way that it was put by one of his team-mates, but he did have the ability to get on the wrong side of his strict taskmaster. Yet although Stein twice gave him a club suspension and dropped him countless times for indiscipline, he was always very careful not to antagonise Jimmy completely. Johnstone would now and again throw a tantrum and ask for a transfer. Jock would not play ball with that idea as he knew how valuable Jimmy was to the club. He also, from a wider foot-balling perspective, knew that Jimmy was far too engrossed in Celtic to do a job for anyone else. Nevertheless, Stein would often say that his greatest achievement was not so much winning the European Cup or nine League championships in a row as keeping Jimmy Johnstone in the game.

But it would be wrong to say that he kept everybody happy. Tommy Gemmell, John Hughes, Charlie Gallagher – good players all – he fell out with, and very often the falling out led to a permanent rupture in relationships. Tommy Gemmell, for example, got himself sent off while playing for Scotland in a World Cup game against West Germany in 1969. Stein, although having no direct dealings with Scotland at the time, felt that he had let his club down as well as his country and dropped him for the League Cup final the following Saturday. Relationships were never quite the same again after that, and John Hughes was never forgiven for missing a chance in the 1970 European Cup final. Charlie Gallagher's Celtic career had come to an end, and he was lining up for Dumbarton when he was appalled to hear his direct opponent, Davie Hay, being encouraged to "break his legs".

Stein also had a problem with goalkeepers. He never understood that breed, and the only one of his many custodians that he could be said to have established a modus vivendi with (and even that one had a sticky start) was Ronnie Simpson, whose sheer length of experience in the game demanded respect. Apart from that, goalkeepers came and went, errors were not forgiven, and there never was (apart from the aged Simpson) any great Celtic goalkeeper in the Stein era. John Fallon, Evan Williams, Ally Hunter, Denis Connaghan, Peter Latchford and Roy Baines all tried, but Jock was never entirely happy with any of them.

STEIN'S LIFE CHANGED RADICALLY for the worst in summer 1975. Early in the morning on the A74 he was involved in a head-on collision while returning from holiday along with some friends. He was seriously injured, and out of action for about a year. During his absence, Celtic suffered, but then we had one brilliant season of Stein before a major misjudgement led to his downfall at Celtic Park.

Season 1975/76 was spent in hospital. It was hardly a surprise that this was the first trophyless campaign for Celtic since 1963/64, the one before his arrival. But in 1976 Stein returned, and in the same way as he re-created Celtic in 1970 after the loss of the European Cup final, he did the same with the dispirited Celtic of 1976. In particular, his judgement in the transfer market was spot-on. The signing of Alfie Conn, as well as being a major embarrassment to Rangers and a further consolidation (if any were required) of the moral high ground, was also a brilliant piece of footballing judgement. Joe Craig had been bought from Partick Thistle as a centre-forward, and all Scotland was amazed by the signing of Pat Stanton from Hibs. Stanton had been indelibly linked with Hibs for over a decade and was clearly coming to the end of his career. But Stein had always admired him and bought him to win the only Scottish League medal and Scottish Cup medal of his career.

These additions, plus the development of young talent like Tommy Burns and Roy Aitken, contributed towards what, in the circumstances, was a fine season for Celtic. The summer of 1977 was passed in contentment. There was the feeling that Jock was now back in charge after his unfortunate acciden,t and that further glory beckoned for as long as we cared to contemplate. After all, Jock was not yet 55, and seemed to have loads of mileage left in him.

But his nemesis came in the shape of Kenny Dalglish. The relationship between Kenny and Jock was complex. It was Jock who had discovered him and made him the idol of the Celtic support, and now he had a virtually automatic place in the Scotland side. But Kenny was not happy at Parkhead. It cannot have been money, as he was surely earning enough with Celtic; it cannot have been the fact that he came from a Rangers-supporting background, as he was hardly the only one who had that problem, if problem it was. It may have been an inability to put up with the growling dictatorship of Stein, and in particular it may have been a lack of confidence in Jock's ability to win another European Cup.

Celtic were involved in a gratuitous and really rather pointless tournament in Australia in summer 1977. Dalglish, recently back from a Scottish tour of South America, was not keen on going, and ended up not, leaving a rather large question mark on his Celtic future. This was now the acid test of Stein. He had done well in years gone by to retain men like Jimmy Johnstone when they turned awkward. How would he react to this latest threat?

This time the magic did not work, and Kenny, to the distress of Celtic fans everywhere, was on his way to Liverpool for a huge transfer fee of £440,000, a British record. It was possibly true that nothing Stein could have done would have kept Dalglish, and there may be something in the school of thought that says the directors were, not for the first time, more interested in the money than they were in the building of a great team.

Other problems hit the team as well, in the shape of early-season and serious injuries to Pat Stanton and Alfie Conn, and then Danny McGrain went down with a mysterious foot injury. But it was the loss of his young protégé that hurt Stein. He lapsed into a depression which contrasted so starkly with his exuberant joie de vivre of a decade earlier. The team's form suffered, the season was over almost before it began and Celtic went out of Europe to a mediocre Austrian team, after which Stein, that notorious prowler of hotel corridors on previous trips, retired to bed, thus abdicating his responsibility and abandoning himself to self-pity.

The transfer of Dalglish, however distressing it was to all concerned, need not have been the cataclysm that it was allowed to become. There was now money in the bank, and there would have been no lack of talented young men currently playing for other clubs in Scotland and England who would have jumped at the chance of coming to Celtic. But big transfers never came, and Stein, giving the impression that he was only doing this to get the fans off his back, bought several low-key players, or men who were clearly well past their best. In fact, they disgraced the Celtic jersey which Stein had always claimed "did not shrink for inferior players". One player was bought from England, was made captain immediately and then scored an own goal on his debut!

This was desperately awful stuff, and although a brave and unlucky effort was made in the Scottish League Cup, the team, virtually leaderless and dispirited, went nowhere. Celtic finished 1977/78 in disarray, and it was almost a relief when Billy McNeill, who had had a great season as manager of Aberdeen, was made manager at Celtic Park in the May. Stein was not sacked, but was humiliated even more by being offered the job of organising the Celtic pools! This was not likely to last, and Stein accepted the manager's job at Leeds United for a brief spell before becoming manager of Scotland.

This was 1978, the year that still causes Scottish hearts to recoil in horror at the thought of Argentina. Stein was not involved in this fiasco, but was employed by the BBC to sit in the studio and analyse. It was curious to see him in this role, now no longer the man who mattered at Celtic. But there was the elder statesman look about him as he sympathised with Ally MacLeod, saying things like: "Once they cross that touchline, there is nothing you (the manager) can do". Clearly he shared the national agony as penalties were missed, games were lost to no-hopers, drugs were taken and players disgraced themselves and their country. His pain was our pain, but his pain was also greater, as he had now lost his own empire as well.

He would serve as manager of Scotland from autumn 1978 to autumn 1985, when he collapsed and died tragically at Ninian Park, Cardiff, seconds after his team earned a play-off for a place in the World Cup finals. His international record was respectable, but no more than that. He deserves credit for winning back some credibility for Scotland after Argentina, but he was unable to lift his country on to the top rung of the world game.

IT WAS WITH CELTIC that Jock Stein was the cult hero. A stand, the one which replaced the traditional Celtic End, where supporters used to stand at Old Firm games, is named after him. There is inside Celtic Park a bust of him inside the foyer. Even this is inadequate. More appropriate would be a full statue outside the stadium, beside that of Brother Walfrid. A statue of Willie Maley, Celtic's other great manager, should also be there, and possibly one of Fergus McCann, who re-created the ground in the 1990s. But no-none has ever done more for the club than Jock Stein. No-one can match the enormity of his achievements of turning a decade of mediocrity into European glory and domestic domination.

It is often worth while considering what might have happened if Stein had not gone to Celtic in 1965. There would have been no European Cup, and the game in Scotland would have been stagnating towards part-time football at home and oblivion abroad, as Rangers won everything in Scotland but nothing in Europe. Celtic's vast support, frustrated and angry, would have given up watching the game, choosing instead to cause trouble in Scotland's towns of a Saturday afternoon and perhaps turning to paramilitary organisations to express, in a thoroughly deleterious and subversive way, their Scottish-Irish identity.

Such Scottish players as did emerge would have been immediately signed on by English clubs, and Scotland, in short, would have become similar to what Ireland is today – with loads of interest in football but loyalties given to English teams like Manchester United, Liverpool and Arsenal rather than the indigenous ones. It was just as well, was it not, that Bob Kelly admitted he was wrong in 1965?

PAT CRERAND

'PADDY'

1958-1963

BHOYS CAREER

Games	120
Goals	5
Caps	16

MAGIC MOMENT

The Scottish Cup final replay of 1961 when Crerand's visionary passing was described as "world class" and "superb". His play truly deserved to win the Scottish Cup but feckless finishing let him down.

IT is generally agreed that the early 1960s were good times. The Welfare State was now kicking in, as it were; slums were being demolished, unemployment was minimal and prosperity was visibly a factor of life. On the football field, things were good and there was now the luxury of being able to watch the highlights of a game on television; occasionally (very occasionally) a live match was offered. Attendances were still high, and the interest, the obsession even, with football in Scotland had not abated.

But it was not the same for Celtic. In the grip of the Kelly dictatorship, with Jimmy McGrory as the nominal manager, the team and club were going nowhere. But there was a youth policy. As long as Jock Stein was there as a coach for the youngsters, there was a chance, but Stein left to become manager of Dunfermline Athletic in the spring of 1960 and things stagnated.

But Stein had left behind some good youngsters. One of them was Pat Crerand. He was a Gorbals boy, born at the start of 1939, and had cut his teeth with Duntocher Hibs before being called up to join the club that he had always supported. His love of the club would become a matter of some doubt and dispute in years to come, but the Gorbals was a Celtic-mad area where there had been widespread dancing in the streets on that never-to-be-forgotten night in 1953 when Celtic beat Hibs to win the Coronation Cup.

It was immediately apparent that Pat Crerand was blessed with wonderful talent. He was a right-half with a superb ability to pass a ball, knowing exactly the right kind of weight to put on his delivery so that it reached its destination. He thrived under the coaching and direction of Jock Stein, and made his debut for the first team in October 1958 in a game against Queen of the South, which Celtic won comfortably. His first-game nerves were barely visible and the general consensus in the press was that he was worth another chance.

Seasons 1958/59 and 1959/60 were chaotic at Celtic Park, as various youngsters were tried. The team was never really in contention for any honours, losing in consecutive years in the semi-finals of the Scottish Cup by heavy margins to St Mirren in 1959 and Rangers in a terrible replay after a respectable first game in 1960. Celtic's right-half was a journeyman by the name of Eric Smith. Those who watched Crerand in the reserves thought that he was better, but it was not until the start of the 1960/61 season that Pat made the right-half position his own.

At 5 feet 8 inches he was not particularly tall, but he was sturdy and well built; he was no greyhound but quick enough to the ball when required; he was a good team man, but not without the ability to snarl at team-mates who, he felt, were not pulling their weight. He had a good understanding with his friend, Billy McNeill, who had quickly developed into the best centre-half in the country. Pat was about to do likewise with the right-half position.

But the key word with this young Celtic team was inexperience. Young John Hughes had broken into the team as well, and he was gloriously productive on some occasions, but as yet he lacked the required consistency. It was at this point that the folly of not promoting Jock

Stein to be manager and allowing him to leave to join Dunfermline began to be apparent. It would hit Celtic hard at the end of the season.

The team was picked by chairman Bob Kelly, a tough man with a laudable desire to see Celtic at the top and for them to play good and sporting football. Many a time the players would hear homilies about how the game should be played, but very little instruction in how to actually set about doing this. Training sessions were badly organised and dull, consisting of endless running round the track, and such tactical instructions as were given were left in the hands of Jimmy McGrory and Sean Fallon.

McGrory was a Celtic legend, but he was never really cut out for management. In particular, he had little understanding of the modern footballer's mindset, and although he knew more than anyone what Celtic meant to the fans, he had little ability to impart his knowledge or to understand the modern game, in which the players were all better fed, fitter, faster and more athletic than ever before. Or at least they ought to have been. Certainly there was no lack of enthusiasm about the players, but there was often a lack of tactical nous or ability to pace themselves.

Sean Fallon had been a good reliable full-back for Celtic. Once again, he was a man who knew what Celtic meant to everyone, but he was a man who lacked any great flair, either as a player or as a coach/manager. He was very much a Bob Kelly protégé, and would conscientiously carry out his duties, but what was required was someone with presence and with charisma. He would in time become an excellent assistant manager to Jock Stein, but at this point Sean's influence was steady rather than inspirational.

Captain Bertie Peacock had been a fine player, but at this stage of his career, the likeable 32-year-old Irishman was beginning to struggle with his own form. The other veteran of the team, Neil Mochan (not always persona grata with the establishment), could not always be guaranteed a place and went to Dundee United halfway through the season. By October of that year, Willie Fernie had been brought back from Middlesbrough with the idea of calming down the "eager beaver youngsters" as they were frequently called by the press. But with all these youngsters about to ripen at the same time, the outlook seemed bright for Celtic, and the supporters, ever-optimistic and loyal, picked up on this enthusiasm. Very soon the sheer talent of Pat Crerand would become apparent, and the supporters would have a new hero.

The team's lack of experience was immediately apparent in the League Cup campaign of 1960/61. Most unusually it was an all-Glasgow section of Rangers, Partick Thistle and Third Lanark. Crerand started at right-half in the first game of the season as Celtic beat Third Lanark, drew with Partick Thistle and then achieved their best result for some time when they beat Rangers at Ibrox (this was their second defeat of Rangers this season, as they had already knocked them out of the Glasgow Cup).The fans began to appreciate this young side and questions were now asked about whether we were on the brink of a great Celtic team. Certainly everyone was impressed by young Crerand, whose powerful play, command of the midfield and visionary passing were a revelation. When they beat Third Lanark again, confidence and euphoria rose astronomically, such was the tangible desire for success.

Came the dawn . . . Celtic went down to Partick Thistle on the Wednesday and then Rangers at Parkhead on Saturday after having scored an early goal. This particular game was the start of the Rangers complex, and Pat would never again be on a winning side against

Rangers in a national competition. The first League game of the season, for example, saw a dismal 5-1 thrashing, and New Year's Day threw up similar distress. The Glasgow Cup final against Partick Thistle was also a disappointment.

It was soon obvious that there was to be no Celtic challenge for the League that season, because the form was so inconsistent. The problem was that although Crerand was learning the game fast, others, particularly the youngsters in the forward line, were not making similar progress. In particular, they found it difficult to "read" him and be in the proper place for a pass. This is where a good manager might have worked on the problem and solved it by assiduous training and advice, but guidance came there none.

Still, after the turn of the year it began to look as if there might be a chance of winning the Scottish Cup. It was often considered to be Celtic's favourite competition, with 17 wins against Rangers' 14. It had last been won in 1954, seven years previously, and (allowing for wartime) this equalled their longest gap between Scottish Cup wins in the 20th century. Supporters began to feel that this might just be the year, with Pat Crerand on board, to lift the trophy again.

The feeling of optimism grew when Rangers went out at an early stage to Motherwell, and Celtic had good wins against Falkirk, Montrose and Raith Rovers. But then Hibs came to Parkhead on 11 March in the quarter-final. Some 56,000 were there in good voice, singing the praises of Pat Crerand, but for a long time it looked as if Hibs, with goalkeeper Ronnie Simpson in inspirational form, would win the day. They also had Joe Baker playing for them, and after scoring early in the second half, they began to look comfortable.

But this Celtic team, who might have given up, now had Crerand urging them on, cajoling, gesturing and making space. They kept on pressing and gradually they wore down the Hibs defence. The Edinburgh men had looked as if they had weathered the storm until Steve Chalmers equalised within the last five minutes. Such were the scenes of ecstasy behind the goal that in the BBC highlights programme that night, the cameras did something most unusual for 1961 – they turned and captured those scenes, which "beggared description".

Crerand was also well to the fore as Celtic beat Hibs the following Wednesday night at a dangerously overcrowded Easter Road. It was a thrilling Cup tie with Celtic's goal coming in injury time from the young John Clark, who was playing in one of his first games for the club. The feeling now grew that this was to be Celtic's year; all that stood between them and their 18th Scottish Cup were Airdrie in the semi-final and the winners of the St Mirren and Dunfermline Athletic encounter in the final. On 1 April Airdrie were comprehensively put to the sword in a devastating first half-display organised by Celtic's "veteran and novice", Willie Fernie and Pat Crerand.

By this time people were beginning to talk about the possibility of a Scotland cap for the prodigiously talented 22-year-old, even against England at Wembley. He did not make that (just as well as it turned out, as 1961 was the year of the 9-3 hammering!) although he had been awarded a cap for the Scottish League against the English League on 22 March at Ibrox. That day the Scots beat their counterparts 3-2, and Crerand once again impressed.

The Scottish Cup final was fast approaching. Dunfermline Athletic had absolutely no pedigree in this (or any other) competition, and it was confidently expected (far too confidently) that Celtic merely had to turn up to win. The Pars, however, had one great asset. He was called Jock Stein.

What a catalogue of woe must now be recalled by the Celtic chronicler as he details these two dreadful Cup finals of 1961! Virgil's *Aeneid* tells the story of the Trojan hero Aeneas, who reaches the shores of Carthage and meets Queen Dido. She asks him to tell her about how the Trojans came to North Africa after the Greeks had captured their city by means of the wooden horse. Aeneas pauses and says:

Infandum, regina, iubes renovare dolorem

translated as: "Oh queen, you order me to renew unspeakable grief". Unspeakable grief is hardly an exaggeration as we deal with 1961.

The first game, watched by 113,000, was a goalless draw in which according to the *Glasgow Herald*: "Left winger Byrne was the recipient time and again of magnificent passes from Crerand, but rarely turned the defence". It was a frustrating experience for the fans and even more so for Crerand, one feels. Dunfermline, the country cousins, had done well and earned the respect of the Glasgow public, but the replay on Wednesday night would be different.

It was a dull spring evening and there was a 6.15pm kick-off in the days before Hampden had floodlights. It was 26 April 1961, about the same time as the extent of the USA disaster in Cuba was becoming known. Events had unfolded dramatically on the world stage the previous week as the USA had launched an appallingly botched and half-hearted invasion of Cuba at the Bay of Pigs. There would be repercussions about this high-handed and incompetent behaviour, but for the moment the world laughed at the useless Americans – but no more than Celtic's enemies laughed at Celtic that night!

Oh what agonies and torture were endured by those who loved the Celtic. Pat Crerand was once again superb, by some distance the man of the match, but the Celtic forward line were "much too individualistic" according to the *Glasgow Herald* – a tactful way of saying they were useless. Celtic fans in the 87,000 crowd and many more listening to the radio commentary on the BBC Scottish Home Service groaned when Dunfermline went ahead halfway through the second half, and the Scottish Cup now seemed as if it were slipping away.

Crerand now became even more dominant as Celtic pushed towards that Mount Florida goal in that melancholy second half. Sleeves rolled up, his pants rolled at the waist, he took charge, spraying passes to both wings and down the centre – then enduring the frustration of chances going a-begging. The Pars goalkeeper Eddie Connachan, himself a great Celtic fan, ironically enough, had an inspired and lucky night, but feckless finishing was the main cause of the Celtic downfall. In the final minute with Celtic now over-committed, a goalkeeping error allowed Dunfermline a second goal and the cause was lost.

One felt, from the top of that King's Road terracing, that Crerand was going to punch his goalkeeper Frank Haffey. It was a sign of his exasperation and chagrin, shared sadly by some of the Celtic support who began to throw empty beer bottles to express their anger. Dunfermline collecting the Cup that should have been Celtic's, Jock Stein watching in his white raincoat, Pat Crerand and some others collapsing in grief at the full-time whistle – these are sights that remain with one all one's life. Almost 50 years later, the wounds have not yet healed.

The press, while clearly enjoying Celtic's debacle and lauding Dunfermline's one and only night of glory in a hitherto barren history, nevertheless praised Crerand, who was so far above everyone else. It was about this time, too, that the first hints began to appear that Pat might one day go to England, a sure sign that Celtic had a class player, sadly in the midst of so many others who had not yet done so well.

More tangibly, Pat was rewarded with his first cap for Scotland. He had done well to avoid the 9-3 Wembley cataclysm of April 1961, but such had been his form in the two high-profile Scottish Cup finals that he could not be ignored by the selectors for the World Cup qualifying fixtures. There was a double header against the Irish Republic in which Crerand played brilliantly and Scotland won both games with a degree of comfort, but then came the encounter with Czechoslovakia in Bratislava on 14 May.

Down 2-0 to a couple of early goals, Scotland were becoming frustrated. They had talent but things were not going well on a difficult pitch with the referee and the crowd against them. Nearing half-time Andrej Kvasnak and Pat had what the papers euphemistically called a "clash". Pat was fouled, but retaliated and the two of them were ordered off. Pat could not believe this was happening to him, for in these days before the use of red cards, the referee pointed the wrong way, having lost his sense of direction.

INCREDIBLY, PAT'S SUMMER OF 1961 began with a sending-off, and also ended with a sending-off. Equally incredibly, the second dismissal was in a five-a-side pre-season tournament at Falkirk. He was suspended for this, and even after his suspension was finished, chairman Bob Kelly imposed a further club suspension as he felt that Celtic's good name had been tarnished by Crerand's conduct. Supporters, at this point, began to feel that Kelly did not like Crerand.

It was a costly suspension, as by the time that Crerand returned, Celtic were already out of the Scottish League Cup, thanks to an inability to beat St Johnstone on two occasions on which Crerand's presence was sadly missed. But his return in September coincided with his best form for Celtic, and the team started to impress.

At the same time, Rangers had unearthed a great left-half in Jim Baxter. Crerand and Baxter were therefore seen by the media as a great counter-balance for each other – they both, for example, "wrote" a ghosted column in the *Evening Citizen* and they were looked upon as symbols of the new age, as footballers began to be personality figures in the same sense as pop stars were. It was part of the new affluent society, and as more and more people began to aspire to a better lifestyle, who better to symbolise it than the two young lions of Scottish football, who fortunately happened to be one on each side of the Glasgow divide?

These were heady days for Crerand. Playing well for Celtic, even winning some reluctant admiration from the stern Bob Kelly, and then being on the winning side in three consecutive Scotland games, Crerand was not slow to play along with this adulation, and even seemed capable of coping with it. The Scotland wins were against Czechoslovakia at Hampden (revenge for Bratislava and enough to earn Scotland a play-off for a World Cup place), Northern Ireland and Wales.

The Northern Irish game was played in Belfast and was won 6-1 by a rampant Scottish team. Rangers players scored all the goals, and although the *Evening Citizen* raised not a few hackles by having "Ireland 1 Rangers 6" as its headline, it also indicated that Pat Crerand was the star man. The Sunday Post the following day remarked that it must have been galling for the Irish supporters to realise that the architect of their destruction was a "callant with the illustrious name of Pat".

One of Scotland's pivotal games in the early 1960s came on 29 November 1961, when they lost their play-off to Czechoslovakia in the neutral venue of Brussels. Scotland were ahead but conceded a late goal. They then went down in extra time after an extraordinary incident at the end of 90 minutes, when Crerand and Baxter were seen to be grabbing the water bottle for the first use of it. This defeat meant that Scotland and Crerand would be absent from the 1962 World Cup, an occasion which they would certainly have graced.

MIDWINTER 1961/62 SAW THE best of Crerand in a Celtic jersey. Three good wins in December lifted Celtic to the crest of the wave, but unfortunately bad weather descended and knocked out a few fixtures, including Rangers visit to Parkhead on New Year's Day. Celtic never really recovered from that, but finished a respectable third in the League behind Dundee and Rangers, from both of whom they took points in the run-in.

But it was the Scottish Cup once again that would determine Celtic. Crerand was heavily involved in two epic ties, a 4-3 win at Tynecastle in which he scored the winning penalty, then a game against Third Lanark at a full Parkhead when Celtic recovered from being 1-3 down to go 4-3 up before losing a late equaliser. The replay had to be held at Hampden rather than Cathkin for safety reasons and Celtic swept the Thirds aside to win 4-0.

Pat was quite clearly the "blue-eyed bhoy" in all this. He played blatantly to the gallery in his pre-match loosening up exercises, and made a point of talking to supporters, giving autographs and letting everyone know that he was one of them. Some supporters made up an anthem to hail their Celtic hero, singing: "with heart and hand and Pat Crerand, we'll cut off King William's balls".

But if there was one game that changed all this, it was the Scottish Cup semi-final against St Mirren. Once again "unspeakable grief" is renewed when one recalls this occasion. Celtic were very firm favourites for this game. They had beaten St Mirren 7-1 at Parkhead in November, and then 5-0 at Love Street on the Monday night before the semi.

This result, however, was an ambush. St Mirren, who now had Willie Fernie in their ranks, had deliberately held back on the Monday, lulling the young Celts into a false sense of security, and allowing the feelings of euphoria, over-confidence and carelessness to take over Celtic's approach to the big game. All the while, St Mirren themselves concentrated on spotting a few Celtic weaknesses.

One such weakness was the self-destruct tendency of the Celtic youngsters to argue among themselves. Incredibly this happened before kick-off at Ibrox on that fateful day of 31 March 1962. It may have been because some disagreed with captain Dunky McKay's decision of what way to play after he won the toss, or it may have had some other genesis, but the Celtic fans were treated to the bizarre sight of their players shouting at one another before the game started.

Celtic never really did get started, and by half-time, to the astonishment of all of Scotland, St Mirren, playing with the wind, were 3-0 up against a lethargic Celtic side. The Celtic fans were aghast at all this, but cheered themselves up by saying that there had to be some recovery and that "Paddy" would rally the troops in the second half now that the wind was on their side. There was some kind of improvement, but no goals as the second period wore on, and fans became even more despondent and nasty. Bottles were thrown, the pitch was invaded and the referee had to withdraw the players to the safety of the pavilion. By the time the players were back and Alec Byrne scored a late and irrelevant goal for Celtic, the club's directors had conceded the game.

This whole episode was one of the saddest in Celtic's long history, and may well have been the beginning of Crerand's reckoning that his beloved Celtic was not necessarily the best option for his career. In truth, the team, talented and enthusiastic, lacked any kind of guidance or control, something that could only have been imparted by someone like Jock Stein. Pat had a low opinion of some of his team-mates, a factor that would soon be leaked to the press, and he must often have wondered if Celtic were ever going to win anything again.

Two contrasting weekends in April must have rammed home this point. On 21 April, while Celtic were losing pathetically to Raith Rovers at Parkhead before an angry crowd which was only marginally over 10,000, ten times that number were less than a mile away at Hampden to see Rangers win the Scottish Cup by beating St Mirren 2-0. This was yet another low point for Celtic and Crerand, yet only a week earlier the famous Scottish half-back line of Crerand, McNeill and Baxter had orchestrated a famous 2-0 win for Scotland over England. Pat had been outstanding in all that, and must have wondered why his career was being retarded at Parkhead in such a shambles of an organisation when he himself was openly being described as world-class in so many newspapers.

Yet he had such a strong emotional pull for Glasgow Celtic. Ironically, so too did one of his admirers, Matt Busby, the manager of Manchester United, now patiently rebuilding a great side to replace the one which had perished in the Munich air crash of 1958. The newspapers screeched about the interest from Old Trafford and many other English teams, but Pat, for all his hot-headedness, remained committed to Celtic. He must, however, have begun to think.

The heartbreaks would continue in the 1962/63 season. The League Cup section was a difficult one with Hearts and the two Dundee teams. Celtic beat all three comfortably at home, lost narrowly and unluckily at Dens Park and Tynecastle, then broke their supporters' hearts at Tannadice Park on the last day of the section. Any sort of win would have ensured qualification, but it was the re-run of so many occasions in the early 1960s in which Celtic dominated and played brilliantly but simply could not score. Pat Crerand was immense, but chance after chance was missed by an inept forward line, and the game petered out into a 0-0 draw. Life might have been different if just one of those chances had gone in, or if the referee had seen that the ball was a good foot over the line on one occasion in the first half, but it was another major disappointment to Pat.

The following week in the Old Firm derby at Celtic Park, the gods were once again not on Pat's side as he missed a penalty after a piece of gamesmanship from Jim Baxter, and Celtic had the mortifying experience of dominating the game, but losing 0-1 to a deflection. On the following Monday, Real Madrid came to Parkhead for a friendly, and although Celtic lost, Crerand found himself waking up the following morning to all sorts of headlines about how he was the best right-half in the world.

It was thus a crazy, rollercoaster sort of life for Pat in late 1962. Round about the time of the Cuban missile crisis in October, the team hit a purple patch, putting Airdrie and St Mirren to the sword, but then unaccountably lost to Queen of the South at Parkhead, and the season disintegrated into a series of lacklustre draws and further defeats.

Crerand was now in despair. In autumn 1962 he had produced another two fine international performances against Wales and Northern Ireland, and there was no shortage of neutral observers who were in no doubt that he deserved to be called world-class. However, the unpalatable truth was that he was being held back at an under-performing club. He loved Celtic, but had little respect for the chairman and was openly critical about some of the forwards. There did not seem to be any great desire to win trophies if that meant spending money for a classy striker.

The fans, though still loyal, were severely tested. A win over Rangers, admittedly in a Glasgow Cup match on a foggy Wednesday afternoon, lifted them, but then the team collapsed against Partick Thistle on the Saturday. Pat, being a supporter himself, understood what they felt. He, however, was a young professional footballer whose ambitions were being thwarted. He had an escape route to get away from the repressive, stifling and depressing atmosphere that was Celtic Park in 1962.

New Year's Day 1963 was the end of the road for Pat and Celtic. The scene was Ibrox on a cold, frosty day. Celtic were 0-1 down at half-time, a position from which recovery was still possible. The Celtic dressing room, however, was downcast, and when Sean Fallon, the assistant manager, took Crerand to task for a few mistakes, all the frustration and anger that had been boiling within Pat for many months erupted. Stories emerged about Celtic jerseys being thrown, about impossible biological suggestions being made, and how it took all the diplomacy of Billy McNeill and a few calmer members of the team to persuade Pat to go out for the second half.

Throughout Celtic history, dressing room disharmony has always led to disaster. One thinks of the events at Arthurlie in 1897, at Airdrie in the League Cup in 1998, and at Parkhead against Inverness Caledonian Thistle in 2000. On this occasion in 1963 the team went out for the second half and collapsed to lose 0-4 in circumstances which had the press and the supporters on the freezing terracings puzzled about the lack of effort. Pat would never play for Celtic again.

He was dropped for the trip to Aberdeen the following Saturday – ironically Celtic won 5-1 in brilliant fashion – and then the big freeze of 1963 descended. What happened in early February 1963 depends on what spin one reads. We are asked to believe that Pat came home from Mass one Sunday to discover that everything had been agreed with Manchester United. What is more likely is that the persuasive Matt Busby held out the attractions of more money, a chance of playing for a successful team and even (as a Celtic-lover himself) holding out the possibility of some "Celtic in exile" situation in England, quoting the precedent of Jimmy Delaney, who had joined Manchester United from Celtic in remarkably similar circumstances in 1946.

Celtic fans everywhere were devastated. With a ferocity which astounded his mother, this author tore down the pictures of Pat Crerand which adorned his bedroom. Older fans shook their heads and thought that Celtic were finished. A few more perspicacious ones remarked that things would have been different if Jock Stein had not been allowed to go to Dunfermline in 1960.

THE LOSS OF A cult hero is always a bad blow. Celtic fans do not cope well with anyone not wanting to play for the club, no matter what the circumstances were. Pat would actually win an English Cup medal that year with Manchester United, but that was little consolation for the broken green-and-white army.

All that frustration was expressed tellingly at the bottom of the terracing steps at the Celtic End of Hampden on 15 May 1963. The occasion was the Scottish Cup final replay, and Celtic supporters were vanishing as fast as snow off a dyke after Rangers had scored their third goal against a dysfunctional Celtic team. In an almost unprecedented sight, 60,000 had turned their backs on Celtic. "Unspeakable grief" did not even begin to describe things. A sullen mob was heading home, too numb to say anything until this man at the bottom of the terracing steps, a middle-aged, respectable, sober man, suddenly dissolved in tears and shouted: "Pat Crerand! Pat Crerand! I hope you're f***in' proud o' yourself!"

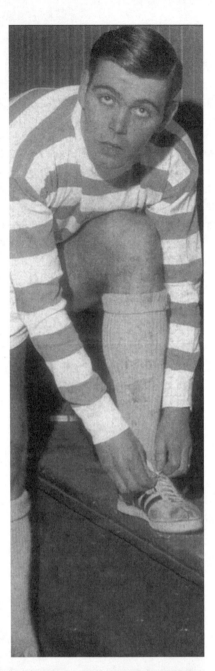

JOHN HUGHES

1960-1971

BHOYS CAREER

Games	416
Goals	189
Caps	8

MAGIC MOMENT

With the club on its knees at the lowest point of its history on 30 January 1965, Celtic amazed the world by beating Aberdeen 8-0. John Hughes (wearing sandshoes on the hard pitch) scored five.

'YOGI BEAR'

'For spontaneous, original brilliance, there is no-one better than John Hughes. If we could only add consistency to that list of qualities...'

Sunday Mail

JOHN Hughes was an enigma. No player had the ability to split the Celtic support to the same extent than he did. Arguments would rage in the stand, the terracings and supporters' buses about the value or otherwise of John Hughes to the cause. Jock Stein himself did not seem able to make his mind up about him, and to this day, it remains difficult to assess John.

Born in 1943, John joined Celtic as a teenager in 1960 from Shotts Bon Accord, making his debut at the start of the 1960/61 season. Part of Hughes's problem was that his start was a whirlwind one, and that the support kept expecting him to live up to this high standard, forgetting that he was merely a teenager, and a rather vulnerable one at that. With his huge physique and his hair sticking up, he very soon earned the nickname of "Yogi Bear", a cartoon character of the time. Stories about him getting lost in a wood on a European trip in 1963 and earning the "bear" nickname on that occasion are false. He was called "Yogi" from a very early stage, and it was a nickname that he shared with his great opponent, Ian Ure, the centre-half of Dundee.

The Celtic team that he joined was young, enthusiastic and recognisably "Celtic" in the desire to attack and entertain the crowds, but crucially the players all lacked experience. The fine, experienced Celtic team of the middle 1950s had beaten Rangers 7-1 in the Scottish League Cup final of October 1957 but had evaporated almost immediately, leaving a youth policy in place. The trouble was that, although the players were good, there was by 1960 when Jock Stein departed to be manager of Dunfermline Athletic, no great guidance.

John scored on his debut as centre-forward in August 1960 against Third Lanark in the Scottish League Cup, then a week later played absolutely brilliantly as Celtic beat Rangers 3-2 at Ibrox. Cyril Horne in the *Glasgow Herald* talks about "much football ability" and a "splendid temperament" (he did not retaliate to much fouling from Doug Baillie). Then Cyril gives us the first Yogi Bear reference when he says "bigger- than-average man" and "better-than-average footballer". This was because Yogi Bear would always say that he was smarter than the average, so naturally John was better than the average Ranger. Yogi Bear had come to Glasgow.

Sadly it did not last. Rangers beat Celtic in the return match in the League Cup, then in the League game, and Celtic imploded miserably. Hughes soon found himself out of the team, whether through injury or being dropped, and it began to look as if he was about to disappear. But by the turn of the 1960/61 season, Hughes was back in action and although League form was inconsistent and patchy, a Scottish Cup run restored the spirits of the support. Hughes was beginning to play well, scoring freely, including two memorable efforts in the semi-final against Airdrie. There was some experience in the forward line as Willie Fernie had returned from Middlesbrough, and he was able to slow the game down and direct the enthusiasm of youngsters like Hughes.

THE SCOTTISH CUP FINAL was against Dunfermline Athletic, who had never been in a final before. But their manager was Jock Stein, who not only knew football, but knew the Celtic team and managerial set-up as well. Yet with their huge support, and free-scoring John Hughes in the centre-forward position, it was difficult to see any other result than a Celtic victory.

Even though almost half a century has now elapsed since these two dreadful Cup finals (the draw and the replay) the Celtic chronicler finds it difficult to contain his emotion as his team's forwards, Hughes in particular, missed chance after chance, then the slick professionalism of Dunfermline gained two goals in the latter stages of the replay. It was a profoundly depressing experience and what this did to the 18-year-old Hughes can barely be imagined. The supporters turned nasty, threw bottles (as they did rather too often in those dreadful days) and singled out Hughes for abuse as he collected his loser's medal in the gathering murk and gloom which symbolically engulfed Hampden on that desperate night.

A more sober and reasoned reflection a day or two later would have found excuses in the youth of Hughes. The trouble was, however, that the team was in the iron grip of chairman Bob Kelly who, using the genial and legendary Jimmy McGrory as his shield, indulged his futile whims in team selection. The support remained large and committed, but there were clear signs that they had taken a great deal more than they were prepared to do. Often the frustration exhibited itself in the singling out of players for abuse. John Hughes, the speedy, powerful but sometimes clumsy centre-forward, was the obvious target on occasion.

THE EVENTS OF 1961/62 were mitigated for the support only by the fact that Dundee, rather than Rangers, won the League championship. The characteristic of Celtic was inconsistency in everything – team selection, performance and achievement. John Hughes played in the centre-forward position virtually all season, and had some really good days cheering up his fans. But on occasion he was disappointing, not least in the disastrous Scottish Cup semifinal against St Mirren, in which the whole team let the support down, but no more than the support let the team down with a late invasion of the field in a misguided crazy attempt to stop the game.

Such a background was hardly what Hughes needed. What was really required was a period of stability in which the young man could learn his trade. But the atmosphere was frenetic, the support was unforgiving and the back-up from the top of the club was virtually non-existent. Sometimes John had great days – there was a fine hat-trick against Stirling Albion in October and two terrific goals in the quarter-final replay against Third Lanark – but at other times he was leaden-footed, clumsily ineffective and seemed to give up far too easily.

Yet it was obvious from the way that he was marked by the opposition that he was very highly rated, and that the potential was certainly there. Season 1962/63 opened brightly, with Hughes scoring seven goals in the first six games, including two fine ones against Ian Ure of Dundee at Parkhead. But, crucially, he failed to score in the game against Dundee United at Tannadice Park that Celtic needed to win to qualify from the League Cup section, and depression set in again. Indeed, without Hughes, Celtic went through a purple patch in the autumn, hitting six against Airdrie and seven against St Mirren. Hughes was back in the team for the New Year, and had the misfortune to be part of the line-up that collapsed ignominiously 0-4 to Rangers at Ibrox.

Pat Crerand left Parkhead in the wake of that disaster. Indeed, he had been at least partially responsible. Pat had no great opinion of John, and in the game immediately after the Ibrox disgrace, Pat was left out and John flourished, scoring a hat-trick on a frost-bound pitch at Aberdeen. This was a feature of Hughes – he was a good player on bad pitches, whether they were frosty or waterlogged. He was such an unpredictable performer at the best of times, and problems with the pitch created even more problems for defenders in trying to read him. That day at Pittodrie, it was a perfect tonic to see the way that Hughes could run through defences. Perhaps the season could yet be saved.

But two things characterised early 1963. One was the big freeze which severely curtailed football for many weeks, and the other was the perpetual chopping and changing of the Celtic team. Hughes played only sporadically, but the side, although reducing their supporters to despair in the Scottish League, reached the final of the Scottish Cup. It was the first Old Firm Scottish Cup final for 35 years. Like the Dunfermline game of two years previously, the 1963 Final went to a replay after Celtic had deservedly earned a 1-1 draw. Hughes had played tolerably well in the first game at centre-forward, then found himself on the left wing for the replay, in which he hardly kicked a ball as the team collapsed to a 0-3 defeat, which could have been even heavier.

The 60,000 Celtic fans who disappeared home that night blamed Hughes as much as anyone, but there would be little relief the following season for the club. That said, Hughes enjoyed some very fine moments during 1963/64. He started off that season in the centre, where he persisted in trying to run through a defender rather than beat him, but then he was moved to the left wing and began to enjoy the extra space. He scored at least two wonderful goals that term – a tremendous solo effort in the Scottish Cup against Morton at Cappielow in January and a great goal in Bratislava to guarantee passage to the semi-final of the European Cup Winners Cup.

But he and the team collapsed miserably against the Hungarians MTK Budapest away from home after being 3-0 up from the home leg. Meanwhile on the domestic front, Celtic could not shake off their Rangers complex, giving every impression of believing that they were not allowed to beat their city rivals, so paralysed and mesmerised were they by the impressive (but by no means) insurmountable skills of Jim Baxter, Willie Henderson and Ralph Brand.

Yet in spite of all this, the fans of Hughes (and there were many) did notice an improvement. He was still only in his early 20s and he had learned as well as he could in that dysfunctional Celtic organisation. When at last Celtic did beat Rangers, in the rain at Parkhead on 5 September 1964, Hughes was magnificent, netting what would have been one of his best ever goals in the first minute, only to find it disallowed for some mysterious infringement on the halfway line after he had run all the way from there to shoot. He did not let that upset him, however, and continued to play brilliantly that day.

BUT THEN IT ALL stopped again. The loss of the League Cup final (against Rangers yet again) was hard to bear, but after that the team collapsed more or less totally. John was out for a while but then came back as centre-forward, and began to play well for the team in what became commonly known as the "one-man forward line". Defeats were common, and people were now beginning to ask the question: "Are Celtic finished?"

In some ways, John Hughes typified Celtic in those years. No-one doubted his ability and potential, but ability and potential were all that we were getting. Consistent success seemed a long way off for both Hughes and the club. He was, of course, the marksman that Celtic needed. A great Celtic team usually has a great personality centre-forward – Quinn, McGrory, Larsson – and poor Celtic teams are characterised by the lack of one. Yet while this may have been a poor Celtic side, there were some fine players there, for all their lack of success.The problem was that they were being led badly.

January 1965 was the turning point. The first few weeks of that year were the absolute nadir, including an infamous day at Parkhead when Hearts fans outnumbered the home contingent. But then it all turned on 30 January. While Sir Winston Churchill was being buried in London, Celtic met Aberdeen at Parkhead on a frosty pitch before a paltry crowd of 14,000. Hughes, wearing sandshoes (as he had done against Motherwell on Boxing Day and scored twice) suddenly turned on the magic and scored five as a not-insignificant Aberdeen side containing fine players like Ally Shewan, Dave Smith and Ernie Winchester, were put to the sword to the tune of 8-0.

Bertie Auld had already returned to the fold, and his influence was important, but the following day came the really crucial announcement that Jock Stein was to take over as manager. The players had already known about this, of course – something that perhaps explains the zip in the performance against Aberdeen – but for the fans, it meant that in the course of one weekend, things had changed completely.

For several players, this meant that their futures would be on the line. A new manager always will make changes, particularly in the circumstances at Parkhead, where changes were so obviously necessary to bring the success that the desperate supporters craved with such intensity. Some players, like Hugh Maxwell, John Divers and Jim Kennedy, did not long survive the arrival of Stein. Jimmy Johnstone was removed from the team, and it looked as if he might not survive the "Big Man" either.

But how would Stein react to Hughes? Would he lose patience with the loveable Yogi Bear, whose performances caused such divisions in the support? Would he off-load him to a team like Newcastle, who would have paid a king's ransom for his services? Or would Jock be able to bring out the best in Hughes, and add consistency and reliability to the cocktail of brilliance and flair that we already knew he possessed?

The relationship between Stein and Hughes was complex, but initially, at least, all went well. John earned a cap for the Scottish League against the English League at Hampden in March and roasted Jack Charlton of Leeds United. Then, under Stein's guidance, Celtic's trophy famine ended on 24 April 1965 when they won the Scottish Cup in an epic final against Dunfermline Athletic. John did not necessarily star in that game, but he was a fine team man, a "rumble-them-up" centre-forward with a fine shot and the ability to draw men out of position, and to lead his own line brilliantly.

WITH STEIN IN TEMPORARY charge of the Scotland team, John won the first few of his eight Scotland caps, playing particularly well in a creditable 1-1 draw in Poland. Things were going well for the 22-year-old and, in retrospect, 1965 was the peak of his career. At long last, he seemed to have matured, to have grown into a good, consistent player, and the word "great" was even beginning to be applied to him.

Certainly destiny called on him to deliver the Scottish League Cup in 1965. This was a vital tournament in the context of the long-term history of Celtic, as a failure to deliver would perhaps have indicated that the Scottish Cup triumph of the previous year was a fluke, and that the "Celtic Revolution" was an illusory, transient thing. On at least three occasions in that tournament, John Hughes delivered the goods.

With Joe McBride now at Parkhead, Yogi was played more on the left wing. Whether he was happy about that was unclear, but Celtic were having a dreadful struggle to qualify in a strong section containing Motherwell and the two Dundee teams. Celtic faced the last game of the section at Dens Park, needing a draw to qualify. Dundee were a good side, with men like Andy Penman, Stevie Murray and Charlie Cooke, and although Celtic scored first through John Divers, the issue was in doubt until John Hughes's wonder goal, which even had the Dundee season-ticket holders joining in the warm applause.

The memory remains bright even after 40 years, of how John got the ball on the left wing, halfway inside the Dundee half, then beat Scotland international Alex Hamilton, charged across the field with Hamilton and another defender in hot pursuit, suddenly turned and fired home a brilliant unstoppable shot from at least 25 yards. As often happens in such cases, there was a moment's pause to allow the 28,000 crowd to take in what had happened before Dens Park exploded in appreciation for such brilliance.

His second contribution came at Stark's Park, Kirkcaldy, when he scored a late hat-trick in the quarter-final first leg against a sadly outclassed Raith Rovers, who were defeated 8-1. It was not so much the hat-trick that is recalled as the breathtaking football played by all the Celtic forward line, with Hughes very much part of it, as if to prove that he could be a team man as well as a brilliant individualist.

Then, after a couple of games to beat the strong Hibs team in the semi-final, came the final against Rangers. This was to be the acid test of the new Celtic. Victory would send out signals to Ibrox and elsewhere that Celtic had arrived; defeat would perhaps signal a backward slide and indicate that the bad old days of the Rangers phobia had not entirely gone. Rangers had the psychological advantage with a 2-1 win in the League a month earlier at Ibrox, and a record League Cup crowd of 107,609 were in attendance.

Reports of this game centre on the crude tackles and the pitch invasion at the end, and thanks to hyperbole like "orgy of crudeness" and "X-certificate" and "war correspondents rather than sports correspondents should have been there", the Celtic victory tends to be ignored. In particular, little credit has been given to the ability of John Hughes to hold his nerve. A quarter of an hour had gone when Rangers centre-half Ron McKinnon inexplicably handled in the box. Ron did not even argue, so clear cut was it. We Celtic fans behind that goal saw the burly figure of John Hughes lumbering up to take the penalty. We held our breath, for although John's record with penalties had been good, we had seen rather too much of his tendency to blow up under pressure. No fear of that, though, as he beat Billy Ritchie from the spot.

Ten minutes later it happened again. This time Davie Provan brought down Jimmy Johnstone, and there ensued a long argument about it, partly, one felt, deliberately prolonged by the Rangers defenders with the express purpose of unsettling John. He stood calmly, the ball under his arm, then placed it on the spot. Once again, we held our breath, and once again John scored, although this time Billy Ritchie got his hand to it.

Two goals up after half an hour, and Yogi was the hero of the Celtic End. But anxiety crept into the battle hymns during the second half as Rangers pressed and pressed, and Yogi played as the one-man forward line while everyone else was back helping out the beleaguered defence. Rangers did, in the event, pull one back but it was Celtic who won the League Cup.

Some misguided youths invaded the field at the end, trying to attack the Celtic players. It was perhaps as well that such idiots, undernourished in both body and mind, did not get anywhere near Big John. What that fit physique might have done to the physically and spiritually derelict of Govan and Larkhall really does not bear thinking about.

But Celtic fans, admirably restrained and without feeling that they had to retaliate, would sing for months after:

"We won the Cup, we won the Cup
High–oh–my-dadio, we won the Cup!
And who scored the goals, who scored the goals?
High-oh-my-dadio, big Yogi scored the goals!

Life was sweet for Celtic and for big John Hughes.

The Scottish League was won that year for the first time since 1954, and only bad luck prevented the lifting of the Scottish Cup. In addition a far too energetic linesman denied Bobby Lennox the goal at Liverpool which would have beaten the home side in the European Cup Winners' Cup. Hughes had played in most of the games that season, and had every reason to feel confident about the future.

The problem was that this was a very strong side, and the following term, 1966/67, saw six forwards vying for five places. Johnstone, Wallace (after McBride was injured), Chalmers, Auld, Lennox, and Hughes would have been an embarrassment of riches for anyone. Hughes was injured in the League Cup final in October – he was replaced by Chalmers, the first substitute in a major Cup final in Scotland – and was out for some time after that. He returned on Hogmanay to play against Dundee United at Tannadice, but unfortunately that was one of the few games that Celtic lost that season, and thereafter his place was in doubt.

He did play off and on, including a few of the vital European games, but for the two biggest games of that season, the Scottish Cup final against Aberdeen and the European Cup final against Inter Milan, John found himself on the sidelines. There were at last two reasons for this. One was that Lennox was a far better player down the left in dry, hard conditions, although perhaps Hughes had the edge in the wet. But the main reason was that this Celtic team, the greatest in their history, was recognisably a combination who played cohesively, who fitted into a system, who read each other and who relied on each other.

John was far more of a loose cannon. Jimmy Johnstone was similarly unpredictable, and possibly Stein felt that one brilliant individualist in the team was enough. John, on his day, could be unbeatable. Fast, powerful, strong – he had all these attributes and he had improved dramatically with the arrival of Stein and the coaching methods of Neil Mochan, but he still remained far too unreliable at producing the performances. On his day, he could beat the world. Sadly his days were not as plentiful as Stein and the fans of Hughes would have liked.

It is important, however, to retain a sense of perspective in all this. Being a reserve for the Lisbon Lions did emphatically not mean that Hughes was a bad player. Indeed, had Stein been allowed substitutes, there is little doubt that he would have featured at some stage of the action in Lisbon, or indeed any other game where Stein felt that a touch of the unpredictable was called for. Hughes remained one of Scotland's great players, and there was no shortage of interest in him from English clubs, particularly Newcastle United, who repeatedly asked about his availability for transfer.

Things would have been different if John had gone south in the mid-1960s, but he stayed as part of the excellent Parkhead set-up, very much in the squad for Lisbon and clearly seen on the lorry going round Parkhead with the Cup the following night. But he would always say that it hurt not being in the actual team, and it was perhaps the beginning of the end of his good relationship with Stein, who may well have handled Yogi's omission from the biggest game in Celtic history in a none-too-tactful fashion.

But his value to the side was seen in the following season, particularly in the latter half. Then the left wing of Charlie Gallagher and John Hughes (neither of whom had been on the field in Lisbon) carried all before them as Celtic, after a series of misfortunes and a long time to recover from disasters in the Ukraine and in South America, rallied to win the League with some absolutely breathtaking performances, particularly away from home at traditionally difficult places like St Johnstone, Dundee United, Hearts and Aberdeen. He was also good enough to earn a cap and to score Scotland's goal in the 1-1 draw against England, but to all intents and purposes the draw was a defeat as it deprived Scotland of qualification for the European Nations Cup finals. John would have graced that stage in 1968, one feels.

The sight of John Hughes rampaging down the left wing, cutting a defence to ribbons and leaving defenders sprawling in the mud was the sight which inspired the song:

> Feed The Bear, The Bear
> He's every-f***ing-where
> Feed the Bear!

This song earned official disapproval in *The Celtic View* and elsewhere because of its offensive lyrics, but it was sung universally and with gusto as Celtic kept winning, and Rangers visibly cracked under the onslaught, even though the direct matches between the two teams had been played to Rangers' advantage.

Yet there was a down side to Hughes as well that season. His er . . . challenge (some might say attack) on the goalkeeper in South America thoroughly merited his sending-off, and there was at least one other time when the referee might have pointed to the pavilion. This was against Hibs at Easter Road in January when John's admirers in the 38,077 crowd found it hard to justify his tackle on Arthur Duncan, which saw that very fine player taken off.

Earlier in the season, on the eve of the trip to South America, he had won his third League Cup medal in a hard-fought final against Dundee in which he scored early, but that League Cup campaign will be remembered most vividly for his goal in the semi-final against Morton. The Ton were already beaten thanks to a fine team performance in the first half, when

Hughes, having done the "team bit", now showed his individual flair with a run from about the halfway line, the waltzing round of several defenders, then a screamer of a shot which had his fans in raptures. If only he could have done that oftener, Celtic could win the European Cup for years to come, we felt.

John had real bad luck in April 1969, as an injury sustained at St Johnstone prevented him from taking part in that magnificent April in which Celtic, uniquely, lifted all three Scottish trophies in a calendar month. It was a shame because he had performed so well that season, scoring goals at the vital times and teaming up so well with others in a side that, in the opinion of many observers, played even better football than they did in 1967, the only blot in the copybook being an unfortunate defeat to AC Milan in the quarter-final of the European Cup.

In August 1969 John was at the centre of a major incident. In an Old Firm League Cup game at Parkhead eventually won by Celtic, Willie Johnston of Rangers was seen to go down following a clash with Hughes. Hughes had already been booked and marching orders seemed to be the inevitable consequence, but to the astonishment and anger of Rangers' players, directors and supporters, Hughes remained on the field. The consequences for the referee were dire, as he found himself suspended for failing to take action, but Hughes escaped any retribution.

There were several mitigating factors. One was that Johnston, who holds the Scottish record for being ordered off most times, was no angel. He had fouled Hughes originally, and he could certainly retaliate himself and fake injury on occasion. The incident had taken place in front of the Jungle, where stood the seething mass of Celtic fans. It could well be that the referee decided to take no action in view of the threat to public order if the hero of the Jungle was sent packing.

CELTIC'S SUCCESS CONTINUED. Hughes was playing in the centre-forward position when the League Cup was won for the fifth year in a row against St Johnstone (where he had a reasonable-looking goal disallowed for a mysterious infringement), and in spite of a few injuries, he played his part in another League championship win. But he will be best remembered in season 1969/70 for his brilliant header against Leeds United at Hampden, which helped propel Celtic to their second European Cup final.

This time Hughes was in the team, but there was clearly an attitude problem with the players before and after their game with Feyenoord. Perhaps it was just complacency and over-confidence, or perhaps there was something else happening, but there can be little doubt that this was a woeful display and that on the night the Dutch team were far superior to a Celtic side which lacked application, zest and flair.

John collected much of the blame (certainly in the eyes of Jock Stein, if not in the opinion of the disillusioned support) by missing a chance in the first minute of extra time in that dreadful final, and it was from that day that the relationship between Hughes and Stein, which had never been close or warm, and had been deteriorating for some time, took a marked turn for the worse.

Stein was clearly rebuilding that season and Hughes, like a few others, was not guaranteed a place. Stein felt that the player exaggerated an injury – even though he needed stitches in a leg wound – in a game that Celtic lost at Muirton Park, Perth, in February 1971. Hughes was off the field, leaving Celtic with only ten men at the time St Johnstone scored their second goal, then he insisted on returning before having to come off again five minutes later. A month after that, when he was left out of the team for a Cup tie against Raith Rovers, Hughes and Stein had an almighty row and Hughes either walked out of Parkhead or was sent home by Stein, depending which story one believes.

The feud continued. Hughes was taken down to Kilmarnock to be told he was not playing in a reserve match, something that he found deeply humiliating, and it did indeed look more than a little like sheer spite on the part of Jock Stein. At the end of the season when Celtic won a League and Cup double, Hughes did not feature. He did not help matters by asking for a pay rise, but it was now clear to all concerned that this feud helped nobody. It was also clear that John Hughes's days at his beloved Parkhead were more or less at an end, even though he was still some two years short of his 30th birthday.

A temporary truce of sorts was patched up at the start of the 1971/72 season, but when Crystal Palace offered £50,000 for Hughes and Willie Wallace in October, both Stein and Hughes accepted the opportunity. He scored one spectacular goal for the Palace against Sheffield United, akin to the famous ones at Cappielow in 1964 and Dens Park in 1965. But he did not sojourn long at Selhurst Park, moving on to Sunderland for a spell to play alongside his brother Billy. Then he returned to junior (non-League) football north of the border, at one point being the coach of the Scotland Junior team.

John remains a curious, difficult-to-understand character. He is an archetypal Celt with loads of flair, individuality and class. He deserves respect for the way in which he came through the dreadful barracking and abuse that he suffered from so-called supporters in the bad days. On his day, like the little girl with the curl on her forehead, when he was good, he was very, very good, fully deserving comments like "unbeatable", "world-class" and "great Celt". What a pity it was that we cannot add the word "consistent" to his many other attributes.

JIMMY JOHNSTONE

'JINKY'

1963-1975

BHOYS CAREER

Games	**515**
Goals	**129**
Caps	**23**

MAGIC MOMENT

Johnstone was devastating as Celtic beat Red Star 5-1 in the first leg of a European Cup tie, ensuring he would not have to fly to Belgrade as Stein had agreed that Jinky could stay at home if Celtic led by four goals.

WHILE one may not necessarily agree with the contention that Jimmy Johnstone was the greatest Celtic player of all time, it is true that he remains, without much doubt, the most talked-about and written-about. Johnstone's continuing high profile, even some time after his death on 13 March 2006, is the result of many factors.

In the first place he was a superb player. He was a great dribbler, a crowd-pleaser, an excellent user of the ball, and a not-infrequent goalscorer. There was a particularly spectacular example at Ibrox in the rain in early May 1967 on the day that Celtic won the Scottish League and, as a bonus, for a little man he was surprisingly good at netting with his head. The art of the dribbler has now gone from football. In truth, it was going, and almost gone, when Jimmy was in his prime. Jimmy, however, did keep it going for several more years than might otherwise have been the case.

Like so many other Celtic heroes, Jimmy was small, and thus there was an instant subliminal identification with the Celtic support. For good reasons or bad, Celtic fans have frequently seen themselves as victims of the system, the downtrodden, the poor people apparently helpless in the face of the discrimination of the establishment. Such a philosophy is dated today, and even in Jimmy's day it was only partly true, but he was seen as the "wee man" whose sheer skill and trickery could beat the system, often represented by Rangers' left-backs.

If Jimmy was the "wee man", there were also dealings with the "big man", Jock Stein. They had a complex relationship which has not become any easier to analyse since the passing of both. Jock was once asked what his greatest achievement was. Most people would have expected him to talk about the 1967 European Cup triumph or the nine League Championships in a row, but rather to the surprise of his interlocutor, he said that it was "keeping Jimmy Johnstone in the game".

It was as well that he did so, because football would have been so much the poorer without him. It was in Europe that he had a particular attraction. Small red-headed people may be common enough in the West of Scotland – an astonishing amount of Celtic supporters have a vague resemblance to him – but in other parts of Europe, red hair is virtually non-existent. Any red-haired boy or girl in the tourist resorts of Spain, Italy or Greece will not lack admirers among the native population. When red hair is combined with such spectacular, individualist football skill, there is bound to be a stir.

Another great media attraction of Jimmy Johnstone was his inability to be far away from trouble of one kind or another. It may have been trouble with referees, it may have been silly things that he did, it may have been his fear of flying, it may have been his attempt to row the Atlantic, it may have been his illness and death in the most dreadful of circumstances through a horrendous disease, but whatever it was, trouble buzzed around Jimmy Johnstone like bluebottle flies around a jampot.

SO WHAT SORT OF a man was this character who was the talk of Scotland and a great part of the football-playing world for well over a decade? Jimmy's book, *Fire In My Boots*, published in the late 1960s, is an extremely candid piece of writing. He describes himself as neurotic, tells how the girls at school all thought he was ugly and how this insecurity caused him to assault a teacher. He pulls no punches, but then again he never did. He was a lovely, transparent sort of character. What you saw in Jimmy was what you got.

"He was not daft, but he occasionally did daft things" was said about him by one of his team-mates and that seems to sum him up. He never seemed very good at resisting temptation. There were times when, by his own admission, he swallowed rather too much alcohol and he was the carefree, gallus, West of Scotland character that he appeared to be. He was once seen at Aberdeen station before a game with his arm round the neck of his good friend Bobby Lennox, singing Roll Over, Beethoven while Stein glowered, but then put on that philosophical expression which seemed to say: "What can I do about that?".

Stein was still manager of Hibs when the two men had their first real conversation. It was in the toilet after a reserve match. Stein said: "What are you doing here? You're far too good a player to be in the reserves" and did not wait for an answer. That comment in many ways showed that Stein had already summed up Johnstone. Jimmy was a great player, but for character reasons, was not, at that point, performing in the Celtic first team.

Born in 1944 in Uddingston, not too far from the home of Scotland's infamous murderer of the 1950s, Peter Manuel, Jimmy was of a Catholic family and therefore there was no great doubt about which team he would support. Indeed, as early as 1958 he was a ballboy at Celtic Park, but it was clear from those who saw him play the game that there was a certain talent. He had read a book about Stanley Matthews, and spent many a long winter night in his kitchen honing his skills in ball control and dribbling. Yet everyone at St Columba's Boys Guild and Blantyre Celtic kept saying things like "He'll be okay – once he grows" or "He's far too slight".

He was, however, called up to Celtic Park and considered good enough to be blooded in a couple of League games at the end of the 1962/63 season. His debut was one of Celtic's greatest ever disasters, a 0-6 defeat by Kilmarnock on Wednesday 27 March 1963. A Scottish Cup tie was looming and several players were rested. Johnstone was one of the cannon-fodder replacements. No tactics seemed to be forthcoming from the Celtic management for the youngster's debut, and a humiliating catastrophe was the inevitable outcome.

Next he was given a game against Hearts on Monday 29 April. Once again the circumstances were similar, as the Scottish Cup final was to be played on Saturday 4 May, and injuries were to be avoided. This time, although the team lost 3-4, they did play well and the minuscule red-headed Jimmy Johnstone showed a few good touches, and even scored a goal.

But then Celtic shocked the footballing world by picking Jimmy for the 1963 Scottish Cup final against Rangers. It was his just third game for the club, and the 130,000 crowd gasped in amazement at the sight of this tiny wee boy with the mop of ginger hair. In the first half, on several occasions, he got the better of Rangers' Davie Provan, and the Celtic fans, whose team had been given little chance in the opinion of the pundits against the rampant Rangers team which had already won the Scottish League, began to have a little hope that miracles might happen, that this little boy might yet bring to an end their trophy famine which had now gone on for six years.

More than 40 years later one recalls vividly standing in the rain on that wet Celtic End, being now and again lifted to unfulfilled hope as the youngster showed what he was capable of, never more so than the moment near the end when a lob from a long distance missed the Rangers goal by inches. It was felt that a star was born, but such were the ways of Celtic management in 1963 that Johnstone was dropped for the replay after having done so well in the 1-1 draw. Celtic lost the replay 0-3.

Yet there was a touch of humour about Jimmy's introduction as well. The Saturday after the first Scottish Cup final and a few days before the disastrous replay, Celtic were at Tannadice Park to play Dundee United. All the local support were there to see this new phenomenon of the small stature and the red hair. Celtic ran on to the field and among them was a three-year-old boy with red hair. Everyone stood in astonishment, asking themselves: "Is he really as small as all that?" But then another slightly larger redhead appeared, and everyone realised that the first one was merely the Celtic mascot!

THE FOLLOWING SEASON, 1963/64, saw Johnstone consolidate his position with a few tremendous performances, notably in Europe against Slovan Bratislava when he won over the whole Czech crowd by his trickery. But still success proved elusive to Celtic, who seemed in those days to believe that they were not allowed to beat Rangers, such was the paralysing effect that the Light Blues held over them. In the Scottish Cup game against Rangers at Ibrox that season, Johnstone on several occasions showed Jim Baxter a clean pair of heels, but Rangers scored before and after half-time and Celtic collapsed.

Celtic's death wish extended to the following season, although Johnstone was good enough to win two Scottish caps in the autumn of that year. But with Celtic, he had really hard luck in the Scottish League Cup final against Rangers in October 1964, when he scored Celtic's only goal, missed a sitter and really should have earned a penalty when he was cruelly brought down by Davie Provan. The League Cup defeat was the catalyst for an almost total collapse of Celtic and Johnstone. Things reached a nadir for Jimmy at Ibrox on New Year's Day 1965. Repeatedly fouled by Rangers' Theorolf Beck, Johnstone cracked. Beck was laid out; Johnstone had made a good job of it, and had to be sent off. Referee Tom Wharton asked his name, and Jimmy said "Roy Rogers", the famous cowboy singer. Tom pointed to the tunnel and said: "Away and join Trigger (Roy's horse) in the dressing room".

Celtic were now at rock bottom. When this happens, the only way one can look is up, and Jock Stein arrived. For a spell, Jimmy did not seem to figure in Jock's plans. Indeed the Scottish Cup was won that year without Jimmy in the team, and he may have wondered about his future under Stein. It may be that had a transfer bid come in for Jimmy Johnstone in the first few months of Stein's reign, it might have been accepted. The manager, in spite of that conversation in the toilet, was far from convinced that Johnstone had a future in this team.

Johnstone was in at the start of the 1965/66 season, but was dropped after a poor display against Dundee at Parkhead in the third game. This was Stein's determination to teach him a lesson and a few weeks later, Jimmy was back – and there began the tremendous contribution of Jimmy Johnstone to the great Celtic team. By the end of the season he had won a Scottish League medal, a Scottish League Cup medal and had scored twice for Scotland against England at Hampden in a game where he had been one of his country's few stars.

By this time he was a more thoughtful, controlled player. He had silenced his doubters and charmed the North American continent on the tour of summer 1966. He was, however, allowed to fly home early to be married to Agnes, and it was on that flight that there occurred the incident that was to cause his permanent fear of flying. The plane hit an air pocket in mid-Atlantic and the impression was given that it was about to crash. The pilot rescued his aircraft from what was not too uncommon a phenomenon in the 1960s, but Jimmy Johnstone got a fright.

Fear of flying affects everyone to a greater or lesser extent. But if you are one of the best players in the world, neurotic wheengings tend to be taken a little more seriously. Heavily involved in European football, Johnstone most of the time had to grit his teeth, take a deep breath and get on with it. But on one occasion, Stein offered him a deal to the effect that if Celtic had a commanding lead at Parkhead over Red Star Belgrade, Jimmy would not have to go to the return leg. Whether Jock meant this seriously or not is not clear, but Johnstone roasted the Yugoslav defence that night in November 1968, Celtic won 5-1 and Johnstone ran off the field shouting: "I'll no need tae go".

And he didn't. Appeals from Stein, the Celtic chairman and even the Red Star chairman, who thought that the people of Belgrade should have a chance to see Jimmy Johnstone, had no effect on Jimmy. He stayed in Glasgow as Celtic went to Belgrade and drew 1-1. Stein never made such an offer again, and Jimmy went on all subsequent European trips. It was not unknown for the flankman to make much of an injury to avoid a trip, but if Jock said "Get on that f***in' plane!", one usually did so, even Jimmy Johnstone.

He was also more than a little neurotic about security from being shot. In 1974 when Celtic played Atletico Madrid, a death threat was issued. This was in Franco's Spain, and it had to be taken seriously. Jokes along the lines of "Dinnae worry, Jimmy. You'll be too fast for them" had no effect on Johnstone. In the same year he was with the Scotland World Cup squad in Germany and again vague death threats were issued. These had to be taken seriously as there were Arab terrorist movements like Black September, who had made such a deadly strike on the Israeli athletes in Munich less than two years previously. Although security was stepped up at Scotland's training ground, Jimmy was always glancing nervously up at trees in case there were snipers.

But if Johnstone was a little neurotic about such irrational matters, one thing that certainly did not bother him was the more tangible danger of serious injury from brutal defenders. The hard men of Scotland paled into insignificance with some of the "clug" men that he met in Europe and South America. Yet the amazing thing about Jimmy, and something that drew admiration from his team-mates, was his ability to be fouled, pick himself up and run at them again. Spanish, Argentinian and Czech defenders were detailed to do nothing other than take out Jimmy Johnstone. But one of the key things about being a tough wee guy in Scotland is that "Ye dinnae let them ken ye're feard o' them". He never did, even though his injuries were terrible.

His relationship with Stein, as we have seen, was complex. Stein knew that he was the best player in the world, but on at least two occasions, Johnstone found himself suspended by the club. One was in a Scottish Cup tie against Queen's Park in March 1967, when Jimmy committed a violent indiscretion unnoticed by the referee, but seen by Jock Stein. He did not play in the next game. Another was in a game against Dundee United in October 1968 when he was substituted to his obvious displeasure, and 46,000 saw an exchange of pleasantries with Jock Stein before he rushed up the tunnel followed by the irate manager. Once again he did not play in the next game.

On many another occasion Johnstone would find himself dropped, and the press and public would be left to speculate on the reasons why. What was notable, however, was that Stein was always very reluctant to sever his connection with Johnstone in a permanent sense. Other men who had given him grief, notably Gemmell and Auld, were dispatched elsewhere by 1971. Johnstone, on the other hand, lasted until summer 1975, with only Bobby Lennox of the Lisbon Lions surviving him at Parkhead.

In another sense, too, Stein gave Johnstone far more latitude than he would other players. Spectators arriving late for the 1967 Scottish Cup final against Aberdeen, for example, would be amazed to discover that Johnstone appeared frequently on the left, then in the centre, then on the right. "Big Jock's gaen wee Jimmy a roving commission the day" was the accepted wisdom of the Celtic support. The late Bobby Murdoch put it differently when he revealed how Stein, before a game, told every player in detail what he wanted and expected of him. No mention of Jimmy who, neurotic and fearful as always that he had been dropped, asked in the plaintive tones of a Victorian orphan addressing the parochial governor: "What aboot me, boss?" "You – I'll just gie you the jersey, the boys'll gie you the ba' and you can dae whut the hell ye want!"

With Scotland, Jimmy was involved in many incidents. The attempt to sail the Atlantic in a small boat in 1974 has passed into legend, but there were other times when Billy Bremner and Denis Law led Jimmy into mischief – or perhaps he led them into it. On one occasion in 1968 before the European Championship qualifier against England, when the gentlemanly Bobby Brown was the manager, the team had been picked for a practice game against some Celtic reserves, and Jimmy was not in the side.

This did not sit very well with Jimmy, and matters were not helped when Walter McCrae appeared on the scene. McCrae was the trainer of Kilmarnock and Scotland, and although a knowledgeable and hard-working character, he was occasionally rather brusque with people. Without handling the matter any too tactfully, Walter approached Jimmy, put a linesman's flag in his hand and told, rather than asked, him to do the needful. Jimmy's explosion was immediate and foul-mouthed, and unfortunately overheard by a newspaper reporter.

The matter was blown up out of all proportion, but Jimmy did not play in the Scotland v England game of 24 February. He did, however, play for Celtic against Kilmarnock the following week, inspired Celtic to a 6-0 victory and rather than ask after Mr McCrae's health, said that his performance was "no bad for a linesman, eh?"

Jimmy played 23 times for Scotland. It should, of course, have been a great deal more, but there were problems of attitude, and in the early years some severe competition from Willie Henderson of Rangers, another fine winger and, like many Rangers players, a good friend of Jimmy behind the scenes. There was, in addition, one aspect of playing for Scotland, in the mid-1960s in particular, that Jimmy found very difficult to handle and this led him, unwisely, on several occasions to say that he did not want to play for his country.

There was a certain identification of Rangers and Scotland in the eyes of Rangers supporters. In the early 21st century this attitude has changed completely, but in the 1960s some Rangers fans felt that they owned Scotland, and that any non-Rangers player in the team was only there on sufferance. As well as Jinky, Davie Hay would be subjected to this nonsense as well, as would Tommy Gemmell, Billy McNeill and Jim Kennedy from this idiotic but vocal minority, which congregated at the Mount Florida end of Hampden. It all got too much and after one game in particular, against Denmark in November 1970, Johnstone announced his resignation from the Scotland team – until he was talked out of it!

Arguably his best game for Scotland came in 1974, a few days after his infamous attempt to row the Atlantic at Largs. Scotland beat England 2-0 and Johnstone was seen quite clearly on television making gestures to the press box after the roasting that they had given him, about how he was "unsuitable to play for Scotland" etc. It was a shame that he did not get a game in the 1974 World Cup. The final game in particular, against Yugoslavia, looked as if it would need a magician to break the deadlock. Manager Willie Ormond had such a magician on the bench. Sadly he was not deployed.

IT WOULD BE WRONG to say that Jimmy always played well in every game for Celtic. In particular, he often found it hard to resist the temptation of beating an opponent again, and again, and then again. Willie Mathieson, who played left-back for Rangers against Johnstone on many occasions, was asked who was his most difficult opponent. He said that the honour would go to Tommy McLean of Kilmarnock. He could beat an opponent, reach the dead-ball line and cross. Johnstone, on the other hand, was so affected by the cheers of his Celtic crowd that he would always try to humiliate his man, thereby giving the full-back a chance to play him into touch.

One recalls an occasion at Parkhead when something like this happened. From the Jungle, there was a clear view of Jock Stein in the Celtic dugout. Jimmy beat one man, then another, then yet another, and with at least three defenders out of position and three Celtic forwards virtually unmarked waiting for a pass, Jimmy cut back and beat one of his defenders again, choosing to entertain his fan club rather than create a goal for Celtic. Jock's reaction was violent and fearsome, pointing, gesticulating and shouting the odds. It was as well that one could not hear Jock.

But there was often little a defender could do to stop Jimmy. Once at Pittodrie, he rounded the full-back and left him sprawling on the wet ground. In a move which would nowadays earn a yellow card, or perhaps a red one, the full-back put his arms round Jimmy's leg and held him back. The Pittodrie crowd, even the Celtic supporters, had to laugh at this.

Jimmy's most famous good day was not so much in Lisbon – although Stein had given orders to Celtic to give Johnstone the ball in the first minute so that he could run rings round a few Italians and win over neutral opinion in the stadium and in living rooms throughout Europe – but in the European Cup semi-final of 1970 at Hampden, where Leeds United's Terry Cooper, generally accepted as being the best in England, was shown a thing or two by the "mighty midget" or the "human flea" as the press were calling him. To his credit, Cooper never resorted to dirty tactics, but that was only because, as the unkind put it, he couldn't get near enough to Johnstone to do so.

In Johnstone's second European Cup final, he had a few good runs, but seemed to be affected by the lethargy that had unaccountably settled on the Celtic team, who lacked the hunger to win the game. Hunger was a quality which had been very obvious in their first European Cup final of 1967, and Johnstone was as upset as anyone by what went wrong in the San Siro of 1970. Even after an interval of almost 40 years, the lack of fight remains a puzzle.

It had all been so different three years earlier. Johnstone's contribution to that season was enormous. It would be wrong, however, to claim that he did more than anyone else. In truth, everyone played their part – Johnstone, for example, had a superb game in the semi-final against Dukla Prague at Parkhead – and the winning of the European Cup was essentially a team effort. Johnstone was very much part of that team.

From time to time, stories would emerge in the press that Johnstone was on the point of a move away from Celtic Park to Tottenham Hotspur, Manchester United, Newcastle United or whoever one cared to mention. Even foreign clubs would be mentioned. These stories have always bedevilled Celtic and are sometimes the wicked creation of a malignant journalist, or simply a journalist under pressure on a dull day to fill up his space. In Johnstone's case, they all ignored one thing. Johnstone was a West of Scotland boy, and a Celtic boy. He had in common with Jock Stein the feeling of homesickness whenever Glasgow receded into the background, and it really was difficult to imagine him with anyone else. In any case, playing for a foreign club would have involved flying!

JOHNSTONE'S AFFINITY WITH THE Celtic support was based simply on this. He was, indeed, one of them. They did very much understand him, and they were particularly sympathetic and appreciative of his attempts to control his temper. Several times, for example in the 2 January game against Rangers in 1968, he was felled by a succession of Rangers players who seemed to be taking it in turns to do the hacking, lest one of them was sent off. Oddly enough, the times that he did lose the place were for irrational reasons. In September 1967, for example, he raised his fists to Kenny Aird of St Johnstone. There had been a minimum of provocation, certainly, but he would later say that it was because he was "moving house" and worried about forthcoming flights to Kiev and South America.

The Argentina trip was a fiasco. Johnstone was one of the sinners, but it is hardly surprising that he retaliated when the Celtic crowd at Hampden Park saw what the Argentinians were prepared to do in Glasgow, let alone in their own country. Johnstone was clearly targeted by the hatchet men of Racing Club – something that might have been taken as a compliment to Jimmy's talent, had it not been for the sinister, cynical side of football that this World Club Championship threw up.

It was often said that Jimmy was not the best of team men. If this means that he found it difficult to adhere to some methodical plan, worked out on a blackboard and with dossiers on opponents, this was true. But Stein realised this, threw him the jersey and told him to play. He was able to adapt to any team that he played in. In 1971, for example, Celtic might have hit a trough, but along came Dixie Deans, with whom Johnstone established an immediate rapport and understanding. Others too – Harry Hood, Willie Wallace, Lou Macari, for example – all owed a great deal of their success to Jimmy Johnstone. He could lose the rag on the field, and in true Glasgow fashion would on occasion want to make something more of it with fisticuffs, but Jimmy could never sustain anger. He was basically such a nice person.

JIMMY EVENTUALLY PARTED COMPANY with Celtic in June 1975. He was still not yet 31 and he felt he had a few years of football left in him. He tried his luck with San Jose Earthquakes, Sheffield United, Dundee, Shelbourne and Elgin City before finally packing in a fine playing career in 1980. He never really settled with any of these clubs, mainly because he was a West of Scotland boy and also because he needed "Big Jock" as he affectionately called him, to keep him on the straight and narrow.

He helped out with coaching at Celtic, and was frequently seen at Celtic games, usually talking to supporters, for indeed he was one of them. His red hair had virtually all gone, but the cheeky smile, the impish grin, the penetrating but never cruel sense of humour, were still all there. His opinions on the current players were always forthright, and his views on the way the club was going in the bad days of the early 1990s were even more so.

Early in the 21st century Jimmy was diagnosed with motor neurone disease, a horrible, crippling, degenerative illness which attacks the nervous system. It is common enough among sportsman: Don Revie, one-time manager of Leeds United and England, and Chris Anderson, a fine player and administrator of Aberdeen, both suffered from it. It did not stop Johnstone from attending functions, receiving awards – he was once voted by Celtic supporters as the greatest player of all time – and appearing at games. However, there was one occasion at Parkhead when he appeared, ready to be introduced, and he bowed to the crowd, sadly unable to raise his arms to wave back at those who still adored him.

His death at the tragically young age of 61 in March 2006 came a matter of days before Celtic played Dunfermline Athletic in the Scottish League Cup final. This game immediately became known as the Jimmy Johnstone League Cup final. Appropriately enough, Celtic won 3-0, something that Jimmy would have been happy about. An amazing feature of the occasion was the amount of banners with Jimmy Johnstone's name on them and the amount of times that the Celtic fans sang the praises not of Maciej Zurawski, Shaun Maloney and Dion Dublin, who scored the goals but:

" Celtic, Glasgow Celtic with Jimmy Johnstone on the wing"

a ditty whose banal and repetitive lyrics seem to go nowhere other than exulting the presence of Jimmy Johnstone.

JIMMY JOHNSTONE DOES, indeed, belong to the superbly great. There was a down side to him, no-one can deny – his short temper, his problems with accepting authority, his inability to resist temptation when led astray and, on the field, his tendency to overdo the fancy stuff. But such faults are dwarfed by his immense good points. On the ball he was, quite simply, a genius. Put the ball at his feet and he would do anything with it. His good friend Bobby Lennox was far more direct and needed the ball a yard or two ahead of him so that he could use his speed. Jimmy, on the other hand, although not without speed, was more of a corkscrew, an old-fashioned dribbler, a trickster of the type that we seldom see nowadays, or even in Johnstone's own time.

He was part of a tremendous time in Scottish football. When Johnstone played his first game for the club in 1963, we had the phenomenon of Celtic going nowhere, badly organised, with a dispirited and sometimes frustrated and nasty support who expressed their feelings in hooliganism and thuggery. Along came Jock Stein and very soon he added all the ingredients to the Celtic cake. The spiciest one of them was Jimmy Johnstone, a quintessential Celtic character.

DIXIE DEANS

'DIXIE'

1971-1976

BHOYS CAREER

Games	184
Goals	124
Caps	2

MAGIC MOMENT

Only 17 days after missing a crucial penalty kick which put Celtic out of the 1972 European Cup semi-final, Dixie scored a hat-trick in the Scottish Cup final.

"DIXIE"

Deans was a very special footballer, the sort of personality player that the Scottish game frankly lacks at the moment. He was given the nickname of Dixie in conscious imitation of his near namesake William Ralph Dean, who played for Everton and England between the wars. Dixie Dean did not like being called Dixie. He felt that it smacked of the Negro slave trade of the 18th century, and that he had been given this nickname because of his swarthy complexion and his curly hair, as if one of his forebears had been a black slave. In Liverpool, of course, that was possible. But William Dean had become Everton's greatest player of all time.

It was, therefore, no disgrace to be given the same nickname as this great man, and John Kelly Deans, born at Linwood in 1946, was the sort of player who developed an instant affinity with the fans, a particular achievement for Dixie, whose background was anything other than Celtic minded. Not to put too fine a point on it, he was a Rangers supporter, or at least was widely suspected of so being, but was hardly the first or the last with a supposed Ibrox-inclined childhood to perform outstandingly at Parkhead. Indeed, in the team that he joined, Danny McGrain, Kenny Dalglish and a few others (not least Jock Stein himself) "suffered" from that "handicap". It was, of course, no handicap at all.

Dixie claims that he was a St Mirren supporter in his childhood. He admits that he came from the wrong side of the city and went to a different type of school (i.e. a non-Catholic one) from the majority of the Celtic fans but, if there was any kind of problem with being accepted by the support, it was never obvious. The legend that Deans was wearing a Rangers "bunnet" at the Linwood engineering works on the day that he joined Motherwell in 1965 is related in the excellent Rhapsody In Green by Woods and Campbell (published 1990) and has never been denied. Yet he is adamant that St Mirren were the team that he loved as a boy.

He was a player whose career was going nowhere fast in the autumn of 1971. Aged 25, he had been with Motherwell for five years, but had been plagued by injury and a bad disciplinary record. He was a fine player, capable of scoring goals, but performing in a Motherwell team whose performances were mediocre, to put it kindly. He did also have a reputation for self-indulgence, a matter which became obvious when he was once dropped for a game against Aberdeen in 1971 because he "overslept". He might have earned a transfer to Rangers in 1968, but the Ibrox men, deterred presumably by his bad disciplinary record, went to Hibs for Colin Stein instead. In 1971 his career was fizzling out to a premature ending, so much so that he was considering emigration, reckoning that in Scotland he was a marked man in the eyes of referees.

He might even have gone to Celtic earlier, had Jock Stein not decided to go to Hearts for Willie Wallace instead. This was on 6 December 1966. On 10 December, when Wallace made his debut at Parkhead, the visitors were Motherwell. The 40,000 crowd were happy with their banners of "Oor Wullie" to celebrate Wallace's arrival, and saw a good Celtic side beat Motherwell 4-2. They would hardly have noticed that a Motherwell man called Deans was sent off after a tussle with Jimmy Johnstone, and they would certainly never have guessed that this insignificant youth would one day become one of their greatest legends.

The catalyst for Dixie's transfer was the shocking League Cup final on 23 October against Partick Thistle. This 4-1 win for Thistle was one of the most famous games in Scottish football history, peppered with myths like the Rangers supporters departing Ibrox at half-time in order to be at Hampden at the end to gloat. Anyone with a knowledge of Glasgow geography and transport on a Saturday afternoon will realise the logistic impossibility of all this, but the myth persists.

Certainly, however, it was a shocker. It was caused by two factors. One was the absence through injury of Billy McNeill and the other was sheer complacency, both in the defence and in the attack. Stein may well have regretted his precipitate decision to offload Willie Wallace and John Hughes to Crystal Palace, but he decided that something had to be done to shock Tommy Callaghan and Harry Hood, whose contribution in the League Cup final had been, to say the least, disappointing. No second-half comeback had happened, and new blood was required.

Dixie Deans was the target. By the following Saturday, the Celtic team bus arrived back from a lacklustre 1-0 win at Ayr to find Dixie Deans waiting at Parkhead to sign. Dixie hadn't been playing for Motherwell that day because he was serving a six-week suspension, a factor which had no doubt helped to reduce the transfer fee to £17,500. Celtic fans were glad to see that Stein was taking action after the humiliation of the League Cup final, but they were possibly a little underwhelmed by what they knew about Dixie Deans. A stocky, chunky sort of character who could score a few goals for Motherwell, certainly, but he didn't always look fit and he clearly had a bad disciplinary record. At 5 feet 7 inches, he also lacked height for a centre forward, it was felt.

Apparently Celtic were breaking some sort of regulation by signing a player who was under suspension, and were fined the not particularly inordinate amount of £50 for this breach of regulations. Clearly Stein thought that it was worthwhile, but he was determined that from now on, Deans' discipline, both with referees and in the wider sense, would improve. This was a success, for Deans was never ordered off with Celtic, apart from once in a reserve game towards the end of his Parkhead stay and when he was sorely provoked.

STEIN WAS JUST THE right type of manager for Dixie. Jock's strict, even obsessive teetotalism was exactly what was required for a man who might have strayed in the company of some of the wilder elements of the Celtic team. Deans, indeed, had an early taste of Stein. Even though he was not eligible to play, Dixie was taken to Malta the following midweek to soak in the atmosphere of Celtic playing a European tie, and to get to know the other players. If Deans had ever thought that he was in for a good time on the Mediterranean island, he was quickly disabused of the notion. He was made to train hard with the rest of the squad, and the night before the game, the social event of the trip consisted of being taken to the cinema where all the players were seated in one row, with trainer Neil Mochan at one end and the stern Jock Stein at the other. This was to make sure that nothing other than orange juice and Coca-Cola were consumed during the showing of the western Eldorado. Even a visit to the toilet was looked upon with grave suspicion!

It is often said that Stein could spot a good striker. He had less success with goal-keepers, but in the forward line, he had already chosen well with Willie Wallace and Harry Hood, and Dixie, he felt, might be what Celtic required. Deans would provide strength and aggression in the forward line, team up with the young but fast-developing Kenny Dalglish, and provide a foil for Jimmy Johnstone, with whom he would develop a friendship and affinity. In the meantime, however, the priority during what remained of Dixie's suspension was to get himself fit. This would be achieved by the strict but enjoyable training regime for which Stein and his worthy assistants, Sean Fallon and Neil Mochan, were famous.

His suspension served, Dixie played his first game for Celtic on 27 November and scored a late and irrelevant goal in a 5-1 tanking at Firhill of Partick Thistle, ironically the team which unwittingly provoked his arrival. From then on, he was a regular goalscorer that season, slotting in perfectly with the rest of the forwards, and almost instantly earning the love of the Celtic fans for his wholehearted approach to the game. He may have worried that "going to the wrong kind of school" might have alienated some Celtic fans from him. This was, and always had been, rubbish. Celtic fans will always accept as one of their own a player who gives his all for the club.

He scored in his next five games, one against Kilmarnock, two against East Fife, one against his old team-mates at Motherwell, then one against Hearts during a Merry Christmas followed by two against Clyde to make it a Happy New Year. The New Year of 1972 would bring immortality to Dixie Deans for the right reasons and for the wrong reasons, but it was already clear to Celtic fans that Jock Stein had turned up trumps once again in his choice of striker.

Celtic won the League very comfortably in season 1971/72 for the seventh year in a row, thus beating the record set by the great Edwardian Celts from 1905 to 1910. The actual winning of the title was at East Fife on 15 April, although another four games yet remained to be played. Dixie scored two that day, and his celebrations at Methil showed that there was, indeed, a great relationship between the player and the fans. He had played a great part in the club's success and Jock Stein was fulsome in his praise of his prolific goalscorer.

But Dixie's relationship with the fans would soon be put to the test, only four days after the capturing of the Scottish League. It was one of the most memorable nights in Glasgow's long football history, but for Dixie it was memorable for all the wrong reasons. It was the night when two European semi-final second Legs were bring played in the city (such was the strength of Scottish football in 1972) – Celtic against Inter Milan in the European Cup, and Rangers against Bayern Munich in the Cup Winners' Cup. Rangers duly won through, but for Celtic it was all frustration.

"Stalemate" and "war of attrition" were the phrases used, as the two teams who had drawn 0-0 in the San Siro also drew 0-0 at Parkhead, even after extra time, neither team having been able to pierce the other's defence. Deans, often under-employed by Stein in European football, was only brought on late in the game for the tiring Kenny Dalglish. Arguably, Stein made a mistake there, because if Dixie had been on from the start he might just have upset the tight Italian defence. As it was, with the nation and the continent watching on televi-sion, the game went to Parkhead's and Celtic's first penalty shoot-out in a major tournament.

Ten players took penalties. Mazzola, Facchetti, Frustalupi, Pellizzaro and Jair did the business for the Italians, as did Craig, Johnstone, McCluskey and Murdoch for Celtic, while Deans was the only man who missed. He took Celtic's first penalty but sent the ball over the bar, not "ballooned" as some glory-hunting newspapers said, but over the bar nevertheless. How Dixie suffered on that dreadful night of 19 April 1972, particularly when some morons in the crowd booed and jeered him. The emphasis is on "some" morons, as the rest of the Parkhead crowd were sympathetically, albeit silently, supportive.

Naturally the Rangers fans enjoyed this – understandably for they had had little else to cheer about for many years – but so too did some of the Scottish media, with all sorts of jokes about how Houston Space Centre had phoned Parkhead to say that they had got the ball, and a particularly unkind ditty based on Jesus Christ Superstar went along the lines of:

"Dixie Deans, Superstar
Kicked the ball over the Inter bar".

It is the easiest thing in the world to miss a penalty. One could make a long list of players, particularly Celtic players, who have missed penalties at crucial times. Dixie's sad miss prevented Celtic's third appearance in a European Cup final, this time against Ajax of Amsterdam. One recalls the distraught Paul McStay in the League Cup final of 1994, and in 2006 Gary Caldwell, Kenny Miller and Evander Sno all missed penalties in a League Cup penalty shoot-out against Falkirk. And, of course, World Cups have been won and lost on penalty shoot-outs. It is the sort of thing that can ruin careers, and it is certainly a circumstance that will take a great deal of living down, particularly when the media refuse to allow the matter to go away.

But Dixie had the character to come back. He actually made the matter go away, thereby relieving a great deal of pain and hurt from himself and the Celtic fans. In the first place, on the following Saturday before a cheering crowd, Dixie scored twice against his old team Motherwell in a 5-2 win. Celtic were awarded two penalties. On both occasions, the crowd chanted his name, wanting him to exorcise the ghost of Wednesday night, but Bobby Murdoch did the needful on both occasions as Dixie politely declined.

BUT IT WAS ON 6 May 1972, only two and a half weeks after Dixie's European nightmare, that immortality beckoned. The Celtic team in the late 1960s and early 1970s were openly being compared to what was generally reckoned to be Scotland's greatest ever team, namely Willie Maley's Edwardian Celts of Adams, McNair and Weir; Young Loney and Hay; Bennett, McMenemy, Quinn, Somers and Hamilton.. Now, in a very real sense, was there an opportunity to mention Dixie Deans in the same breath as the immortal Jimmy Quinn!

It was the Scottish Cup final against Hibs, a fine team in those days with Stanton, Brownlie, Blackley, Edwards and others. Dixie scored a hat-trick against them. Only Jimmy Quinn had done that before in a Scottish Cup final, and even Jimmy's ghost would have marvelled at Dixie that day. There are times in Celtic's history that some unseen power seems to be at work. Billy McNeill claims that Dixie had said the night before that he fancied himself to score a hat-trick, and that if he did, he would do a somersault. He did both.

The first and third goals of the hat-trick were superb, good, strikers' goals showing his strength and accuracy, but "divine" is hardly too strong a word to describe his second. He rounded goalkeeper Jim Herriot, seemed to lose the ball, then regained it, beat Herriot again, then another defender, and slammed home before doing the famous somersault which endeared him even more to the exultant green-and-white hordes behind that King's Park goal. Fortunately, in this age of videos and DVDs, this goal can be enjoyed time and time again.

Jimmy Quinn's Scottish Cup final hat-trick had happened as long ago as 1904 in a 3-2 victory over Rangers. In addition, it was claimed half-heartedly that a few players had done the same in the 19th century, including Sandy McMahon in 1892 (depending on how one reads the newspaper reports) but these claims were difficult to prove. Quinn's was for definite, while great strikers like Jimmy McGrory had failed to emulate that feat. Now, in 1972, there could be no argument – Celtic had another Cup final hat-trick hero to boast about.

Dixie scored 27 goals for Celtic that season, more than one per game, but it was that hat-trick in their famous 6-1 win over Hibs to win the Scottish Cup for the 22nd time which erased from most memories his penalty miss. Not only that, but Dixie had also made everyone forget the Partick Thistle fiasco, and one wonders what the people in Motherwell thought of all this. A fee of £17,500 hardly made up for what they were missing.

In the following season, he hit the net 32 times. That term, 1972/73, saw the narrowest title win of the famous nine in a row. A rebuilt Rangers side, winners of the European Cup Winners' Cup in 1972, pushed Celtic hard, and it was often Dixie Deans who would notch the vital goal, frequently at crucial times of the game when the opposition were threatening to equalise, or even go ahead. Many goals were simply the tap-ins of a born poacher, but Deans could head a goal, had a devastating shot and, surprisingly for a man of his build, had an unexpected turn of speed.

Round about February, Celtic were suffering from a crisis of confidence. This was obvious in a game at East Fife in which three separate players – Dixie was not one of them – missed penalties. As a result East Fife were winning 2-1, but just at the death, Dixie appeared on the right to beat his defender and score the goal which gave Celtic a crucial point. As spring arrived Celtic's last seven League games were all won. Just as well, as Rangers were breathing down their necks. Apart from the game against St Johnstone in which Deans was injured, he scored in every one of them.

As the season reached its breathtaking climax, Deans scored twice in the game at a packed, and not particularly well behaved Easter Road, and the title was clinched. The first was in the first half, he helped Dalglish score a second, then Dixie himself scored the goal which induced sheer delirium as the fans celebrated Celtic's eighth successive League championship, and turned Edinburgh green and white. On the train back from Edinburgh that night, fans sang:

"Is it true what they say about Dixie?
Does the sun really shine on him?"
or the less wordy:
"Oh, Dixie, Dixie, Dixie,
Dixie Dixie Dixie Deans."

But if there was euphoria about the Scottish League, there was unhappiness in all three Cup competitions that year. Injuries to Dixie – a bustling centre-forward like Dixie is always likely to pick up knocks – robbed Celtic of his services on two vital occasions. On 4 November against Dundee United, Deans was substituted by Harry Hood, and the slight injury to Deans persuaded Stein to go for a defensive formation on the following Wednesday against Uijpest Dosza in Hungary – a type of game for which Celtic are temperamentally unsuited when guarding a narrow 2-1 lead – and Deans was only brought on when the damage was done. Had he been fit, Stein might have gone for an early away goal to ease the pressure. As it was, Celtic simply did not cope with the loss of an early goal, and never came to terms with the game.

There was a similar tale of woe in the League Cup final where Celtic faced Hibs on the ridiculous date of 9 December 1972, far too late in the year for a major Cup final. It would have been nice to see Dixie's hat-trick heroics of May repeated in the winter gloom. However, he had been taken off in the 6-0 defeat of Dumbarton the previous week, and was not risked for the final in which the good Hibs team got their revenge over a Celtic side deprived of their main striker, and relying too much on the as-yet-unripened talents of Kenny Dalglish to do the needful.

Hopes that Deans might reproduce his hat-trick in the 1972 Scottish Cup final a year later were to prove unfounded against Rangers on 5 May 1973. Deans had a fine game, and indeed the rest of the Celtic team had little reason to reproach themselves, but it was Rangers who scored three against Celtic's two – and the Celts were just a little short of luck at vital points of the game. So 1972/73 came to a close with only the Scottish League on the sideboard. This was actually considered a failure!

The following season, 1973/74, Dixie even made Jimmy McGrory tremble, but with anticipation rather than fear. Jimmy had held the record for goals scored in a single match since 1928, when he had notched eight against Dunfermline. On 17 November 1973 in a game against Partick Thistle, as "Dixie! Dixie!" resounded around Parkhead, Dixie scored six, and frankly, it might have been more. McGrory, watching from the stand, would have been delighted to see his record broken, but it was "just" six. In a rare and perhaps unprecedented burst of extravagance, the Parkhead "biscuit tin economy" allowed Dixie to keep the ball and perhaps even provided the pen for the players of both sides to sign it!

The enthusiasm engendered by this fine performance had a touch of escapism about it, for late 1973 was a difficult time for the world. A Middle East war led to the price of oil being quadrupled and there was a threat of petrol rationing. In the meantime US President Richard Nixon, around whom the noose was tightening for his role in the burglary of his political opponents' office, namely Watergate, showed every sign of cracking, putting his troops on a low-key state of nuclear alert. If this was not enough, the miners in Great Britain were on an overtime ban and threatening an all-out strike against the Conservative government. Football, and the goalscoring talent of Dixie Deans, provided some sort of welcome relief. But even in that area, the crowds were dwindling, possibly as a protest at the poor facilities and the problem of hooliganism, which no-one seemed prepared or even willing to tackle.

Dixie was injured in a League Cup quarter-final at Pittodrie, and the tragedy was that he did not recover quickly enough to be fit for the final against Dundee. Thus for the second year in a row, Celtic went into a League Cup final without their star striker. For the second year in a row they lost, this time in the surreal atmosphere of a virtually deserted Hampden, hardly assisted by an unplayable pitch and a kick-off at 1.30 pm so that floodlights would not have to be used in the energy shortage. The Scottish League persisted in their moronic belief that December was a good month for a Cup final.

He celebrated his return with four goals against Falkirk on 22 December and from then on played his full part as Celtic surged to their ninth League title in a row, this time with remarkable ease as their challengers Aberdeen, Hibs and Rangers all collapsed woefully. Dixie also won his second Scottish Cup medal that season in a campaign in which he made three notable contributions – a hat trick against Clydebank which included the first goal scored in Scottish football on a Sunday, the only goal of a tight contest with his old mates Motherwell in a replayed quarter-final, and a goal almost at the death in the Scottish Cup final to make it 3-0 against an outclassed and overawed Dundee United.

EUROPE WAS A DISAPPOINTMENT. A tense and spirited performance against the Swiss club Basle saw Celtic through to the semi-final against Atletico Madrid. On one of European football's saddest nights, the Spanish side kicked Celtic off the park, being prepared to lose three men in the circumstances. Sadly their tactics worked, as Celtic were so put off by the violent tactics that they could not score, and the first leg finished 0-0. Deans did not play in the return leg, and the intimidated Celtic went down 0-2 in Madrid.

Deans scored 33 goals that season, and it remains a sore point that Scotland's manager Willie Ormond did not employ him in the World Cup finals of 1974. Perhaps Ormond felt that Dixie's disciplinary record counted against him, but Celtic supporters were mystified, particularly when Scotland went out, simply because they did not score enough goals that summer. It is hard to believe that the presence of Dixie would not have helped. Possibly he was a tad slow for international football, but on the other hand he was an unorthodox striker who might well have unsettled the Brazilians. It is certainly true, one feels, that had Deans been playing against Zaire, the goalscoring tally would not have been restricted to two.

Finally, he was given two Scottish caps the following season. He played well enough against East Germany at Hampden in October but fatally did not score in the 3-0 win. Then when Scotland lost the next game to Spain, Dixie was substituted halfway through the second period, was subsequently made one of the scapegoats by the press, and was never picked again. Dixie himself also felt that there was the influence of Jock Stein, who as Celtic's manager was never too keen on his players risking injury with Scotland.

It was often Hibs who bore the brunt of Dixie's scoring talent. He earned the title "the Hammer of the Hibs". Indeed, he scored 19 times against that good Hibs defence in 14 appearances, saying that he did not "like the green jersey". Significantly, when Hibs beat Celtic in the League Cup final of December 1972, Dixie was not playing. But he had another hat-trick to dish out to them in a Cup final, this time the League Cup final of autumn 1974. Two of the goals were strikes to be proud of, but one of them was truly phenomenal. A corner-kick came to Jimmy Johnstone at the edge of the penalty box. Jimmy drove hard for goal, the ball cannoned off a defender at full speed, and Dixie catapulted forward to head home the deflection. Exactly how quick Dixie's reactions must have been, we do not know, but the reactions of the crowd were a little slower. There was definitely a split second on the terracing before the fans could actually believe what they had just seen.

A feature of that game was the understanding he displayed with Jimmy Johnstone. Indeed, they were very similar characters, neither of them exactly choirboys on the field or off it, but both with a heart of gold and both rejoicing in a tremendous rapport with the adoring Celtic fans, who chanted "Jinkie" and "Dixie" ad infinitum that crisp autumn day as Celtic lifted the Scottish League Cup. Dixie made a point on that occasion of talking to Joe Harper of Hibs. Like Dixie, Joe had scored a hat-trick that day, but poor Joe had ended up on the wrong end of a 6-3 scoreline.

IT WOULD TURN OUT to be Dixie's last big day. Injury plagued him during the 1974/75 season. He missed the Scottish Cup final against Airdrie, dropped to his intense disappointment in favour of Paul Wilson, and that was the campaign in which Celtic finally lost the League championship which had been theirs since 1966. All good things must come to an end, but the feeling was frequently expressed that if Dixie had played more games than his 18, the championship might well have been retained for yet another year, thus establishing a world record of ten in a row. He missed, for example, the crucial New Year game at Ibrox when Rangers won 3-0, and the game at Pittodrie when Celtic slid to a 2-3 defeat. On several occasions, he played only half a game, having to be withdrawn because of injury or the loss of form and fitness that being injured often brings. Europe, too, was a disappointment that year, with Celtic going out as early as October to a Greek team, Olympiacos, with whom the better Parkhead combination of a few years previously would have wiped the floor.

In the summer of 1975 Jock Stein was involved in an horrendous road accident, which he was lucky to survive. Thus he was out of action for a year. This was clearly a problem for Celtic, and particularly so for Dixie Deans, who lacked the firm guidance of Big Jock. Captain Billy McNeill had also retired. Assistant manager Sean Fallon tried hard, but something had gone from Celtic. The moment had passed, the magic had evaporated and Dixie was part of the general Celtic decline in 1975/76, the season in which Rangers won a treble that they would hardly have hoped to achieve over a sterner Celtic side.

Deans was unlucky to miss through injury the League Cup final, and he would surely have made a difference to that dysfunctional Celtic forward line in the 0-1 defeat. Following the defeat in the Scottish Cup in January to Motherwell, the decline was steep, with Deans scoring only two goals (one of them a penalty) for the rest of the season. In the summer of 1976, Deans was off to Luton Town for £20,000 and then he played fitfully for Partick Thistle and Carlisle, and had a spell in Australia.

He will always be remembered, however, for his brief but phenomenally successful spell with Celtic. Indeed, it is salutary to remember that he played for less than five seasons as a Celt. He did seem to have been around for a great deal longer than that. He scored 125 goals for Celtic, many of them great individual efforts, more of them through the striker's predatory instinct of being in the right place at the right time. He had speed, determination and strength – some of these qualities not immediately obvious from his somewhat chunky frame.

The memory will always remain of Dixie's characteristic celebration, with arms raised and fist clenched, in the style of a Victorian boxer who had just knocked out an opponent. Perhaps he did not start off life as a Celt, but he very soon became one, acknowledged, accepted and admired. It was just as well, maybe, that Partick Thistle did win that dreadful League Cup final of 1971, otherwise Dixie Deans might have slowly disappeared onto the sunset, perhaps to Australia, but certainly to oblivion. He had much for which to be thankful to Jock Stein. But then again, we all have.

ROY AITKEN

'THE BEAR'

1975-1990

BHOYS CAREER

Games	667
Goals	55
Caps	57

MAGIC MOMENT

The 1985 Scottish Cup final; with Celtic 0-1 down to Dundee United, Roy was moved from the defence to the dysfunctional midfield, took the game by the scruff of the neck, and won the Cup for Celtic.

ROBERT "Roy" Aitken was, by no means, Celtic's best ever player, but there was never any doubt about his commitment, determination and leadership. He fought, he battled, he scrapped and he won more often than not - and in football these qualities are inestimable. In the 15 years that Roy was at Parkhead, from 1975 until 1990, his influence was decisive on many occasions. He led the team to many successes but also steered them through many troubles in the 1980s, until in 1990 things eventually got too much for him. His departure in the early part of that year was sad, and a certain amount of Celtic left with Roy Aitken.

The departure needs to be analysed. Roy left his spiritual home in a cloud of unhappiness, alleging all sorts of unfair treatment at the hands of referees, media and his critics on the terracing. Referees are referees, and a totally committed player like Roy Aitken is often liable to be in trouble. As we shall see, the 1984 Scottish Cup final against Aberdeen involved a piece of over-reaction from a referee to a robust challenge from Roy, who saw a red card five times in his Celtic career. The media were frequently on his back. In particular, there was a none-too-subtle personality clash between himself and journalist Gerry McNee, who saw fit to single Roy out for a few disappointing performances for Scotland and lost no opportunity to do Roy down.

Yet referees and the media, like the poor, are always with us. It was the third source of Roy's problems, the boo boys on the Parkhead terracings, which caused the most distress. To an outsider the thought of the wholehearted Aitken being jeered by his own fans was more than a little incomprehensible. True, Roy could be careless and his ball distribution was not always of the best, but these were honest errors, such as could be made by anyone. Why then did the Parkhead crowd, in that awful season of 1989/90, turn on Roy, someone who was so recognisable as one of their own, and to whom they owed so much?

THE ANSWER CAN ONLY be seen in the context of what had happened at Celtic Park in the previous year and a half. The centenary season, 1987/88, had been a great experience for the Celtic fans as a League and Cup double had been landed. Aitken had not only been part of that, he had driven Celtic to it, rescuing lost causes, and cajoling, bullying and forcing the rest of the team to perform. "The man's unbelievable" said Paul McStay.

Things had looked good in that glorious summer of 1988 as the Glasgow Garden Festival, within spitting distance of Ibrox, had featured Celtic flowerbeds to commemorate 100 glorious years of the club, in the same way that the Empire Exhibition of 1938 (and its trophy that Celtic had won) had done so much to typify the first great 50 years. The future had looked fine. Sadly it did not work out that way, as Celtic suffered a major setback early in the following season with a 1-5 defeat at Ibrox. Defeats, even 1-5 defeats, had been sustained before and had been got over. This one was different, though, because the team plunged into a lethargy and depression which could not be understood or rationally explained. Bright hopes of Europe were dashed, any League challenge fizzled out piteously, and what was more and more apparent was that Celtic FC were in the hands of people who seemed to lack the will or the resources to tackle Murray and Souness's millions at Ibrox.

There had been one bright moment in the winning of the 1989 Scottish Cup, a 1-0 victory over Rangers. Roy had played well that day and it had been he who had collected the Scottish Cup for the 29th time in the club's history, the TV cameras catching him winking to a fan in the crowd as he ascended the steps. But it had been no accident that the one isolated and spectacular success, however welcome, had come on the one weekend of 1989 when Celtic had, politically and diplomatically, seemed to get the better of Rangers. It was the day after Maurice Johnston had declared himself a Celtic player. He said he was glad to be back and, yes, famously, he described the Celts as "the only team I ever wanted to play for". A month or so later, Johnston had joined Rangers, to the fury of the Celtic fans and to the visible distress of the Celtic players, Aitken as much as anyone.

So at the start of season 1989/90, Celtic supporters were pessimistic and unhappy. That their mood was justified was soon apparent when on two successive midweeks in September, Celtic crashed out of the League Cup and European competition. For both these disasters, Aitken must take a share of the blame. In the semi-final of the League Cup against Aberdeen, Roy was sent off for over-commitment and a certain amount of rashness. That was bad enough, but worse came the following Wednesday night when Celtic went out of Europe to Partisan Belgrade on away goals when the final aggregate score was 6-6. The defence was non-existent at times, and it was the old, old story of naïve defending. Fingers were justifiably pointed at Roy that night.

Thus as winter approached, gloom was the order of the day. There was the odd good result to show what life might have been like, but the main fare was mediocrity and poor defending. Everyone knew that Rangers were going to win the League. The fault lay with the Celtic directors, who had singularly failed to invest in the team. In fact, we were seeing the first stages of the disasters that were to lead to the board's ignominious collapse in 1994, but the fans, embittered and disappointed in the events of the past 18 months, were looking for someone closer at hand than the distant directors. Roy's unfortunate run of form came at exactly the wrong time.

There was too, it must be said, an element of paranoia in Roy's attitude about all this. Although there was an element of "Roy must go" in some of the support, particularly those who wrote volubly and persuasively in Celtic fanzines, the majority of the support still wanted him to stay. Disappointment at what was seen as a temporary loss of form was certainly not the same as wanting him to leave the club. The complaints of a friend are very different from the invectives of an enemy, after all. But for one reason or another, Roy decided that enough was enough and went off to Newcastle United in January 1990, leaving a support even more bewildered and upset than previously.

THE SUPPORTERS HAD EVERY reason to remember Roy Aitken's Celtic career with pride and gratitude. He had served the team for well over a decade. He had never given less than total commitment. There had been at least two games in which Roy's performance had been the difference between victory and defeat. One such occasion was the Scottish Cup final of 1985. It was in this game that we saw, not for the first time, the true grit of Roy Aitken. It is necessary to examine this game in perspective.

The previous two years had been disastrous. Since the departure of Charlie Nicholas, then manager Billy McNeill in 1983, Celtic had struggled. 1984 was George Orwell's vision of a dreadful impersonal world in which Big Brother watched everyone, and 1984 for Celtic was scarcely any better. Two Cup finals were lost, one affecting Aitken intimately; Celtic were cheated out of Europe by a dreadful outfit called Rapid Vienna, and in both 1983/84 and 1984/85, Celtic finished up second best to Alex Ferguson's Aberdeen in the Scottish League.

There remained the 1985 Scottish Cup final to save the job of manager Davie Hay and, indeed, the Celtic careers of many players. The opposition were Dundee United, Jim McLean's well drilled and boringly effective side, who knew how to kill a game once they went ahead. Early in the second half, this was exactly what happened, with Aitken at least partly to blame for Dundee United's goal.

The second half continued with Celtic, predictably, unable to break down the Tannadice men's stubborn defence. Hampden had lapsed into brooding, introverted silence, the green colours and favours sagging in tune with the fading hearts. The songs of triumph were no longer heard, even the anthems of defiance had disappeared. Watches were looked at, and a few of the weaker brethren were beginning to think of an early departure.

Tommy Burns had already been taken off, and with only 15 minutes to go, Davie Hay took a desperate gamble. He took off Paul McStay and replaced him with the little known defender Pierce O'Leary. This move flummoxed the TV and radio commentators until the lumbering frame of Roy Aitken was seen to be moving forward to the centre of the field. The supporters booed at the loss of Paul McStay (in truth, it had not been one of Paul's better performances) and Davie Hay was reviled even more than he had been previously. His predecessor and successor as Celtic manager, Billy McNeill, in the BBC commentary box said: "There are times when a manager just has to be unpopular . . . he's gambling now".

Aitken's arrival in the midfield immediately galvanised the dysfunctional Celtic side. Within a minute, a free-kick had been won on the edge of the penalty box. Davie Provan took it and scored. Aitken was now like a man possessed as he charged about the Hampden turf, shouting, cajoling, encouraging, gesticulating. Five minutes remained when Aitken picked up a loose ball on the right, made ground and crossed a ball right on to the head of Frank McGarvey to win the Scottish Cup for Celtic.

It was very definitely Aitken's Cup and he revelled in it all, speaking in that fast staccato way of his ("he speaks as if someone had stuck a red-hot poker up his bum" a veteran supporter said) to the reporters and TV commentators, as the supporters sang his praise. "Look round the stadium and see what this Cup means for Celtic" said Roy. But the previous year it had been a totally different story.

Aitken had been sent off. It was not the first nor the last time in his Parkhead career, but this dismissal was high-profile, controversial and, in view of later events, redolent with irony. The Scottish Cup final of 1984 was played between Celtic and League champions Aberdeen. The Dons, under Alex Ferguson, were tough and brutally professional, not without a touch of cynicism. The referee was Bob Valentine of Dundee, the same referee who had awarded Celtic a crucial penalty in Aitken's first Cup final, in 1977 against Rangers, and who was so unpopular with Rangers supporters as a result that he was called "Bob Vatican".

The game was, as one would have expected, fast and furious. Aberdeen went ahead through Eric Black, a goal which video evidence would indicate had at least two things wrong with it. Celtic were clearly nursing a sense of grievance as half-time approached, as a few other decisions seemed to be going against them. Aberdeen broke and the ball came to Mark McGhee. Aitken crashed into him. It was a foul, and possibly even a yellow card for Aitken's over-enthusiasm, but McGhee knew what he was doing and stayed down. At this point, Gordon Strachan appeared on the scene, told McGhee to stay down and persuaded Valentine that the tackle was worth a red card. Valentine obliged and Roy walked.

One could not, in all honesty, say that Valentine was outrageously wrong in his decision, but in a Cup final a little discretion might have been used. The decision gave the Scottish Cup to Aberdeen, because although Celtic, even without the inspirational Aitken, fought bravely and equalised in the 90th minute, Aberdeen's 11 men were too much for Celtic's ten in extra time. McGhee, having marvellously recovered after seeming half dead an hour previously, scored the winner. The sight of him charging up the field in triumph was particularly difficult for the lovers of Roy Aitken.

It was only the first in a series of ironies. McGhee joined Celtic some 18 months later, Aitken himself joined Aberdeen as player and manager a decade or so down the line, and then two decades on Gordon Strachan became manager of Celtic. Bob Valentine retired, became a referee supervisor and is generally regarded (rightly) as being one of Scotland's better referees. Those of us, however, who loved Roy Aitken felt that Bob Valentine may have made a mistake that day.

This was the only Scottish Cup final that Roy lost. He pocketed a winner's medal in 1977, 1980, 1985, 1988 and 1989, in each game playing a heroic part. Three of his victories were against Rangers, nerve-tingling games for the supporters, but Aitken was a man who seldom showed the slightest sign of nerves. The 1989 Cup final was coming to an end with Celtic holding on grimly to a 1-0 lead. Aitken, by now the captain of the team, had won a free-kick near the Rangers corner flag. The Celtic end fully expected that he would hold on to the ball, possibly trying to win a corner, but suddenly Aitken belted the ball over the touchline to give Rangers a goal kick.

For a while, the Celtic fans wondered if he had taken leave of his senses, but then realisation dawned that it was all to win Celtic more time. It took a while for the ballboys to get the ball back. By that time Aitken himself was back on the halfway line to marshall the defence and crucially to win the ball. Had he not done that, he might have lost possession and he himself would have been stranded down by the corner flag while Rangers might have run up and scored.

A year previously, Roy had received the Scottish Cup from Prime Minister Margaret Thatcher after beating Dundee United in a replica of the 1985 Cup final. In 1988, of course, Celtic celebrated their centenary, and how fitting it was that Roy Aitken led the club to a glorious double. Mrs Thatcher, not exactly the most loved Prime Minister in Glasgow, had bravely attended the game – say what you want about the old dear, but she did not lack courage – and stooped briefly as she handed the Cup to Roy Aitken. It was a fine moment, but one had to spare a thought for a man who had managed to wangle for himself a hospitality ticket and was seated yards away from the Cup presentation. You see, not only did he support Rangers, but he was also a member of the Labour Party. Margaret and Roy were not a good combination for him!

ROY, (OR TO GIVE him his proper name, Robert) was born in 1958 and joined Celtic in 1975. He was a talented young man gifted in other things as well as football. He was a more than competent piano player, having gained a diploma from the London Royal Academy of Music, a body which did not exactly throw its diplomas around like confetti. He was also a basketball player, having captained his school St Andrews Academy, Saltcoats, to victory in the Scottish championships of 1973 and represented Great Britain schoolboys at that sport.

Jock Stein had been very impressed by the youngster, but it was not Jock who gave him his debut in September 1975. The manager had been involved in a nasty road accident in the summer of 1975 and was out of action for a year. Thus it was Sean Fallon who was in charge, and Roy made his debut for the first team at the unlikely venue of Ochilview Park, Stenhousemuir, in a League Cup game in September 1975. It was in February of the following year that Roy became a regular. It was an unfortunate season for Celtic, as they were in transition, and had no Jock Stein. They had already gone out of the Scottish Cup and the Scottish League Cup, and stuttered badly towards the end of the League campaign. It was the first year since 1964 that Celtic had ended the season trophyless.

A certain amount of humour in an otherwise grim experience was engendered in the trip to East Berlin to play Sachsenring Zwickau. Aitken, not yet 18 and still a schoolboy, was technically a minor and the very strict East Germans, ever worried about things like child abduction, insisted that the young man was "adopted" by Sean Fallon!

Yet even though 1975/76 was a dismal season, Aitken was young enough to learn. He made his mistakes, but these were forgiven by the Parkhead crowd, who sensed that in this youngster Celtic may have found someone special. He was tall (and one could see why he was good at basketball) but he was not unduly thin, and he looked as if he wanted to play the game and to play it well. It was immediately apparent to opponents that the young Roy Aitken was no pushover who could be easily bullied. He could tackle courageously and fiercely.

It was the following season that made Roy Aitken. Jock Stein came back and liked what he saw in the strapping Ayrshire lad. Jock also had one of his brainwaves in going to Hibs for the ageing but still superbly organised Pat Stanton. It was Stanton's job to prevent goals being scored, thus allowing Aitken to move further forward. All through Aitken's career, he could play either in defence or in a more aggressive midfield position. Jock decided that, at this stage, Aitken was a better midfielder.

There were disappointments in the early stages of the season in the shape of a European exit and a gallingly unlucky defeat in the League Cup Final to Ally MacLeod's Aberdeen. But slowly the Celtic team took shape and soon after New Year they began to exert dominance. Aitken had played brilliantly in a 4-3 win over Hearts in November at Tynecastle, and soon afterwards one began to hear the Celtic fans calling him "The Bear". He was so called because of his size and his frizzy hair, presumably, and he was flattered to have the same nickname as John Hughes. Less pleasant or wholesome were the words of the song:

Feed The Bear, The Bear, He's every f***in' where, Feed the Bear!

But no-one judged Roy by the inanity of the words of his song. They were far more impressed by his play.

That Aitken had arrived as a true Celtic great and cult hero was proved by his superb performances against Rangers in 1977. On 11 January, he pulled off a magnificent goal-line clearance at Parkhead to deny Rangers a draw, and then he scored both goals at Ibrox on 19 March to earn Celtic a 2-2 draw. This was the game that Rangers really needed to win to give themselves any kind of chance in the League race. It was fast and furious, as such games invariably are and should be, and in this case moronic crowd behaviour added to the cocktail of tension and excitement.

Rangers had gone ahead 2-1 with ten minutes to go. A certain amount of ill feeling had been engendered by what looked like a foul on Celtic's goalkeeper Peter Latchford, and there had been a pitch invasion by the less well educated elements from the Celtic end. After a delay in which the police and the Celtic management team persuaded everyone to resume their places, Celtic won a free-kick. Johnny Doyle took it and Aitken was on hand to hammer home.

The BBC footage of that goal is priceless. It was scored at the Rangers end of the ground. The backdrop was one of blue scarves in the air and throaty singing. The ball hits the back of the net and the terracing behind the goal goes immediately and deathly quiet as the blue scarves come down and are stuffed into coat pockets as complaints about the inadequacy of the Rangers team take over. A gleeful shout of "No Defenders" permeates the Glasgow air from Celtic throats and Aitken is feted as the new hero.

The League championship was won, as was the Scottish Cup in 1977 in an Old Firm Final. This was no showpiece occasion, however, in the Hampden rain. Once Celtic went ahead, they defended with fierce determination and stern concentration. Aitken's role was an unspectacular one, but the game itself was anything but spectacular. It was Celtic, however, who collected the Scottish Cup for the 25th time, and Aitken now had his first Scottish Cup winner's medal.

Next season would see the other side of the coin. It would be a salutary lesson for the young Aitken that success, even at a club like Celtic, does not come automatically. Celtic shot themselves in the foot even before the season started by selling Kenny Dalglish, a blow from which they never recovered. Stein, perhaps feeling guilty at the blunder he had committed, lapsed into what looked to all outsiders very like a depressive illness, and Celtic never really got going that season. Injuries came early on as well, and at one point Aitken was made captain as most of those bought to replace Dalglish flopped miserably.

That the young Aitken was not yet up to the captain's job was proved in the infamous Scottish Cup tie at Kilmarnock, in which he was sent off. A few days after that, just to prove that it never rains but it pours, Celtic lost the League Cup final to a Rangers team who were scarcely their superiors but who managed a goal in extra time, putting an end to a game universally described as mediocre.

Had 1978 been a more successful season for Celtic, Aitken might well have made it to Argentina for the World Cup. He probably did well to avoid that disaster, and his moments of Scotland glory were not far away, but for the present, he took all the misfortunes on the chin and buckled down to his task. It seemed likely that 1978/79 would be a similar dismal flop for Celtic, until the very end of the season when Roy took charge and played his greatest 90 minutes in a Celtic shirt.

The Scottish League campaign, much punctuated by postponements, had been a mundane and uninteresting one until the very last game on 21 May. A win for Celtic over Rangers at Parkhead would mean that the League championship went to Celtic Park. Any other result would favour Rangers. On occasions like this, greatness and destiny beckon. Ian Paul in the *Glasgow Herald* states quite blandly: "… they (the fans) had seen a performance by Roy Aitken which must rank among the finest by any Celtic player in a 90-minute spell".

That simple tribute by Ian Paul, extravagant and lavish though it was, was no hyperbole. Aitken really was immense, and Gallacher and McGrory of old would have been delighted to have been linked to him in this way. The facts of this tremendous encounter, famed as the "Ten Men won the League" game, are well known. Celtic one down, Johnny Doyle sent off, then equalise, go ahead, Rangers equalise, then Celtic score twice to send three-quarters of Parkhead into delirium and the other quarter into catatonic silence. What is more difficult to quantify is the sheer, almost superhuman effort that Aitken put into that game. He revelled in it, he relished the fight, and he won the day in a way that almost defied analysis.

A foolish union dispute prevented even highlights of the game being shown on either STV or BBC, so we are dependent to a large extent on still photographs to re-create that glorious Monday night. Surely the best photograph of them all is Aitken coming off the field with a supporter's tammy on his head. In a picture taken in the dressing room, the tammy is still there. Could there be any greater indication of the symbiosis between Aitken and the support? The fans went home that night, many of them having to work the following day. Work would be a glorious experience that day, not only because of a brilliant performance to win the League over the great rivals. More importantly, they had a new hero. And unlike Dalglish, he had no desire to move. He loved the Celtic.

BY 1981, AITKEN, ALWAYS a home-loving man, was telling Rodger Baillie of the *Sunday Mirror*: "If everything goes alright, I would be quite happy to stay at Parkhead. By that I mean as long as I was still playing first-team football. But really the thought of moving anywhere had not crossed my mind, and I mean anywhere, not just England. At the end of the day I reckon Celtic will look after a player as well, if not better, than any other team". Comforting words they were for the Celtic fans, and a total contrast to the mercenary behaviour of so many others.

Aitken and Celtic won the League championship in 1977, 1979, 1981, 1982, 1986 and 1988. Three of these titles "went to the wire", as the pundits would have it, in that they were won on the last day. Seldom, however, can the last day of a League season have produced such excitement as 3 May 1986. Celtic, frankly, had little chance. They had to beat St Mirren at Love Street by four goals and hope that Dundee could beat Hearts at Dens Park. Aitken, who now shared the captaincy with the venerable Danny McGrain, realised that, football being the psychological game that it is, if Celtic played well in the first half and were well on top, this would create panic in the Hearts ranks. He hammered home this message to his men.

By half-time, Celtic were 4-0 up. The goals had been superb, Aitken had been inspirational and Celtic, playing in their lime-green strip, looked unstoppable. The news was, indeed, relayed over the air waves to Dens Park, hard though the Hearts management team tried to stop it reaching their players. It was still goalless on Tayside. Concern first, then uneasiness, then panic began to set in for a team which had not won anything for 24 years.

Meanwhile at Love Street, Celtic had scored another and then eased off. Their job was done for the day. There was nothing more that they could do – other than support Dundee! The crowd grew quiet as the standard of play visibly dropped, with one or two Celtic players asking fans if it was still 0-0, and the St.Mirren players, many of them unrepentant Celtic fans, clearly wanting to go home. Home was where some of the spectators were beginning to troop as well, when the crowd erupted in glee at what looked like a perfectly ordinary picking up of the ball by St Mirren's goalkeeper Jim Stewart. BBC Radio Scotland had told Love Street that Albert Kidd had scored for Dundee.

Aitken's face relaxed as he exchanged a few glances with other players. Then he remembered that he was a professional, and he returned to the game in hand. The crowd roared again – Albert Kidd, the angel of deliverance, had scored another. Aitken now smiled before resuming the fray. Then the crowd, now in uproar, raised the roof, as the full-time whistle had gone at Dens Park and Dundee had won 2-0. A minute or so later, the game at Love Street finished, and Aitken's Celtic were champions.

This was unbelievable, romantic stuff that really belonged to the world of Boys Own, with its "thrilling ties" and "gnawing anxiety" and "rip-roaring action". One would not really have been able to make this up, but it had happened. Instead of Roy of the Rovers, the legendary star of Melchester Rovers, being the hero, this was our own intrepid Roy – Roy Aitken of the Celtic, who was being feted and honoured for bringing glory to his side.

ROY DID PACK A great deal into his years with Celtic. European forays were generally a failure, although Celtic did beat Real Madrid in the Parkhead leg of the European Cup quarter-final in 1980. The Scottish League Cup was never a favourite trophy of Celtic's. Aitken has only one winner's medal in that tournament, although he took part in another four League Cup finals, three against Rangers and one against Aberdeen, all of which resulted in narrow, unlucky defeats after which Aitken shared the despondency of the fans. He also managed to play 57 times for Scotland, although his last few caps were after he had moved on, participating in the World Cup finals of 1986 and 1990. Those who had no reason to love Celtic would often single out Aitken for censure after a bad Scotland performance, but Roy had nothing to be ashamed of in his games for his country, which he served with as much passion as he did his club. It was clear from the position that Aitken played for Scotland that Jock Stein believed he was a better midfielder than a defender. It was an opinion shared by many Celtic fans, but it mattered little, as Aitken gave his all wherever he played.

After the sad departure of Aitken from Celtic Park in early 1990 to Newcastle United – another club who crave a cult hero to bring them some success – things were never quite the same again. His years at Newcastle and St Mirren were not as happy as his time at Celtic. When he moved to Aberdeen as manager, he was responsible for their capture of the League Cup in 1995, but he very soon went the way of all Aberdeen managers since Alex Ferguson, unable to satisfy the demands of a potentially very large support.

In recent years he has worked at both Leeds United and Aston Villa, before in January 2007 becoming assistant manager to Eck McLeish in the Scotland job during the national team's heroic push for Euro 2008 qualification. In November 2007 he moved with Eck to Birmingham City as the pair opted to try their luck in the English Premier League. But to those who saw Celtic in that tumultuous decade of the 1980s, with all its glories and disasters, Roy

Aitken will always be associated with no team other than Celtic. He was, and remains, a Celtic cult hero.

CHARLIE NICHOLAS

1979-1983
1990-1995

BHOYS CAREER

Games	236
Goals	124
Caps	20

MAGIC MOMENT

A marvellous goal at Ibrox on New Year's Day 1983 when Charlie passed from one foot to the other before hammering home to give Celtic a 2-1 victory.

'CHAMPAGNE CHARLIE'

CHARLIE Nicholas was one of Celtic's greatest ever players – or at least he could have and, indeed, he should have been. He was recognisably very much one of the Celtic type, very Glasgow and very much one of the Celtic supporters. He was born in 1961, and was in his early years of primary school at the time of the great Jock Stein's Celtic side. He played for a team called St Columba of Iona, Maryhill, before graduating to Celtic via the Celtic Boys club. His first game for the first team was in August 1979 in the Glasgow Cup, and enough was seen of him at that time to indicate that there was something worth preserving in that boy.

But manager Billy McNeill did not rush the starlet, keeping him out of the limelight for the 1979/80 season, while at the same time doing nothing to discourage the stories emanating from those in the know that something special was to be unleashed. The unleashing happened at Kilmarnock on 16 August 1980 when, with Celtic comfortably ahead, the Rugby Park crowd saw the Beatles-style haircut, the fresh face and the undeniable football talent that was Charlie Nicholas come on to take the place of the tiring Frank McGarvey.

The speed with which Charlie became a cult hero was absolutely breathtaking. In the month of September 1980, Charlie scored in every game that he played, and was even entrusted, at the tender age of 18, with the task of taking the penalties. In truth, there was something phenomenal here. The ball control, the visionary passing, the ability to take a goal, the speed and the commitment were all present. Even the veteran supporters of the McInally and Gallacher era were convinced that here was a splendid player.

CELTIC SUPPORTERS OF THAT era needed a hero. They always need someone in any era, of course, but in 1980 football was at a low ebb. Attendances were low, and there was a lack of the players with flair and personality who had so characterised the 1960s. Celtic had thrown away the Scottish League in April 1980 to Alex Ferguson's Aberdeen in a way that had bewildered their supporters. To a certain extent they had redeemed themselves by winning the Scottish Cup against Rangers. But even that success had been tarnished by a disgraceful riot between the fans of the Old Firm, who had battled in front of the world's TV cameras for the right, the acerbic claimed, to be called the thickest in Glasgow. It was clear that day that questions really had to be asked of Scottish society, not least about the palpable failure of the education system.

Scotland's national side had not yet recovered from Argentina in 1978, and Celtic had not yet recovered from the sale of Dalglish to Liverpool the year before that. There was a definite feeling that Celtic were going nowhere. In particular that disastrous selling of Dalglish had clearly sent out the signal that Celtic were not interested in the European Cup any more, an astonishingly pessimistic conclusion when they had actually won the trophy a decade previously. True, they had spectacularly defeated Real Madrid in the European Cup of 1980 – but only at Celtic Park. The return leg had seen the scoreline reversed and overtaken. The team was full of honest, hard-working players, but flair and panache had gone out the window. The supporters yearned for the precision passing of Bobby Murdoch, the trickery of Jimmy Johnstone, the rapier thrusts of Joe McBride and certainly the pure professionalism of Kenny Dalglish, now winning honours galore for Liverpool.

The pall of depression hanging over Parkhead was visible, even tangible. The huge stadium had vast empty spaces on most match days. The fans stayed loyal but had that glazed, abandoned, deserted air about them. They still loved the Celtic, the green-and-white jerseys and manager Billy McNeill. They were less enchanted about the directors. There was quite simply the feeling that if Celtic did unearth another great player, he would be sold. That had happened with Macari, Hay and Dalglish. Celtic supporters did not like that. They could never come to terms with the notion that Celtic were only in business to supply the English teams with talent. There was no excuse for that notion, as Celtic had been the first British team to win the European Cup. Asset-stripping could only be explained in terms of money-grubbing and pocket-lining.

Tied in with this was the broader footballing status of Scotland. The nation had earned deserved worldwide ridicule for the Argentina fiasco of 1978, and had yet to recover its self-respect, even though the great Jock Stein was now the manager. Politically as well in 1980, there was a reason for this massive inferiority complex. She was called Margaret Thatcher, voted in by the south-east of England, which outpopulated and outshone Scotland in terms of wealth. Scotland, already by 1980, was on the receiving end of quite a few rounds of the guns, and unemployment was rising inexorably.

The stage was thus set for a cult hero. Charlie Napier of the 1930s and Charlie Tully of the 1950s had both been sung about – "Clap, clap hands, here comes Charlie". Now a third person of that name entered the scene, and for ever so short a time, brightened Parkhead before plunging it back again into unrelieved gloom.

Inspired by their young genius, Celtic played some fine football in season 1980/81, although until the New Year inexperience was evident in the unpredictability of performance. Also the exit from Europe at the hands of Eastern European unknowns should have been hard to accept. The atmosphere, however, was so pessimistic and demoralised that shoulders were shrugged and a philosophical acceptance was the order of the day. Domestically, the chief opponents this year were not so much Rangers, as the "New Firm" of Dundee United and Aberdeen, where Jim McLean and Alex Ferguson were producing teams who were no longer afraid of a trip to Glasgow. It was Dundee United, for example, who removed Celtic from the Scottish League Cup in the two-leg semi-final. Following a respectable 1-1 draw at the difficult venue of Tannadice, Celtic unaccountably collapsed 0-3 at Parkhead, and then in the week between Christmas and New Year, Celtic were on the wrong end of a 4-1 drubbing from Aberdeen at Pittodrie.

But Nicholas, who had been injured, came on as a substitute that day and scored a consolation goal. It was as if the team had been waiting for his return because, beginning from New Year's Day at Kilmarnock, Celtic went on a tremendous run, never again losing in the Scottish League until the championship had been well won. Nicholas played some tremendous football, and in addition to his own trickery, there now seemed to be a maturity and a development as a team player far beyond what could reasonably have been expected from his tender years. In truth, Celtic had some fine players. There were Tommy Burns, Frank McGarvey, Davie Provan, Murdo MacLeod, good players all, and with Nicholas on song, the form of that Celtic team was a sight to behold, the boys visibly growing in confidence in those early months of 1981.

In January, Dundee United were defeated at Parkhead, then Hearts were demolished at Tynecastle, before 21 February, when Rangers came to Parkhead to be shown Charlie Nicholas in all his glory. Rangers were a goal up at half-time, but then Nicholas, in unstoppable form, scored twice and was not far away when Roy Aitken scored a third.

But the best game for sheer football was the visit of St Mirren to Parkhead on 14 March. The 7-0 thrashing of the luckless Buddies on a dry and dusty pitch was a sight for sore eyes and a perfect antidote to the weaker among us who had reckoned that Celtic were finished. If only that had been against some European opposition, rather than St.Mirren. What a performnce that would have been! And it all came from the young genius, "Champagne Charlie" as he was now called. Manager Billy McNeill was asked if Nicholas was the new Dalglish. Billy replied that Nicholas was the one and only Nicholas.

It so happened that on that remarkable day when St Mirren were put to the sword, League rivals Rangers and Aberdeen both lost points, and seldom have the faithful had such a happy journey home. Yet even at this early stage, before Nicholas had finished his first full season as a Parkhead regular, mischievous journalists were beginning to ask questions about his future, unsettling him with talk of big English teams. Whether this was a deliberate attempt to undermine Celtic and Nicholas, or merely a device to fill newspaper space on quiet days, was unclear, but it was an annoying distraction from some fine football.

Yet at this stage, Nicholas refused to be influenced. On 31 March he was quoted as saying: "I just want to stay with Celtic . . . I don't want to go anywhere else. I've always supported Celtic and they are the only club I've wanted to play for". He was by no means the only player to say "the only club I wanted to play for" cliche, and he may even have meant it at that stage, as everything was going so swimmingly well for the club and for the player.

It was Dundee United who eventually put a spoke in the Celtic wheel. This came in the Scottish Cup semi-final when, after a 0-0 draw, Celtic, in spite of a marvellous Nicholas goal, went down 2-3 to a competent and efficient Tannadice side. Dundee United under Jim McLean presented a total contrast to Celtic. United were well organised and stable, while Celtic were full of flair but often capable of failing on the dynamics of defending. Games between the two of them were always tough but fair, and both sides had a total respect for each other. On this occasion in the replay on a dull spring evening at Hampden, Celtic went ahead through a Nicholas penalty. Then Dundee United scored two in quick succession before, just on the stroke of half-time, Nicholas was on the edge of the penalty box when the Dundee United goalkeeper Hamish McAlpine punched a ball out to his feet, and Charlie lashed it home first time. Sadly, all Charlie's good work was undone in the second half when a defensive error allowed Dundee United a late winner.

The following Saturday, Celtic got over their disappointment at their Scottish Cup exit by beating Rangers 1-0 in a curiously low-key Old Firm derby. Nicholas (who else?) got the goal, and this meant that Celtic would only need one more point to secure the championship. Their opponents on that Wednesday night of 22 April were none other than Dundee United at Tannadice. On this occasion, with late and unseasonal snow in the air, Celtic decided to turn on one of their best performances of the season and defeated United 3-2 to tremendous scenes of jubilation and triumph, not least from the young genius who was not yet 20 and was already being talked about as one of Celtic's all-time greats.

In truth, he had come a long way in one season. Maturity, at least in the football sense, had appeared along with superb ball play. His ability to take a goal was second to none, and he could take a good penalty. The future seemed bright for this young man. His second season would not be quite so good, or so lucky.

CELTIC WON THE LEAGUE championship again in that 1981/82 campaign, but they did so to a large extent without Charlie Nicholas, who played only 14 games. He broke his leg in a reserve game in January at Cappielow. Ironically, he was in the team simply because he was short of match practice, thanks to a severe winter. Effectively Charlie did not play again that season. As a result Celtic departed the Scottish Cup at a comparatively early stage of the campaign, but even in the first half of the season when Nicholas had been available, the form of the team had been disappointing. A miserable League Cup campaign had seen defeats to the likes of St Mirren and St Johnstone. Although the fires burned briefly in Europe after a 1-0 win over Juventus at Parkhead, the team (without Nicholas) went to Turin and obeyed the unwritten law of the 1980s that Celtic must collapse before high-class opposition.

Nicholas had not played as well in the early part of the 1981/82 season as he had previously. He was injured once or twice and there were also signs of "second-season syndrome". The opposition had begun to spot his weaknesses, and had begun to target him for one or two hefty tackles. In addition, he now began to suffer because he was a Glasgow celebrity. The media were very much on his case, and Charlie found this hard to deal with. He was expected to work wonders every week. He could not quite do this.

But Celtic, without Nicholas, did win the Scottish League in 1981/82, and the fans, as they watched the World Cup in Spain that summer or flocked to Bellahouston Park to see the Pope on his tour of Scotland, looked forward to the season that was to come with fevered anticipation. Not only would Celtic be the defending champions, they would also have Charlie Nicholas back.

Another great player had emerged in Paul McStay. Paul was less flamboyant than Charlie Nicholas, but still showed great promise. The future looked more optimistic than it had done for some considerable time, and in early December the League Cup was won. The League Cup was traditionally the tournament in which Celtic did less well than in others, and it had been eight years since the last success. Nicholas was very instrumental in bringing this rare success to Parkhead. He scored at least one goal in every game he played in the League Cup except for one, and he had the ability to be there at exactly the right moment to save the day when things were tight.

The semi-final against old foes Dundee United had been a case in point. Two goals up from the first leg at Parkhead, Celtic had squandered their lead at Tannadice, and the rampant United side, even although they had had a man sent off, looked as if they were to score the winner against a ragged and shaken Celtic side. The Celtic half of the crowd had lapsed into desolate and ominous silence, as they do when disaster seems imminent. Two minutes remained when Tommy Burns broke away and slipped the ball to Nicholas. A lesser man would have tried to round the goalkeeper and risk losing the ball, or he might have blasted over the bar. But Charlie showed all the coolness in the world as he drilled the ball past Hamish McAlpine to put Celtic into the final.

The stage was thus set for Nicholas's best and most famous game of his Celtic career, the Scottish League Cup final of 4 December 1982 against Rangers. The weather hardly graced the occasion, as rain poured down on that dreadful afternoon, particularly on the uncovered Celtic end of the ground. In addition, Hampden was under construction, so that the North Stand area was totally bare apart from items of building equipment and a few men in oilskins. It was the most unlikely setting for a Cup final, held at a ridiculous time of year when conditions were liable to be at their worst, yet for Celtic and Nicholas it was a spectacular and glittering success.

Darkness had already fallen by the time of the 3pm kick-off, but Charlie lightened the gloom. Early in the first half, Rangers won a throw level with their own penalty box. They got themselves into a fankle, and Davie Provan emerged with the ball. He passed to Charlie on the edge of the penalty box on the Celtic right, and with four defenders closing in on him, he slammed the ball home. Football is a simple game sometimes, and when the ball comes to you in these circumstances, kicking the ball once and making a good job of it is usually the best option. It is certainly preferable to trying to beat a man and find a better position, thus giving the goalkeeper and his defence time to organise.

By half-time, it was 2-0 and Nicholas, although having no direct part in the second goal, was simply on fire as he ran at that Rangers defence, passed to colleagues and cajoled, heartened and inspired the Celtic team. To their credit, Rangers fought well in the second half and pulled a goal back, but Celtic continued to dominate with Nicholas leading the way. He actually managed to miss an open goal near the end, but it mattered little, as the game finished with Celtic well on top and winning 2-1.

The rain-drenched Celtic hordes had not been so happy for a long time. One trophy was in the bag, and the prospects of a treble of domestic honours seemed bright. Celtic had a good side, a charismatic, committed manager in Billy McNeill, the man who had lifted that big, beautifully ugly European Cup 15 years ago - and they had Champagne Charlie! The optimism intensified after a good win at Ibrox on New Year's Day, incredibly the first win there on a New Year's Day since 1921, when Joe Cassidy had delivered the goods. This time victory was made remarkable with a great Celtic goal from Nicholas, who feinted to go one way, then the other, passing the ball, as it were, from his right foot to his left, and it was the lethal left which scored the winner.

THERE WAS A GREAT deal of euphoria in the Celtic ranks that January, but already the seeds of destruction had been sown. On days when there was no football, the press began to outdo each other with stories which did not speculate on whether Nicholas was going to England next year, but to whom he was going, with Arsenal, Liverpool, Tottenham Hotspur and Manchester United all mentioned. Some newspapers blatantly told Nicholas to go, and we used to get offensive headlines like "Three million reasons why Charlie should go", a reference to the three million unemployed in Mrs Thatcher's grim Britain. There was nothing logical in all this; it was merely telling the naive young man that he should make all the money that he could.

The traditional Celtic paranoia now began to kick in as well. Celtic supporters often find it difficult to believe that there is not a conspiracy theory behind every headline in the *Daily Record* and the *Daily Express*, and that there is a cell or lodge of Rangers supporters in every newspaper ready to manufacture a story to discredit or to embarrass Celtic supporters. Stories also began to emerge that the relationship between Nicholas and his manager Billy McNeill was not good – that McNeill, for example, disapproved of Nicholas's dress, his wearing of an earring and his unsanitary habit of not wearing socks. Whether these stories were true or not, the damage was done, and many Celtic fans would never be convinced that this was not a deliberate policy.

The problem was that everyone, except Celtic supporters, stood to gain from a Nicholas transfer. Other Scottish teams would be glad to see the back of him, as he was the man who made Celtic operate. For example, he was not playing on a windy day at Fir Park against Motherwell and the team lost 1-2, a point not lost on the rest of the world. The Celtic directors were clearly very keen on the idea of making money from a transfer, and Nicholas himself, already under the baleful influence of an agent – who would earn a large amount from any transfer that he negotiated – began to feel unsettled and unhappy.

On the playing front, Nicholas continued to score the goals and sink the penalties, and Celtic were in danger of becoming over-dependent on him. Jock Stein was sufficiently impressed to award him his first Scottish cap on 30 March at Hampden against Switzerland. He marked his international debut with a marvellous goal, as attention on him intensified. Even foreign teams were now interested in him, and little wonder, as he scored 48 goals for Celtic that season, often celebrating with a curious but characteristic shake of the hand. Yet Billy McNeill was determined to retain him. "He must mature among friends, the terracing and the team", said Billy in a quote in which the words "must mature" actually said an awful lot.

Celtic's season and their chances of a treble hinged on one week in April. They were still ahead in the Scottish League, fending off a strong challenge from the New Firm of Dundee United and Aberdeen, and they were in the semi-final of the Scottish Cup. On 16 April 1983 they faced Aberdeen in the semi-final at Hampden, then they had Dundee United at home in a re-arranged League match on the Wednesday night, followed by a trip to Pittodrie the following Saturday. To the astonishment of all concerned, Celtic ran out at Hampden without Charlie Nicholas. The reason given was that he had picked up an injury and failed a late fitness test. This story was not universally believed, and Glasgow being the place that it was, rumours circulated before half-time in that game. "He has already been transferred to . . .", "He has walked out on Celtic and McNeill", "He has refused to play", "He was arrested last night" . . . all these stories, and many more, went round the Celtic end of Hampden that day.

In his absence, the contention that Celtic were over-dependent on Charlie Nicholas gained credence, as they went down 0-1 to the Dons. Aberdeen scored early in the second half, and Celtic without Nicholas simply did not have the know-how to break down the defence of Miller and McLeish. This was a bad blow for Celtic, and a great deal of damage had been done. Although Nicholas did come back from whatever the problem had been, Celtic proceeded to lose to Dundee United on the Wednesday night and then Aberdeen at Pittodrie on the Saturday. In the space of eight days the season had been well and truly blown. A couple of days after the defeat at Aberdeen, Nicholas was voted Player of the Year. This was hardly surprising, but Celtic fans might have preferred other honours, like a trophy to match the League Cup won with such Nicholas panache in December.

The end came at Ibrox on the day that Dundee United won the Scottish League. Celtic actually had a fine day, beating Rangers 4-2 after falling 0-2 behind. Nicholas, deadly from the penalty spot all season, scored with two spot-kicks and inspired Celtic to a victory. Amidst all the euphoria and banner-waving which one would expect in the wake of an Old Firm victory, there was one banner, simple and poignant, which caught the eye. It said quite simply: "Don't Go, Charlie". The gentleman in question must have seen it. Sadly he ignored it and went, plunging Celtic into a long period of uncertainty and under-achievement.

Since the days of Robert Burns' *A Parcel of Rogues In A Nation*, there has been no lack of English gold to buy and sell Scotland.

But pith and power till my last hour
I'll mak this declaration
We're bought and sold for English gold
Sic a parcel o' rogues in a nation!

The irony here was that Nicholas, although he certainly did earn more in London than he would have in Scotland, would hardly have been a pauper with Celtic, who were offering to make him the best paid player in the club's history. And what he made in money, he lost in goodwill and reputation. Had he stayed, certainly he would have become one of the greatest Celts of them all, on a par with Quinn, Gallacher, McGrory and Delaney.

IT IS STRANGE FOR a group of tens of thousands of people to feel lonely, but this is exactly how Celtic supporters felt during that summer of 1983. A conspiracy of the Scottish press, grasping agents, an English team with too much money, the Celtic directors and, sadly, Nicholas himself had seen Celtic deprived of their star. Against such a powerful combination, the wishes of the Celtic fans counted for nothing. Little sympathy came from anyone. We heard the pious cant about: "He's a professional footballer and is surely entitled to better himself" or "You would accept promotion in your job, wouldn't you?" Such platitudes were harder to accept than the undisguised gloating from our enemies, because they ignored the sheer commitment and emotional investment of the Celtic support and the devastation that they felt. Celtic are no ordinary team.

It was Terry Neill's Arsenal that paid the price of £750,000. Yet they paid the price in another sense as well, as Charlie never performed for them the way that we knew he could, or in the way that Dalglish, for example, had done for Liverpool. The writing ought to have been on the wall after the England v Scotland game at Wembley on 1 June, when Nicholas played embarrassingly badly and had to be substituted. Two nations began to wonder what all the fuss concerning this young man was all about.

A few weeks later Billy McNeill departed from Celtic Park as well. The dispute was about the lack of a contract, but it was hard not to see a connection with the Nicholas transfer. The common factor was a board of directors whose parsimony and misplaced economy beto-kened sheer lack of ambition. The new season opened with the earnest David Hay in charge and the Rangers supporters at a pre-season Glasgow Cup game taunting gleefully: "Where's your Charlie gone?" Season 1983/84 was destined to be a prolonged tale of woe for Celtic supporters. Refereeing decisions and managerial mistakes may all have played their part, but the bottom line was that there was no Charlie Nicholas.

His Arsenal years saw one success, in the League Cup final of 1987 when his goals helped to beat Liverpool, but Arsenal had every right to feel short-changed. He appeared once at Parkhead in a pre-season game, and the booing and hatred were terrifying in their intensity. Celtic fans do not like to feel that they have been betrayed by one of their own kind. Some old timers sagely brought up Tommy McInally, the Cult Hero of the 1920s, and how he had pined for home and returned. Charlie would eventually return as well, but by that time a great deal of damage would have been done.

There was an Aberdeen interlude first. He played well enough for the Dons. whom he joined in January 1988, and he was well respected by the canny folk of the north, but any lingering doubt that "Celtic, Nicholas and unhappiness" were inextricably intertwined, was dispelled by the events of the 1990 Scottish Cup final, clearly one of the most painful in the long and lamentable chronicles of Celtic disappointments. This game was the first Scottish Cup final to go to a penalty shoot-out. If Nicholas had missed his, Celtic would have won, but Charlie was always a great penalty-taker and duly scored. Aberdeen went on to win the shoot-out, and this was Charlie's one and only Scottish Cup medal, for he never won one with Celtic.

It was that summer that he returned, at last, to Parkhead. There was still a great deal of football left in him, but the Celtic team that he joined in summer 1990 was a Celtic team in name only. They were so far behind the money of Souness and Murray at Ibrox, that the Scottish League was hardly a contest at all. The board of directors would collapse in spectacular fashion in 1994, and Nicholas, to his credit, was among the rebel players who advocated change. He did however overuse the phrase "Celtic-minded" to indicate the commitment of men like Paul McStay, Peter Grant, Pat Bonner and himself. There were those among us who felt that we wished we had seen a little more Celtic-mindedness back in 1983.

The board did depart and changes for the better followed. Nicholas had actually been given a free transfer, but was brought back by the new manager, his former team-mate Tommy Burns, for one final season. There would be one spectacular collector's item of a horror show to finish off Charlie's Celtic career. This was the League Cup final at Ibrox on 27 November 1994, when Raith Rovers enjoyed the one and only success in their long and interesting history, and Celtic plunged to depths previously unimagined. It was not as if Nicholas could be blamed for what went wrong in the penalty shoot-out. Indeed, Nicholas had been one of Celtic's stars, scoring the second goal which had seemed to deliver the trophy. But Raith equalised and then Paul McStay had his own personal cataclysm. Celtic, Nicholas and heartbreak now came together again.

CHARLIE WOULD FINISH HIS playing days with Clyde, and then he moved to TV punditry, much caricatured and satirised for his enthusiastic and ungrammatical approach to the game. It is a shame that 1983 went the way that it did. Nicholas had it in him to be one of the greatest Celts of all time, and he might well have been compared to McMenemy, Gallacher, Delaney, Tully and Johnstone, but the problem was that he could only do it for Celtic. He is the reverse of many other players who have come to Celtic Park and have failed to deliver what they did elsewhere. Charlie in 1980/81 and 1982/83 showed the Celtic fans and the Scottish public what football was all about. If only he had paid a little more attention to that banner at Ibrox in the last game of the 1982/83 season which said: "Don't Go, Charlie".

HENRIK LARSSON

'KING OF KINGS'

1997-2004

BHOYS CAREER

Games	221
Goals	173
Caps	93

MAGIC MOMENT

His hat-trick in the 2001 Scottish League Cup final in which ten-man Celtic defeated Kilmarnock 3-0. Larsson's third was an exquisite piece of finishing after running half the length of the field with the ball.

THE Rangers fans in the pub thought it was funny. "Who the f*** 's this they've got noo?" they asked derisively at the sight of Celtic's new substitute. Dreadlocks gave a slightly feminine look to his face, and as he was being brought on as a substitute in Celtic's first game of the 1997/98 season, various homophobic words of scorn were heard from the ill-educated. It was against Hibs at Easter Road, and Celtic were struggling.

Even greater was the scorn of the ill-mannered lads in blue when Larsson conceded possession with virtually his first touch of the ball and Hibs ran up and scored what proved to be the winner. Celtic, who had now lost nine League championships in a row, looked as if they had taken the first step towards losing their tenth. Catatonic despair reigned among the Celtic faithful.

It had been new manager Wim Jansen who had brought Henrik Larsson to the club from Feyenoord, where latterly he had been far from happy. Celtic supporters, who at the beginning of the summer had heard of neither Jansen nor Larsson, were already resigned to a season of frustration, or at least to a long period of adjustment. There had been other buys as well – Darren Jackson, Craig Burley for example – and the new manager had to be given a reasonable chance. But this new centre-forward with the funny hairstyle did not look the part.

It was probably too early for despair, but despondency was in the air. If ever Celtic needed a cult hero it was now. The nine years without a League title had been deeply wounding, and these dreadful times had been characterised by the rise of quite a few "false messiahs" who had threatened to become the new personality that the support all craved – only for personal, emotional or temperamental problems to get the better of them. Paolo di Canio, Pierre van Hooijdonk and Jorge Cadete, talented players all, saw the beckoning finger of Parkhead immortality. One after another, each one of them threw it all away.

So Parkhead in August 1997 was akin to a spiritual desert. Not a physical desert – a new stadium was almost completed – nor a financial one, as Fergus McCann and his share issue were pouring money into the club. What the fans craved, however, was success and a cult hero, a personality to deliver it to them. There were those who said with a straight face that they, literally, could not face the taunts of "ten in a row" that were being rehearsed at Ibrox, and that they would not stand for it. Presumably this did not mean suicide, or even emigration, but it did hint at taking up a new hobby instead of football. The stakes were high, indeed.

Rangers winning ten in a row would have destroyed a great deal of what Jock Stein had done. The great Celtic team had won the championship from 1965/66 until 1973/74, and now craven, spineless and misguided stewardship of the Celtic club had thrown this record away. The stewardship of the club was now much better, but success on the field had not yet arrived. Celtic supporters could not take much more. Where was the Deliverer?

He was, in fact, the man with the dreadlocks. A brilliant flying header to score at McDiarmid Park, Perth, a few weeks after his unfortunate Celtic debut was the launch of a truly great Celtic player and goalscorer. Slowly the team recovered from its dismal start to the season, and by the end of November, silverware returned to Celtic Park in the shape of the Scottish League Cup, won at Ibrox with a competent 3-0 victory over Dundee United. Larsson had excelled that day, scoring one of the goals and always being instrumental in the creation of some fine forward play.

This had followed a European experience against Liverpool in which Celtic had proved themselves to be at least the Merseysiders' equals, even though they had gone out on the away-goals rule. Celtic and Larsson's day against Liverpool would come, but in the meantime there was a thrilling chase for the Scottish League Premier Division title, in which Celtic, Rangers and Hearts challenged each other with spellbinding ferocity.

It was the best Scottish season for some time. Celtic lost to Rangers in the Scottish Cup semi-final, then went down to them in the League the following week in April, and things looked distinctly gloomy. About this time Hearts blew up, as they were always likely to do, but Celtic recovered from their defeats to Rangers, and inspired by Larsson reached the penultimate week of the season needing only to beat Dunfermline at East End Park to win the League. Larsson released Simon Donnelly to put Celtic ahead, but then late in the game, the Pars scored a fortuitous equaliser to deny Celtic.

Thus it was on to the last day of the League season. Celtic still retained the initiative, but to be absolutely sure of winning the title, they had to beat St Johnstone at Parkhead. It was Larsson who scored in the first minute of the game, catching the Perth defence and the Celtic crowd by surprise with a fine goal from the edge of the penalty box, and then as nerves visibly set in among the other Celtic players and the supporters, Larsson came into his own, showing calmness and poise to control the game. In fact, it was Harald Brattbakk of Norway who scored the second and decisive goal, but who was it who was seen on Harald's back, pointing to him and saying: "He's done it! It's Harald!"?

There was thus built up over that tense and exhausting season an affinity between Larsson and the Celtic hordes. Larsson was not ethnically, nor in any other sense, a "Celt" by birth, but he, like so many others, soon became one. The supporters soon got around to making up songs about him. This clearly shows that Henrik was, indeed, a cult hero, and had in nine months come a long way from the diffident Swede who came on as a substitute and immediately gave away a goal. He was even immortalised in a song written about him by the band Fanclub:

Give me the magic, give me the passion,
Show me the lovin', show me the game,
Let's get excited, don't ever hide it,
Star of the moment, whisper his name
Henrik Larsson
Henrik Larsson
Henrik Larsson
Larsson, Larsson, Larsson, Henrik Larsson

But despite this adulation Larsson's mentor Wim Jansen resigned in the flush of victory, for ill-disguised reasons of being unable to get on with another member of the management team, and Celtic then had to begin an undignified scramble for a successor before coming up with former Aston Villa manager Jo Venglos, a likeable Czech whose best days were behind him. Season 1998/99 was a major disappointment, with Larsson still playing well but clearly frustrated and upset at the lack of success.

Venglos departed in the summer and was replaced by John Barnes. Barnes' reign as manager would collapse in ignominy after defeat by Inverness Caledonian Thistle in February 2000, but most people agreed that the real cause of that dreadful winter of discontent happened on 21 October 1999 in Lyon when Henrik Larsson broke his leg. Memories haunt one still of TV pictures of Henrik with his tibia visibly broken and hanging in a sickening position. It remains one of the most distressing sights in a lifetime of that glorious obsession called supporting Celtic.

One would not have been surprised if this had meant curtains for the career of Henrik Larsson, but Henrik was nothing if not determined, and by the end of that season he was able to return to playing for Celtic. By the time he came back, the season had gone, and although the team had managed to win the Scottish League Cup in a dreadful final against Aberdeen, the season 1999/2000 was not a great one in the annals of the club.

It was at this point that Celtic and Larsson were at the nadir of their fortunes, but in these circumstances there is only one way to go and that is up. At long last, Celtic appointed a credible manager in Martin O'Neill, a proven winner, and with a fully fit Larsson and many shrewd buys, Celtic took off to make season 2000/01 one of the best in the long and glorious history of the club.

LARSSON'S STRONG POINTS WERE commitment and professionalism. This was in addition to his undeniable ability. Larsson, who would always give 100 per-cent for any manager, now began to give 110 per-cent for Martin O'Neill. O'Neill's side had bounce, rhythm, determination and passion, and very soon these qualities were mirrored in the stands at Celtic Park, now a ground which could reliably house close to 60,000 every week. Celtic won the treble that year, a feat which put them in the same bracket as the men of 1907/08, 1966/67 and 1968/69, and it was appropriate that this was the year in which the Willie Maley song became common with the lyrics of "to play football in the good old Celtic way".

Larsson simply could not stop scoring that year. Half a century of goals came his way (putting him in the same bracket as Jimmy McGrory in 1936, and that is saying something) and although many of them were tap-ins from the excellent approach play of the others, they were not all like that. For example, one recalls the League Cup final against Kilmarnock when an injury-hit team, reduced to ten men after Chris Sutton had been sent off, still beat Kilmarnock 3-0 with Larsson scoring a hat-trick. His first was a brilliant piece of athleticism, the second perhaps a shade fortunate with a deflection, but the third was sheer class, as he picked up a ball on the halfway line, shrugged off repeated fouls, charged for goal, rounded the goalkeeper, put one foot over the ball and scored with his other foot. For this, Henrik was given the Man-of-the-Match award. It was a silver platter. Several times, Henrik made as if to throw it into the crowd as the team did their lap of honour. It was as if to say: "I am one of you".

The Celtic fans, for their part, were singing his praises, and it was no accident that the song was borrowed from evangelical Christianity:

Give me joy in my heart, Henrik Larsson
Give me joy in my heart, I pray
Give me joy in my heart, Henrik Larsson
Keep on scoring till the end of day!

Henrik Larsson, Henrik Larsson
Henrik Larsson is the King of Kings

It alternated with another ditty, this time a parody of *You Are My Sunshine*:

You are my Larsson, my Henrik Larsson
You make me happy when times are gray
Keep your Shearer, he's a ******
Please don't take my Larsson away!

The offensive reference to Alan Shearer did not rhyme or scan particularly well, and no doubt would have upset the kindly Newcastle United man, who does not hide his affections for Celtic, but the Celtic songwriters, however deficient in talent, did not hide their love for the man who had done so much for them that season.

Then there was the Scottish Cup semi-final against Dundee United, when he scored with a bullet header, and the final against Hibs where he scored a good goal, then a penalty, but sadly could not notch the hat trick in a Scottish Cup final which would have made him the equal of Jimmy Quinn in 1904 and Dixie Deans in 1972. There was not a shadow of doubt about who both the journalists and the players would choose as Scotland's Player of the Year – 2001 belonged to Henrik Larsson. Henrik Larsson was, indeed, the "King of Kings" as the fans now sang repeatedly.

The next few seasons saw Celtic with a superb team. What a joy it used to be to go to Parkhead in those days to see a team playing in top gear with a total understanding of each other and enjoying the total love of their support. Henrik, or "Henke" as he became known, was the jewel in the crown. Supporters began to wear Henrik Larsson masks.

No longer did he have the dreadlocks. He had shed them in autumn 2000, and somehow or other, his lack of dreadlocks seemed to accentuate his lean and lithe frame, especially when a burst of speed was necessary. But his physique was strong as well. A centre-forward must not be pushed around. He must have weight in his shoulders to ward off challenges and to shield the ball when necessary.

He was fortunate in that he had loads of good players around him. He developed an understanding with Chris Sutton, he could use the speed of Didier Agathe, and exploit the fine midfield play of Stilian Petrov and that "little genius" Lubo Moravcik. He was an old-fashioned leader of the line-type of centre-forward who could distribute and feed other players, then be in precisely the right place for the return pass.

His bad days were few. The 2002 Scottish Cup final was, perhaps, one such occasion, when Larsson was less than up to his game and was marked out of the match by Rangers' Lorenzo Amoruso. The result was a heart-breaking loss in the last minute, a disappointment that Henrik would take with him to the World Cup in Japan and Korea. Henrik would frequently say that he hated to let the Celtic fans down. He never did that totally, of course, but there can be little doubt that the 2002 Cup final was a bitter blow. It was, however, more than compensated for by the retention of the SPL Championship in 2001/02. Like the previous year, it was won very comfortably by the beginning of April and was characterised by some phenomenal football, played by the whole team.

AND THEN WE COME to the tumultuous events of 2002/03. Oddly enough, it was a season in which Celtic won nothing in terms of silver (always a hard thing for Celtic fans to accept) but in which they gained everything throughout Europe, in terms of respect, affection, admiration and even love from those who would not necessarily of choice support Celtic.

In the first place they reached the final of the UEFA Cup, going down to Jose Mourinho's Porto team of plausible divers only in extra time and after Bobo Balde had been sent off seconds after a free-kick should have been awarded for a foul on Larsson. Celtic's two goals were scored by the head of Henrik Larsson, and had fortune smiled on Celtic that night, the result would surely have gone the other way.

One recalls the interview given by Larsson in the immediate aftermath of the Seville disappointment. While retaining his dignity, Henrik expressed his own frustration and that of the fans in a way which made everyone realise the depth there was to this man. It cannot have been easy, and the temptation must have been to lash out at the referee or the Portuguese divers or his own goalkeeper, who was badly at fault for at least one of the goals. His sorrow for the fans was so genuine and so apparent.

Yet the fans were happy enough in their own way. Ten years previously, the suggestion of Celtic in a European final would have been bizarre. In 1993 Celtic could not even claim with any honesty to be the second best team in Scotland. Now they were a power in Europe again. The difference was Henrik Larsson.

The final had been reached with many fine performances, not least against the two English sides Blackburn Rovers and Liverpool. On both occasions, patronising comments about Celtic and Scottish football came to sudden stop, as the Larsson-inspired Celtic showed the English Premiership that it had no monopoly on successful football sides. Before one of the games, a pundit had said something along the lines of "men against boys". After Celtic had won, Larsson gently reminded that chap in a TV interview that it might be better in future if he were "to keep his mouth shut".

The Liverpool result was all the more remarkable as Larsson was just back from a broken jaw, sustained in a game against Livingston at Parkhead in early February. As with the broken leg of 1999, determination played a great part in Larsson's return, far earlier than anyone dared hope. In the semi-final against Boavista, Larsson scored in the first leg at Parkhead, then had the mortification to miss a penalty, leading the cynics and the pessimists to believe that Celtic had gone far enough and that the final was an impossible dream. Not a bit of it. Henrik scored again away from home – an untidy but crucial goal, and Celtic were on their way to Seville.

The Seville experience showed Celtic at their best, even in defeat. The Celtic family was in evidence that day as the wonderful fans descended on the Spanish city in a number reckoned to be not far short of 80,000. Deservedly did they win their reward for being the best fans in the business, and it was a fascinating exercise to recall that dreadful night less than ten years previously when a fox ran on the park in a game against Kilmarnock as the previous dynasty came to grief. Things were different now. Apart from anything else, we had Henrik Larsson.

THE HEARTBREAK OF LOSING the UEFA Cup final was compounded by the loss of the Scottish Premier League the following Sunday, simply because Rangers scored more goals against feeble opponents than Celtic did. Yet at a key point, as those who were watching two televisions simultaneously could tell, Rangers scored as Larsson hit a post. There were, of course, other reasons in missed penalties and sheer bad luck, but once again Henrik retained his dignity, applauding the fans who idolised him. While a colleague, not entirely without justification, lashed out at Rangers' opponents for insufficient effort on the last day, Henrik, who must have been hurting just as much, kept silent counsel.

But there was a quiet determination in that summer of 2003 for more success. Henrik had decided that 2003/04, his seventh season at Celtic, would be his last. Despite all the emotional blackmail in the world in the shape of letters to the press, personal appeals and a few banners which said "Don't go, Henrik", he stuck to his resolution, clearly determined that the Celtic fans would have something to remember him by. Clearly he remembered the old axiom that one should go when the fans are still asking "why?" and before they begin to ask "why not?"

Apart from a draw in the first game of the season, League form bordered on the invincible, with Rangers and others regularly taken apart. In a game against Motherwell in September, Henrik's birthday as it turned out, an erroneous, albeit courageous, referee booked him for diving. One well recalls the storm of booing and whistling that greeted this decision – not only for the insult to Parkhead's greatest son, but also because the referee had accused him of doing something that was totally alien to the way that he played the game. Frankly, Henrik was too good to have to cheat.

Europe was a disappointment that season – although there were several superb Larsson performances, not least in a game against Lyon in which he did not score but set up two brilliant goals for Liam Miller and Chris Sutton – and once again Celtic failed to be involved after the New Year, but this allowed more time and energy for the Scottish season. The SPL was never really in doubt and was clinched one Sunday in April at Kilmarnock with loads of games to spare. The day that the trophy was presented was, ironically enough, after a defeat at the hands of Dunfermline. The defeat took some of the edge away from the occasion, it has to be said, but the Parkhead fans exulted in the sight of Henrik Larsson collecting his fourth League medal, and then the sight of young Jordan Larsson, complete in the green-and-white hoops, scoring goals as part of the celebrations.

The Scottish Cup was also a triumphant march that year. Defeats of Ross County, who put up a brave performance at Parkhead, Hearts at Tynecastle and then Rangers at Parkhead, left Celtic to play the semi-final at Hampden against Livingston. Henrik scored at the Celtic End with a deft flick past the goalkeeper, then ran to his adoring fans and did the deft flick again just in case they had missed it the first time round. The opponents in the final on 22 May 2004 were Dunfermline Athletic. It would be Henrik's last big game in the colours that he loved so much – sadly, however, not the hoops, but the change strip, although the hoops would be used if they had to collect the Scottish Cup.

There were still a few who hoped and prayed that he might yet be persuaded to stay for just one more year, but he was inexorable and would go to Barcelona for the following season. Thus the Scottish Cup final assumed great importance. Would Henrik go out with a bang or a whimper? In addition, the historically-minded pointed out that it was exactly 100 years ago in 1904 since the immortal Jimmy Quinn had scored his famous hat-trick in a Scottish Cup final at the same ground. Could Henrik do likewise?

At half-time, depression reigned at the Celtic End, as the Pars were one goal up. It had been a lucky goal, perhaps there had been a foul on the goalkeeper, and Celtic and Larsson should have had one when they were whistled up for offside. But Celtic were now attacking their favourite King's Park end of the ground – and they had Henrik Larsson.

For a spell, all remained quiet as the Dunfermline defence grew in confidence and Celtic seemed to lack creativity. But then, a strange sound was heard as all the seats at the Celtic End of the ground tipped up simultaneously. A long ball had reached Larsson, and the fans all stood up at the same time to see their hero run on and score a somehow typical Larsson goal. We then suspected that it was to be Henrik's day, and he scored another after some fine play. It would have been nice if Larsson had scored yet another so that he could be mentioned in the same breath as Jimmy Quinn, but it was Petrov who grabbed the third goal to seal Celtic's 3-1 victory, and their 32nd win in the Scottish Cup. Oddly enough, perhaps, Larsson won only two Scottish Cup medals in 2001 and 2004, and in both games he scored twice.

And so Henrik was off. He had another emotional farewell in a friendly game, but then he disappeared to Catalonia, to Barcelona. There he played for two years, but was frequently injured, and was never the same player as he had been for Celtic. There were two occasions, however, when he impinged on the life of Celtic.

One was in the following season when Barcelona, as the luck of the draw would have it, were paired with Celtic in the European Champions League. It was Larsson's fortune to score a goal – and a good one it was – against the team and the fans who still adored him. There was something almost pre-ordained about that. Certainly the media had predicted it, but his body language showed as he ran back to the centre of the field, accepting the congratulations of his team-mates in a restrained and quiet way, that he would have preferred the opponents to be someone other than Celtic. The fans reacted quietly as always happens when the opponents score. Stunned silence reigned, until everyone realised that it was Henrik Larsson who had scored, then there was the blasphemous sound of a ripple of applause to hail a goal scored against Celtic. The historically-minded could recall one previous such occasion, and that was in January 1951 when Jimmy Delaney scored for Aberdeen.

The second occasion was a far happier time for both Celtic and Larsson. It was the European Cup final of 2006 between Barcelona and Arsenal. Henrik did not score, but he played a part in both Barcelona goals in the 2-1 win. Celtic fans were obviously delighted for their former hero, but particularly so because, thanks to the labyrinthine and mystifying regulations of UEFA, it meant that Celtic, the champions of Scotland, would qualify directly into the group stages of the Champions League, rather than through preliminary rounds. Thus had Henrik Larsson done Celtic yet another great favour.

HENRIK LARSSON BELONGS TO the supremely great. Celtic have had throughout their history many great goalscorers, but perhaps there are three who stand out above all the others. They are Jimmy Quinn, Jimmy McGrory and Henrik Larsson. The inclusion of Larsson in that elite bracket is deserved. Little gain can be served by arguments about which of the three was best. They played, after all, in totally different circumstances and ages, but the claims of Larsson to be considered one of the greatest worldwide at the turn of the century are substantial.

He was a complete player. He was compact, a thorough professional, a great team man, gracious and encouraging to team-mates, chivalrous to opponents. He had speed, and in particular he had a turn of speed in that he could suddenly step up a gear; he was tirelessly energetic and prepared to forage for the ball if necessary.

His goalscoring ability was phenomenal. A great deal of his goals were tap-ins, but that is the hallmark of a great striker, in that he can be in exactly the right place at the right time, having read the play, then made himself available to pick up a cross from Didier Agathe or a through-ball from Alan Thompson or Paul Lambert. But also he could score spectacular goals, hammered into the roof of the net from the edge of the box, and he had some gloriously headed goals as well. "It had to be Henrik" was the cry of the commentators, as if they could not quite see, at the critical moment, who had scored. But then a split second later, they realised that no-one else could score such a magical goal.

Yet there was more to him that that. He was a good player and has done well for other clubs like Barcelona and (briefly) Manchester United, and Sweden on the international scene, but he has not been great for them. His greatness has been reserved for the seven years that he spent with Celtic. He loved Celtic and he loved Scotland, where his wife and family settled very comfortably. He was able to cope with the ignorance and the bigotry because he had the intelligence to ignore it, and he could cope with the media spotlight because, quite simply, he did all his real speaking on the field, although he interviewed well also.

He joined Celtic at the time when they were at the crossroads. The summer of 1997 was a time when all of Celtic's massive support was beginning to ask whether the club would ever come back, so inured were they to failure and second best. There have been times in Celtic's history when "slave mentality" has taken over the mindset. It happened in the 1940s, the 1960s and certainly in the 1990s. Something extra special is required to convince Celtic and their supporters of their own value and worth in these circumstances. In the middle 1960s, it was Jock Stein who did just that. The late 1990s were characterised by the emergence of a truly great player.

It is also very easy to forget about Henrik's horrendously broken leg in 1999. That would have knocked the stuffing out of many a lesser man, but we are talking here about Henrik Larsson. There was also a broken jaw in 2003, although Henrik was comparatively free of other lesser injuries. Mental toughness is a great thing to have. Henrik Larsson realised that he was lucky to be such a great footballer, lucky to earn such a fine living out of doing something that he loves. Therefore training and dedication, including something that was foreign to Scotland, namely a care about diet and nutrition, were of paramount importance.

Celtic were also lucky in that Larsson was easy to get on with and a good team man. There was one incident in which Tosh McKinlay and he had a violent altercation:

"Oh Tosh McKinlay, Tosh, Tosh, Tosh McKinlay
He pit the heid upon the Swede
Oh Tosh McKinlay"

sang the Rangers fans when news of this leaked to the press, but the general opinion was that it was an isolated incident in which Henrik was less blameworthy than his protagonist. Apart from this, little scandal ever attached itself to Henrik. He was emphatically not a trouble-maker, and also co-operated with the succession of managers that he worked with – Jansen (with whom he had worked at Feyenoord), Venglos, Barnes, Dalglish and eventually O'Neill, who recognised in Larsson something really special.

A total of four SPL medals (1998, 2001, 2002 and 2004), two Scottish Cup medals (2001 and 2004) and two Scottish League Cup medals (1998 and 2001) in seven glorious years could have been more, had he enjoyed a little more luck. But it is the less tangible legacy that is more important – the memory of some tremendous goals and some tremendous football played by this valiant man. Those of us who have followed the club for over 50 years (and more) will always say, presumably, that the best Celtic team would have to be Jock Stein's all-stars of 1967 and the few years after that, but we will scratch our heads and eventually shake them if we are asked to name a better all-round player than Henrik Larsson. "I've seen Patsy Gallacher" said those who were around in the 1920s. Those of us who were around at the turn of the century saw Henrik Larsson.

SHUNSUKE NAKAMURA

'NAKA'

2005-PRES

BHOYS CAREER

Games	76*
Goals	18*
Caps	73*

* as of 1/12/07

MAGIC MOMENT

Injury time had been reached at Rugby Park and still Celtic could not score the elusive goal that would win them the 2007 Scottish Premier League title. Until that is, a free-kick was awarded outside the box...

'Another cracka from Naka!'

Dave Crocker of Setanta Sport

THE Celtic supporters in their thousands at Kilmarnock's Rugby Park and in their millions beside television screens throughout the world were getting impatient. It had been a frustrating afternoon. "Not easy watching" was the phrase which sprung to mind, and often supporters would wonder why it was that they put themselves through the excruciating torture that loving Celtic often is. Why couldn't we have taken up gardening, or played cricket or golf, or chess?

Or even supported someone like Stirling Albion or Forfar or Partick Thistle where the agonies were a lot less acute? Not for the first time did we appreciate the truth of the dictum that one does not support Celtic as any kind of casual hobby. If we do decide to go down that path of life – and very seldom does anyone decide to support Celtic, for usually that green-and-white seductress has us ensnared from a very early stage – then it is a commitment for life. It is also an endogenous, irreversible and, indeed, terminal condition. Such philosophical thoughts were whirling their eddying way round our psyche . . . but the bottom line was that we wanted, we needed, we craved a goal.

A victory was required to win the Scottish Premier League that fateful day of 22 April 2007. The team had played well in the early part of the season, but after the New Year a few dramatic late victories had perhaps disguised some deficiencies in the team. After an unlucky defeat in Europe to AC Milan, the team had stumbled and were crawling towards the finishing line rather than striding purposefully towards it. David Lloyd George, the British Prime Minister in 1918, had described the last few months of the Great War as "a bloodstained stagger to victory". Celtic supporters in 2007 knew what he meant.

On this day at Kilmarnock it was all about anxiety and nerves. The team had gone ahead in the first half when Vennegoor of Hesselink scored from a Nakamura corner, but then Kilmarnock had equalised at the start of the second period. The second half had crawled agonisingly, with Celtic clearly on top but unable to convert their outfield supremacy into the one goal that would guarantee delirium. Seconds before the 90 minutes were up, Derek Riordan put an easy one over the bar, and the feeling grew that it was not to be. A few of the weaker brethren went home, and those watching on the TV began to think that they could vent their frustration outside on the grass by giving it a fierce going over with the rusty lawn mower.

But then a ray of hope appeared, almost like the rising sun does in Orient, as it were. A free-kick was awarded just outside the box, to the right of the centre. This was Nakamura territory. We were well within the three minutes of stoppage time, so it did not take a genius to work out that this was the last chance saloon. Naka had saved our bacon many times this season. Could he do it once more? The *Setanta* commentator drew our attention to the fact, as if we didn't know it, that millions worldwide would now be watching. The thought passed through my mind that it would be about 11 o'clock on Sunday in the United States and Canada (and that people would be going to church), the middle of the night in Australia . . . very early on a Monday morning in Japan.

Naka nodded to someone and after a wee bit of pushing and jostling between Celtic attackers and Killie defenders in what passed for a wall, he ran up to take it. It was absolutely perfect, curling in at the far post and hitting the line as it crossed, so that even if the goalkeeper had been able to get across to the ball, he would have had a job getting down to it.

Cliches like "the terracing erupted" or "the crowd unleashed a tidal wave of appreciation" were somehow inadequate to describe the reaction of the fans. But the joy released behind that goal bore ample testimony to the support's appreciation of what had been achieved. It was simply so fitting, so appropriate, that the man who had saved Celtic so many times over the past two seasons with his brilliant free-kicks should do it again today, on the day that the League was won.

"Nakamura Na Na Na Na
Nakamura Na Na Na Na" etc, ad infinitum

Consisting of by no means the hardest lyrics to learn, this ditty was chanted by the deliriously happy Celtic fans who now knew, if they hadn't known it before, that a new immortal was entering the ranks of the Celtic greats. As he was interviewed that afternoon, his interpreter had to be employed, as Nakamura's English was limited to phrases like "Thank You". That interpreter, a gentleman of Oriental appearance, had a fairly broad Glasgow accent. Shunsuke was very definitely one of ours.

Craig McAughtrie, the editor and webmaster of the Keep The Faith website, was particularly impressed by the emotion expressed by the normally stoic Japanese. "Only once have I witnessed Naka absolutely losing the plot – after his aforementioned fantastic free-kick goal in the 93rd minute at Rugby Park in April 2007, when Naka's sensational strike clinched a 2-1 Celtic win against Kilmarnock and with it the SPL championship. Naka went bonkers! One of the best goalscoring celebrations ever!"

This particular goal has been played many times on TV, and one gets the impression that it has a long way to go yet, rivalling perhaps Patsy Gallacher's goal in 1925 or Dixie Deans's effort in 1972 for the most famous Celtic goal of all time. For once, it can honestly be said that it deserved all its "A goal fit to win the League" sort of hype. Ally Begg on Celtic TV would describe it, with elegance and simplicity, as "Naka's Cracka".

LIKE SO MANY CELTIC cult heroes, Nakamura is a small man. He is not small for reasons of malnutrition, as one could have said of some of Celtic's earlier small men, but simply because there are very few tall Japanese gentlemen. But smallness is something that endears itself to the maternal or matronly among the Celtic support.

In the Scottish Cup final of 2007, a somewhat rash tackle on a Dunfermline player earned Shunsuke a wigging from referee Kenny Clark. Clark is a tall man, and from high up on the Celtic End, the impression was one of a man of huge size in blue rigout towering over a pathetic figure in a green-and-white jersey. A couple of elderly lady supporters were outraged. "That's Naka getting a tellin' aff frae the referee". "Hey, Clark, leave him alane! Pick on someone yer ain size." Then in a fine vignette of affection, possibly hinting at some sort of emotional deprivation, one of the senior ladies said irrelevantly but pointedly: "He's such a lovely wee man. I want tae tak him hame wi me."

Craig McAughtrie, whose Celtic website boasts the most hits worldwide, purrs his appreciation of Shunsuke Nakamura: "Celtic manager Gordon Strachan has described him as a genius, Celtic fans refer to him as 'our Japanese Bhoy', almost everyone in Scottish football agrees he's a magician and one pundit famously said: 'He can open a tin of beans with his left foot'. I admit to having absolutely no idea if Shunsuke Nakamura can open a tin of beans with his left foot, but I dare say that if Naka practised long enough he'd manage. Because it's all about practice, or so Naka insists, and not about genius."

It was Willie Maley, over a century ago, who said: "It's not a man's creed or his nationality that counts, it's the man himself". Such a statement we would like to think is self-evident today, but it wasn't necessarily universally accepted then. Celtic, of course, had a long tradition of being able to accept anyone from Jerome Solis through Gil Herron to Johannes Edvaldsson as long as they could play the game. In recent years the hero had been a Swede by the name of Henrik Larsson, yet more proof of the inexorable spread of the Celtic family.

But a man from Japan was different. It is probably true to say, regretfully, that because of the Second World War, feelings of equanimity and reconciliation towards the Japanese race were harder to achieve than with other previous foes. Films like *The Bridge on the River Kwai* and *A Town Like Alice* had rather emphasised the facile view that the British upper class, with their stiff upper lips, were morally superior to such "barbarians".

Yet there were some justified grounds for bitterness as well. Just too many bad things had happened in the building of that Burma railway after the fall of Singapore for the British to feel otherwise. And the added factor was that Japan was such an unfamiliar country, with its totally different culture (where a lost wallet, for example, is invariably faithfully returned intact to its owner) and its alien language. Very few British people have ever been to Japan. Possibly no more than 100 Celtic fans had been there when Shunsuke joined us in 2005. The Celtic View added to the general air of ignorance of Oriental cultures by mixing up Nakamura with a Chinese player, Du Wei, who had joined us at the same time.

Japan remained a land of mystery, and had always been so. There was, for example, Sumo wrestling, which can entertain the eccentric as they flick through sports channels on days when there is no football. Like Spanish bullfighting, it would be hard to imagine it catching on in Scotland. Gilbert and Sullivan had produced *The Mikado* in 1885, portraying the "Gentlemen of Japan" saying:

Our attitude's queer and quaint
You're wrong if you think it ain't

an attitude which might offend the politically correct brigade of the early 21st century, but it is certainly the case that Scotland and Japan knew very little about each other. Still, it is always said that football can transcend national barriers, as it is the common language of mankind.

Japanese football had been growing. Scotland had played in the Kirin Cup of 1995 and would do so again (winning it!) in 2006, and Japan along with Korea had done an excellent job in putting on the World Cup of 2002. The national team was now a certainty to qualify for the World Cup finals and it was clear that the game of football, which in worldwide terms went from strength to strength, was now developing in Japan in a big way.

Global television meant that Japanese viewers could follow the progress of the Scottish Premier League and the English Premiership. But how would this Japanese gentleman cope with Scottish football, we wondered. Scottish football was, after all, quite different from anyone else's, as indeed was Scottish climate, culture and society. And, of course, football in Glasgow is in a department of its own, different even from the rest of Scotland, let alone the rest of the world.

SHUNSUKE NAKAMURA WAS BORN in June 1978 and had started off his footballing career for a Japanese team called Yokohama Marinos from 1997 until 2002. He won the Japanese Cup with them in 2001. With them, also, he earned many international caps and was part of the Japan side which won the Asian Cup of 2000. Rather surprisingly he was left out of the squad for the World Cup which was held in his own country and this may have motivated him to try his luck in Europe.

He has played for Japan many times since, famously scoring a somewhat controversial goal in the 2006 World Cup against Australia, which led to the sacking of the Egyptian referee, even though the Australian team won comfortably. But the 2006 World Cup was an unhappy time for both Japan and Nakamura himself, and it is probably true to say that he has done better at club level, particularly for Celtic, than he has at International level.

From 2002 until 2005 he played for the Italian side Reggina, but struggled with fitness and form in a team which waged perpetual battles against relegation. He never really settled in Italy, but it was nevertheless clear that he possessed tremendous talent which could be better displayed elsewhere. It was 25 July 2005 that he joined Celtic, very much a Gordon Strachan signing.

It would be fair to say that the Celtic support had not spent a happy summer of 2005. Still shattered by the blow of throwing away the SPL on the last day at Motherwell (albeit partially restored by the winning of the Scottish Cup a week later) and upset by the departure of Martin O'Neill, they were still coming to terms with new manager Gordon Strachan. He was a man whose previous appearances at Celtic Park had been in opposition colours, and his visits had not produced happy memories for Celtic fans. Balm was hardly poured on unhealed wounds when, in Strachan's first game, Celtic went down 0-5 to Artmedia Bratislava in a Champions League qualifier, effectively meaning that there would be no European stage for Nakamura in his first year.

This may have been a financial disaster for the club, but in playing terms it was not necessarily a bad thing to confine one's attention to Scotland while the new manager was finding his feet and the team were in the throes of transition.

But how would this slightly built Japanese chap cope with the rough and tumble of Scottish football? It was a cliché to portray Scotland as the land of tough defenders, heavy November pitches, unremitting rain between October and March, ruthless hard men as referees and grimly unforgiving fans for whom victory was the essence. There is more than an element of truth in this stereotype and how would the balletic splendour of this small and clearly loveable man cope with it all?

It was immediately obvious that the support had taken him to their heart. Very soon the flag sellers of London Road and the Gallowgate took to selling Rising Sun flags of Japan and other Japanese insignia, such as headbands with Japanese writing on them. This was a clear sign that Shunsuke was doing well, as a few years ago such stalls had sold Swedish flags in honour of Henrik Larsson.

The editor of Keep The Faith is emphatic that there was one aspect of his character that stood him in good stead for the stern tests ahead: "Nakamura has become an icon for Celtic fans because of his craft and guile, his passing prowess and that ability to find time and space on the ball, even during the chaos of Scottish football. I admit to also being impressed by his dedication to fitness. It has been calculated that Naka runs 14 kilometres during a single game, yet he heads off to the gym post-match for half-an-hour on an exercise bike as a warm-down whilst most of his colleagues in Scottish football are in the players' bar. He also goes swimming on his days off."

This aspect of his character is also borne out by people who work at Celtic Park. They will attest to the fact that there are times when the stadium is almost deserted in the late afternoon, apart from Shunsuke and his interpreter, who are practising free-kicks, corners and penalties, with the interpreter exercising his goalkeeping and ball-fetching skills while the little genius rehearses his repertoire with all the dedication of a concert pianist or a Shakespearean actor.

Elsewhere we have extolled the virtues of practice. Cricketer Glenn McGrath, arguably Australia's best ever fast bowler, when asked what was the secret of his success, said emphatically that there was no secret. All that you had to do was bowl well, and for this you needed practice. Clearly Nakamura is of the same persuasion.

Nakamura's first few games in season 2005/06 were ordinary but he scored his first goal against Dunfermline at the end of August. This was beamed back to Japan on TV, and very soon after that we saw Japanese tourists appearing at Celtic Park with green-and-white scarves. They were a welcome addition to the Celtic family, something that will very soon be the greatest institution of its kind in the world, if it is not already.

Shunsuke's first great goal was against Motherwell at Parkhead on a Wednesday night in late October. It was a free-kick on the edge of the penalty box at the Jock Stein Stand end of the ground. More than 56,000 people rose of one accord out of their seats to applaud a great goal and to welcome into the Celtic pantheon a new hero.

From then on, free-kick goals came reasonably regularly, but there was more to him than that. He was industrious, a tricky football player, a good passer of the ball, a great taker of corner-kicks, and those who felt that he would suffer because of the difficult Scottish conditions were proved wrong. In addition, the rapport with the fans was there, and it was no coincidence that the only game that Celtic lost in the League between an Old Firm defeat in August and the New Year was the one in which Nakamura wasn't playing, an otherwise inexplicable 0-1 defeat to Dunfermline in late November.

Celtic suffered a disaster early in the New Year of 2006 when they went down to Clyde in the Scottish Cup, but Nakamura rallied the team after that, and by March he had won his first medal in Scotland, that of the Scottish League Cup. This final was played at Hampden against Dunfermline a few days after the death of Jimmy Johnstone. Naka didn't score that day, but received a great compliment from a supporter of mature years sitting near me, who remarked that he was the closest we had had to Jimmy Johnstone since Jinky had given up the game.

A greater prize was forthcoming in early April when the team won the SPL, defeating their closest rivals Hearts 1-0 on a Wednesday night. He clearly revelled in the adoration of the fans, who sensed the great part that he had played in the return of the crown. Such occasions were, of course, beamed back to Japan, which now had its first winner of the Scottish Premier League.

STERNER TESTS AWAITED IN the following season's Champions League. The group stage saw Celtic drawn against Manchester United, Copenhagen and Benfica. This did not look easy, but Celtic delighted their fans by qualifying. The best game was the defeat of Benfica, but the most thrilling games were the clashes with Manchester United. In each of these Nakamura scored with a trademark free-kick. The one at Old Trafford was good and created a little history in that it was the first goal ever scored by a Japanese player in the European Champions' League, but it was not enough to save Celtic from a narrow and unlucky defeat.

It was the goal that he scored at Parkhead when Alex Ferguson's men came to Glasgow that was significant. It was a phenomenal strike. It was late in the game and decided the issue, qualifying the team for the last 16 of the Champions League for the first time since the competition became known by that name.

At such times, Parkhead explodes. A packed Celtic crowd celebrating a decisive goal in a tense encounter remains the greatest show on earth, and it was the man from Japan who brought this about that night. The game had been close and controversial. Nine minutes remained when Celtic won a free-kick some 30 yards from goal. It was slightly to the right of the goal at the Jock Stein Stand end of the ground. It looked as if it were just a little too far out for the "Nakamura territory" description to be applied to it, but we noticed that he was going to have a go. With so little time left in the game, he was as well to do that, we felt. He took the kick and duly delivered.

It was, perhaps, a very significant goal in the history of the Celtic psyche. There has existed for many years an inferiority complex about teams like Manchester United and Liverpool. Scottish slave mentality tends to underplay Scottish achievements and to encourage the belief that if we ever were to defeat an English team, it would be a fluke and that we are not allowed to beat them. In the same way that John Hartson did against Liverpool in 2003, Nakamura knocked that one on its head as far as Manchester United were concerned and showed the world what Celtic could do.

Then in the game against AC Milan (the eventual winners) in Italy, Celtic pressed hard and Milan themselves would admit afterwards that the Celts gave them more bother than anyone else. But how different it might have been if Gordon Strachan had not taken off Nakamura at the beginning of the second half of extra time. To be fair, Nakamura was not having the best of games and was visibly tiring, and Gordon may well have felt that the fast running Kenny Miller might have swung the game.

But just at the death with Celtic trailing to a Kaka goal, the hard-working Scottish team were awarded a free-kick in Nakamura territory. Sadly, Naka was now on the bench and could do nothing other than watch the honest Lee Naylor take the free-kick. Naka might well have scored, and that would have been enough to earn a 1-1 draw and an away-goals victory.

Celtic endured a form slump after this result, but even then, there was still Nakamura about whom it was believed that, as long as he was on the field, anything was possible. Celtic had lost to Rangers, Falkirk and drawn with Dundee United, and now at Parkhead, Motherwell were proving a tough nut to crack. Well into the second half, the score was still

0-0, with Celtic unable to turn their outfield superiority into goals and break down the stuffy and stubborn Motherwell defence. The ball came to Nakamura from a throw-in. With a piece of sublime footwork, he passed the ball from one foot to another to deceive an opponent, then having made some space, he sent over a great high ball for Jan Vennegoor of Hesselink to knock down for Derek Riordan to score what turned out to be the only goal of the game.

FREE-KICKS ARE, OF course, Naka's trademark – shortly before the AC Milan game, he had scored another fine one at Pittodrie against Aberdeen – but it would be wrong to think that was all he could do. He takes a brilliant corner as well, and no doubt appreciates the Japanese-style bowing that takes place among the support as he trots over to take the kick. He is also a fine passer of a ball, a crafty player and the nearest that we are likely to meet in the modern game to an old-fashioned dribbler. He possesses a fine temperament. He is able to take a certain amount of fouling – inevitable in Scotland if you are a ball player – without reacting badly.

Craig McAughtrie is particularly impressed with the phlegmatic nature of the man from Japan. "Nakamura should also be admired for another quality he undoubtedly possesses – bravery. In the madness of Scottish football, the hammer-throwers have lined up in a disorderly queue to boot our Japanese Bhoy up in the air. And yet invariably Naka courageously shrugs his shoulders, gets up, dusts himself down and returns for more. The similarities with Jimmy Johnstone are patently obvious. Only once have I witnessed Naka almost losing the plot and almost retaliating after a series of brutal attacks. That was against Dundee United at Tannadice when, after one bludgeoning too many, Naka appeared ready to administer the death grip to Arabs captain Barry Robson".

In fact, Nakamura had a particularly good season in 2006/07 against Dundee United. There was a free-kick against them in March at Tannadice, a delightful chip to salvage a point on Boxing Day at Parkhead and a stunning hat-trick on the previous visit to Tannadice in October as the Celtic fans began to sing:

It's so Japanesy.

to the tune of *Cuanta la mera*.

It was because of performances like these that Shunsuke won both Player of the Year awards in Scotland at the end of season 2006/07. One was voted for by the writers, and the other, which arguably carries more prestige, by his fellow professionals. This one is perhaps the best indication of how good a player is. After all, the men who have played against you on the field know how difficult an opponent you are, and have, perhaps, a keener insight into the problems and stresses of a modern professional football player. Both awards were won by Nakamura without any great competition.

Craig McAughtrie, like all other Celtic supporters and, indeed, most Scottish football sup- porters, is in no doubt that the awards were totally justified. "Undoubtedly, Shunsuke Nakamura's talent, like his wiry and athletic physique, is God-given, but our Japanese Bhoy has practised this inherent talent to make perfect, thereby explaining how, with one flash of his artistry, creativity, skill and vision, Naka can fashion a goal for Celtic. Be it from a precision perfect set-piece to a team-mate, a fantastic free-kick into the back of the net or a defence-dissecting pass to match a striker's run, Nakamura's worth to Celtic has become incalculable during the considerable successes of Gordon Strachan's managerial tenure."

Craig has just one reservation about Strachan's employment of Naka. "It is . . . undeniable that the Celtic manager has yet to discover a system that fully exploits the genius of Shunsuke Nakamura by providing him with the absolute freedom of the pitch – the 'number-ten role' to which Naka is eminently suited."

One could at this time recall what Jock Stein once said to Jimmy Johnstone as Jinky listened to a team talk in which everyone's role was laid down, but without any mention about what he (Jimmy) was expected to do. Plaintively he asked: "Whit aboot me, Boss?" Back came the growl: "You? Just get the ball and do what the f***in' hell ye want!" Nakamura is like that, one feels. He can do the unorthodox, the unusual, the bizarre – and quite a few Celtic fans feel that Naka (and the team) could benefit from him being given an even freer hand than he has at the moment to express his genius.

He remains a very inscrutable character. This merely adds to the mystery of him. Rightly he is concerned that over-exposure by the media will harm himself and his immediate family. He has seen in his home country how much has been made of wealthy and successful westerners like David Beckham. Yet we did see a small Naka appearing at Parkhead on the day that the SPL trophy was presented in April 2007.

CULTURALLY, NAKAMURA REPRESENTS an important part in the global development of the concept of Celtic. In the early days of the club, the support would have all lived within a few miles of Celtic Park, would have been first, second or third generation Irish immigrants and would have been of the Roman Catholic faith. Early in the 20th century, the play of Jimmy Quinn and the mighty half-back line of Young, Loney and Hay broadened the base to include a wider spectrum of Scottish society, particularly in the East of Scotland. Jock Stein drove a horse and cart through any lingering desire to return to any prejudiced or insular stance; Henrik Larsson and others introduced a European dimension to Celtic, and now Nakamura has linked East and West. Celtic are now big in Asia.

By the summer of 2007 Shunsuke had won four major honours with Celtic. But he has done more than that. He has won the hearts of the fans, and has given the support the belief that the best is yet to come. He and Celtic suit each other. He is the personality player that Celtic have been awaiting for so long. Messianic qualities appear embodied in him. He has been rightly compared to Jimmy Johnstone. There is also a touch of the Charlie Tully and the Patsy Gallacher about him. Success in Europe beckons, and with Nakamura on board, everything is possible.

Bibliography

An Alphabet Of The Celts
Eugene MacBride, George Sheridan and Martin O'Connor
Polar Print, 1994

Celtic - A Complete Guide 1888-1992
Paul Lunney
Stanley Paul, 1992

The Celt fanzine
edited by George Sheridan and Eugene MacBride

The Celtic Football Companion
David Docherty
John Donald, 1996

The Celtic Story
James Handley
Stanley Paul, 1960

Dan Doyle - The Life and Death of a Wild Rover
Marie Rowan
Blakc & White

Dreams And Songs To Sing
Tom Campbell and Pat Woods
Mainstream, 1999

The Glory And The Dream
Tom Campbell and Pat Woods
HarperCollins, 1986

Heroes Are Forever: The Life And Times Of Celtic Legend Jimmy McGrory
John Cairney
Mainstream, 2005

Jock Stein - The Celtic Years
Tom Campbell and David Potter
Mainstream , 1998

The Mighty Atom (The Biography Of Patsy Gallacher)
David Potter
Parrs Wood Press, 2000

The Mighty Quinn: The Biography Of Jimmy Quinn - Celtic's First Goalscoring Hero
David Potter
Tempus, 2005

Rhapsody In Green: Great Celtic Moments
Tom Campbell and Pat Woods
Mainstream, 1990

The Sky Sports Yearbook
various
Stanley Paul

The Scottish Football Book (Nos. 8,9 & 12)
various
Stanley Paul

The Story Of The Celtic
Willie Maley
1938

Willie Maley - The Man Who Made Celtic
David Potter
Tempus, 2003

Additional archive sources:

The Glasgow Herald
Glasgow Evening Citizen
Evening Times
www.keep-the-faith.net
The Celtic View
The Scotsman
Sunday Mail
Weekly News